Mazel Tov!

Mazel Tov!

The Complete Book of Jewish Weddings

LEA BAYERS RAPP

CITADEL PRESS
Kensington Publishing Corp.
www.kensingtonbooks.com

This book is intended, through the best efforts of the author and publisher, to enlighten readers on the subject matter included. It is not intended to represent every interpretation of Jewish law and custom, or to serve in a legal, accounting, rabbinical or other professional capacity.

CITADEL PRESS BOOKS are published by

Kensington Publishing Corp.
850 Third Avenue
New York, NY 10022

All Kensington titles, imprints, and distributed lines are available at special quantity discounts for bulk purchases for sales promotions, premiums, fund-raising, educational, or institutional use. Special book excerpts or customized printings can also be created to fit specific needs. For details, write or phone the office of the Kensington special sales manager: Kensington Publishing Corp., 850 Third Avenue, New York, NY 10022, attn: Special Sales Department, phone 1-800-221-2647.

Citadel Press and the Citadel Logo are trademarks of Kensington Publishing Corp.

Design by Leonard Telesca

First printing: June 2002

10 9 8 7 6 5 4 3 2 1

Printed in the United States of America

Library of Congress Control Number: 2001099894

ISBN 0-80652333-6

For my husband, Stanley
the love of my life and my very special hero
and for Ilana and Justin,
who demonstrate every day that children are indeed
a blessing from God.

Contents

Acknowledgments

THIS BOOK WOULD NOT have been possible without the input of so many people who have generously given of their time, expertise, talent, and insights. I'd like to thank Bruce Bender and my editors Margaret Wolf and Francine Hornberger (who managed to tame the beast) as well as Carrie Cantor, who championed the book at its inception. Thank you to the staff of Kensington/Citadel for all of your hard work. Matchmaker Willa Speiser of *New Jersey Bride,* thank you for thinking of me. Bit-e-Byte, Inc., Somerville, New Jersey, you are the best! What would my computer and I do without you? Justin, Ilana, Stanley, and Lisa Lewis you have been on call for me 24/7 and I'm forever grateful. Miriam and Menachum Golan in Europe, and Lea Erez, Ran Erez, and Dorrit Inbar in Israel, thank you for your help across the miles. Caryn Schloss, thanks for your hand—literally! Malka Izhaky, your input was always on target. I'd like to thank my mom, Adele Bayers. Your eagle eyes and sharp sense of language saved many a page from typo-terrain.

And most important, I'd like to heartily thank all the rabbis, lawyers, accountants, financial experts, vendors, artists, photographers, and government officials who have so generously given of their time and expertise. I'll be forever grateful to the brides and grooms, their parents, and members of their wedding parties who let me into their lives, and who shared their stories and experiences with me. If only I had the space of another book to thank you all individually! And most of all, I'd like to acknowledge the wonders of the institution of marriage—may it bloom and blossom forever!

Introduction

MAZEL TOV! NOW THAT you've become engaged, somehow your entire world seems to have changed. You're living life in a new emotionally charged dimension, in a stratosphere filled with love, joy, and anticipation of your marriage to come.

Under Jewish law, getting married is simple: Before two witnesses, the groom signs the marriage document and the bride accepts an object of minimal value that belongs to the groom (a plain gold ring), while he recites, *"Har'e aht me'kudeshet le, b'taba'at zo, k'dat Mo'sheh v'Yisro'el,"* which means: "With this ring, you are consecrated unto me according to the law of Moses and of Israel." After consummating the marriage, you are officially husband and wife.

But a Jewish wedding can be so much more! Many wonderful, meaningful, and important customs surround this special life-cycle event, which have developed over the centuries, formed by the pulse of the times, the cultures of the communities, and the philosophies of Judaism as practiced around the globe.

As you spread the word of your engagement, plan your wedding, and arrange for your honeymoon, you'll find a dizzying array of options before you. You can maintain current Jewish practices within your community, select customs from a rich Judaic heritage, and combine them with secular events, if you like. You can incorporate traditional methods and invoke new technologies.

Sometime, somehow, in between "regular life," you'll be making up invitation lists, choosing your bridal attire, going for fittings, and thinking about your hair and makeup for the big day. And most likely you and your honey, and perhaps your parents, will be meeting with a magnitude of vendors: jewelers, stationers, caterers, artists and calligraphers, florists, photographers, musicians, transportation providers, travel agents, beauticians, cosmetologists, and many more.

Use this book as your guide throughout the process of planning your wedding. Let it help you sort through your choices and make informed consumer decisions. Take the fun-filled quizzes to test your knowledge and gain a giggle.

Rest assured, something definately will go wrong along the way. And so what! Trust me, it won't be the end of the world. You'll find that all the things that may have worried you will instantly disappear as you take that first step down the aisle!

It's your ceremony, it's your party, and it's going to be your wonderful life together. So relax. Enjoy! And, here's to you both. *Mazel tov!*

Mazel Tov!

1

You're Engaged!

IT HAS FINALLY HAPPENED. You know you love each other and want to spend the rest of your lives together. Whether it's been a whirlwind romance or you've been together for years, the time has come. You've decided to get married. You've decided to make the commitment to spend the rest of your lives together. And it's a heady happening, indeed.

But whether you privately savor the experience for a day or two or can't contain yourself for even a moment, it's time to share your exciting news with the world. And although you may feel compelled to blurt out the news to the first people you happen to see, remember that good news travels fast. You don't want the most important people in your life to hear it through the grapevine. Be sure to tell your parents, your children, if you have them, and other family members about your engagement before you announce it officially. The rest of this chapter will guide you in all the various ways to share your happy news with the world.

From Mouth to Media

Fortunately, there are many ways for you to spread the news and share the *simcha* with your family and others. In this era of advanced technology, there is an arsenal of equipment at the ready to complement the more traditional ways of making the grand announcement.

While "in person" is the traditional, most ideal way to announce your engagement, this isn't always an option. The phone can be a great way to get your news out there. Be prepared to answer a million and one questions if they've never met your honey before:

- 💕 "What's his last name?" (That's a euphemism for "Is he Jewish?")

- 💕 "Is he *a professional?*"

- 💕 "What in the world is a quality assurance automation tester?"

- 💕 "Can he actually make a living at this?"

- 💕 "Is he handsome?"

- 💕 "Where are his parents from? What do they do?" (Translation: "Do they have money?")

- 💕 "Have you met them yet? What are they like?" (Translations: "Shall we be jealous of them now?" "Will they treat you like the princess you are?" "Will we become merry *machetenestas* or outlaw in-laws?")

- 💕 "When are we going to meet our future son-in-law?"

There are several other ways in which to tell your loved ones about your engagement. You can leave a voice-mail message, send an e-mail, send a fax, even set up a Web site that announces your good news. You can then direct friends and family there so that they can be joyously surprised. Another method you might try, especially if your family and friends live far away and it isn't possible to tell them in person, is to make a videotape of you and your fiancé breaking the good news.

Putting It in Print

Now that you've told your immediate family and friends, you or your parents can further spread the word by placing an engagement announcement in the newspaper. You can select your local paper, the newspaper of the largest metropolitan area near you, the one that covers the town where you work, a neighborhood weekly paper that publishes social notices, and/or any Jewish newspapers in your area. If you're really into telling the world, why not go public? Pro: it's an easy way to share your good news with a wider group of people than those you can notify in person or by more individualized methods. Con: you never know who's reading your announcement and what type of information they can glean from it. Con artists and kooks can learn lots of things about you—including what you look like and your background. Another caveat: it seems like every wedding vendor in the world will be calling to sell you something. But hey—you may get some good ideas or deals!

Some newspapers provide instructions right on their social pages that walk you through submitting your announcement. Others mail informational kits upon request. Still others list instructions on their Web sites. The paper may ask that you send in a press release. Be sure to ask whether the paper will print both your engagement and your wedding announcements. Some will only publish one or the other. If that's the case, you'll have to decide which of these you want to run.

Some newspapers only publish a few of the many requests they receive; others print all, but cannot guarantee they will make it into the paper by the dates requested. Some publish the announcements for free, while others charge a fee that varies depending on the length of the announcement and whether a photo is published along with the text.

Just the Facts

Whether your newspaper provides a form to be completed or simply asks you to write your own press release, there are many facts you don't want to leave out. These include:

- ❦ The name or names of the people issuing the announcement
- ❦ Your complete names
- ❦ Your ages
- ❦ City and state where you each live
- ❦ College or university attended and any degrees you each have received
- ❦ Your current occupations
- ❦ Any significant honors you may have received
- ❦ Organizations in which each of you are active, if any
- ❦ Your parents' names and the city and state in which they live
- ❦ Month or season of the proposed wedding (include the year only if it's not the current one)
- ❦ Location of the wedding, if known

These are standard bits of information. If you're paying for the announcement by the column inch, you may want to limit the information you include to help cut costs.

Sending Engagement Announcements

There's something special about receiving a beautifully engraved or thermographed engagement announcement presented on rich, creamy paper stock. *People like it.* In fact, many people collect and cherish these traditional engagement announcements. Somehow, the traditional written announcement, delivered by a uniformed postal carrier, creates added impact.

Although engagement gifts are not mandatory, many people wait to get an engagement announcement before starting to ferret out the location of your bridal registry or searching for the perfect engagement gift for you.

Some brides- and grooms-to-be hesitate to send out engagement cards, worrying that it will simply look like a tacky request for gifts. And some etiquette books may agree. But this is not necessarily the case. Those who want to send gifts, of course, will. But others will be happy to send you a card, or just quietly be pleased that you thought enough about them to keep them graciously informed about an important event in your life.

So, bottom line, it's generally a good idea to send out (or have your parents send) the traditional engagement announcements, even if you've already told some of the people you're sending them to.

Engagement announcements can be designed to reflect your personality, or, as is more often the case, selected as an early sampling of your wedding invitations and the personal style of your forthcoming wedding. There are countless different styles for announcement cards. Many select engagement announcements that are smaller in size than the wedding invitation they plan to send. It can be a single card that fits into a matching envelope, or a card folded in half horizontally. Usually, it will match the stationery the couple plan to use for their wedding invitations. Try to get the best paper stock you can afford, because the announcement and subsequent invitations will set the tone of the entire "marriage event."

If you plan to send engagement announcements to only a small circle of people—say, fewer than twenty-five—it might not be cost-effective for you to order such elaborate announcements. A handwritten note telling your good news is always appropriate.

Another option for a mailing to under twenty-five people is to create beautiful notes on a computer using card- or project-making software. Although scorned by some who feel that anything computerized shows a lack of personal attention, others find that creatively designed computerized announcements show even more effort than standardized engraved ones. In any event, acceptance of personally designed computerized cards is growing.

The key is to making the best announcement of your engagement is to put yourself in the place of the people you're about to contact. How would your mother feel if she learned of your engagement via a mass e-mail message? Or from a phone call from Aunt Gertie, who heard the news from your cousin Mindy? How would his great-aunt Sadie in a nursing home respond to a computer-generated announcement card? Would a phone call to her or possibly an in-person visit serve better?

Ta'na'eem

When couples decide to get married, the bride usually receives an engagement ring, and sometimes prenuptial agreements are drawn up by attorneys and signed by the bride- and groom-to-be. But in ancient Jewish times, traditions were a bit more formal—especially since marriages were arranged by families. During an event, the "match" was acknowledged, the promise of marriage was declared, and the terms of the marriage were hammered out by the families involved in a process called *shidduch*. This included the date and time of the wedding, where it would be held, the size of the guest list, the bride's dowry, and the bridegroom's financial responsibilities toward his wife. Part of the traditional document also stipulated a hefty monetary fee (the *kenas*) that must be paid by the party who—heaven forbid—breaks off the engagement. This is to cover "pain and suffering," humiliation, as well as any expenses already incurred on behalf of the wedding. And the fee was usually hefty indeed, to help ensure that minds weren't changed lightly.

When negotiations were complete, the terms of the contract—called *ta'na'eem*—were drawn up, documented in writing, addressed to the fathers (or other representatives) of the couple, signed by two witnesses, and held legally binding under Jewish law. The ceremony that formalized the deal by signing the *ta'na'eem* was thus called—you've guessed it—*ta'na'eem*.

For the most part, the traditional *ta'na'eem,* if implemented today, is included merely as a symbolic gesture before the signing of the *ketubah* on the wedding day. After all, family-arranged Jewish marriages and dowries aren't all that common these days. And if you're having your wedding in a catering hall, it's more often the availability of space that dictates your marriage date—not an agreement between your father and future father-in-law.

There are, however, modern-day couples who want to return to their roots, and who like the idea of a formal and binding agreement and engagement ceremony, perhaps even officiated by a rabbi. It can prove to be a deeply moving and significant experience. The original *ta'na'eem* can be tweaked to eliminate the customs such as a dowry and the financial penalty for breaking the engagement. It can also be reinvented to include newer versions of *ta'na'eem* that apply to society today.

Just as brides and grooms may incorporate their own wedding vows into their marriage ceremony, the *ta'na'eem* can be drawn up to reflect your own situation and the decisions that are relevant to your lifestyle today. The list could include things such as the approximate length of your engagement period, whether to have a large or small wedding, even whether a spouse will work or attend school or both after marriage. It can include your decision about wanting to have a large or small family, or whether you choose to have children at all. And given today's mobile society, a couple can decide where they plan to reside, at least initially. With many couples living together prior to marriage, the *ta'na'eem* could simply be a pledge to wed at a certain time: when we reach our second year of togetherness, when we graduate from college, before we decide to have children. It can add a level of commitment more comforting than an open-ended "let's just live together" arrangement.

The *ta'na'eem* can be written in Hebrew, English, or your native language if different from these, and may incorporate translations. It can be as simple as a handwritten agreement on a piece of paper, or as ornate as a beautiful piece done in calligraphy.

Although the *ta'na'eem* can be a private agreement, witnessed, signed, and then shared only between the two of you during a quiet moment, you can also choose to celebrate the signing with family and friends. Some may choose to invite a small intimate circle of friends to share this event, while others may feel the ideal way to share the *ta'na'eem* ceremony is to incorporate it into a secular engagement party, adding the richness of tradition and commitment to that party.

During the engagement party, call everyone around a table for the ceremony. Your officiating rabbi can explain the meaning of *ta'na'eem* and address a few wise words to the newly engaged couple. The document can be read by the fathers, the rabbi, the witnesses, or the couple themselves. Traditionally, the two fathers each held the opposite end of a handkerchief, symbolizing their acknowledgment of the terms.

Giving nod to ancient tradition, the document can be signed by the fathers of the engaged couple, along with two witnesses. In a more modern approach, both the bride- and groom-to-be (with or without their fathers' endorsements) can sign it as well, thereby fostering their commitment to their future lives together. As a matter of fact, both the bride and the groom must agree to be married and enter into marriage of their own free will as a prerequisite for a Jewish wedding.

And just as the wedding ceremony ends with the breaking of the glass, the *ta'na'eem* ceremony is concluded with the mothers breaking a plate wrapped in a napkin or a pillowcase. Dancing, singing, and greetings from guests can uplift this moment to be cherished. The engagement is official.

Of course, right now you're probably much too excited to think of all of these details. So go ahead—indulge. Waltz down the street singing. Envision yourself walking down the aisle in the most perfect wedding gown. Give yourself fifteen grand minutes—or perhaps the entire week! Then snap back to reality. From now until after your wedding day, you're going to be very, *very* busy indeed.

2

Financing Your Wedding

YOU'VE MADE THE GRAND announcement, and your life has probably taken on a whole new dimension. Where it used to be "me," you now see life as "we." You're in love, you are loved in return, and you can't help but go through your day with a smile on your face, a twinkle in your eye, and a very amazing feeling inside.

Perhaps, as a bride, you see yourself as the true "Jewish princess" in tons of fabulous tulle, and your groom most elegant in tails and a top hat. Your wedding space is abloom with fresh flowers and rose petals, and the cantor's melodic voice fills the air with song. And there, before three hundred of your closest family and friends, surrounded by a royal roundup of bridesmaids and groomsmen, you and your beloved say your "I dos." Your rabbi's face is beaming. Your aunts, clutching crumpled tissues, are dabbing at their eyes. With great pomp and purpose, your rabbi proclaims you to be husband and wife. After a hearty stomp on a fine crystal goblet, and to joyous cries of *"Mazel tov"* from all, your groom gently lifts your veil. Your lips meet tenderly for your first kiss as husband and wife. And then, on cue, the music rises. Everyone joins in applauding and singing *"Mazel Tov* and *Siman Tov."* With the room pulsating with love and joy, you lift the hand-beaded hem of your designer gown and together with your love, make your way back up the aisle. Now it's on to the big-blast reception that will celebrate the beginning of your wonderful new life together.

But perhaps your wedding vision is a more modest one. In *your* dream, you envision a small, elegant gathering of immediate family and a few close friends. You're wearing the perfect wedding gown or wedding suit, and every flower of your bridal bouquet has been carefully cultivated to join together in perfect harmony. You and your fiancé have spent endless hours discussing the details of the *chuppah* under which you'll be married. You agreed that it should have special meaning to you both. Thus you decided to have it hand-made by a seamstress using the preserved fabric of your grandfather's *tallit* and edged with remnants of your grandmother's lace wedding gown. A string quartet will play enchantingly as your guests arrive, and later uplift in song as you are declared husband and wife.

After an intimate reception resplendent with fine linens, sparkling crystal, gleaming silverware, exquisite candleholders, and artistic culinary delights, you and your love take leave for a quiet honeymoon in a tucked-away corner of the globe. It's a place you have always dreamed of sharing lovingly with each other.

Okay. Stop the video. Because just about now you've reached the moment where fantasy intersects with reality. For most of us, anyway. For every clink of fine crystal, there is the jingle of a cash register.

Even back in Talmudic times, finances played a major role in marriages. Brides came with dowries. Grooms documented how they would support their brides. Getting married was a family enterprise, and it was not unusual for lawsuits to erupt and monetary fines to be imposed.

Today, money still matters.

The "Average" Cost of a Wedding—Not!

Pick up a bridal magazine or turn on a television talk or bridal show and you'll probably hear that the average cost of a wedding today is twenty thousand dollars—or perhaps forty thousand. Maybe even fifty. But think about it for a moment. The "average" cost actually includes the least expensive and the most over-the-top weddings you can imagine—and everything in between—all divided and chopped to statistical satisfaction. Some of these figures represent weddings with 100 guests, others with 150, 200, even 500 or more. Some take place in New York City or Los Angeles, others in small towns where costs can be much lower. Some receptions can be simple and priced at under a thousand dollars—others grand extravaganzas that can cost a million dollars or more.

When Melissa Rivers got married, the reception her mom, Joan Rivers, planned was so lavish that the band reportedly played "Hey, Big Spender" when the mother of the bride walked into the room. And gossip has it that Michael Douglas's wedding to Catherine Zeta-Jones hit the two-million-dollar mark. For most of us, however, our dream weddings might have to be adjusted a bit.

Take those figures of "average costs" and toss them out of your head. No such animal exists when it comes to computing *your* wedding day. Even two very similar weddings can vary in price. Locale makes a big difference. Similar reception menus in the same hotel can vary in price, too—there's always an element here or there that makes the difference.

The quality and quantity of food served; whether you're serving kosher or nonkosher food, buffet or sit-down; the type and amount of liquor; whether your wedding gown is bought or borrowed; the size of your wedding party; your choice of flowers; the type of transportation you use—all of these factors affect the cost of your wedding.

So how can you figure out what *your* dream wedding will cost? And whether or not you can afford it? Perhaps you're the ultimate pragmatist and don't take kindly to dreaming big. You want to know what you have going in and limit your vision to the dollars at hand. There's nothing wrong with that! If this is what makes you comfortable, go for it. Find out how much money you're able to gather; with that amount in mind (and hopefully in hand!), you can contact vendors and deal. In fact, by using this method you can be much firmer on the amount you're willing to spend for each element, and vendors will know that you mean business.

No one is promising that financing your wedding can be easy. You can also work it out in the three-step plan that follows.

Step One: Start Out With Your Dream Intact and a Notebook at Your Side

Divide the pages of your notebook into two columns: one labeled ELEMENTS, and the other DOLLARS.

Next, visualize your wedding as you both agree you would like it to be. Play it out like a movie. You are the directors and can choose the elements that will make up your event. Pan the scenes slowly, viewing them in rich detail, and discuss your visions with each other. (And if your fiancé backs away from wedding plans, it's all yours—so indulge!)

Think of the engagement announcements you plan to use. Write down specifics, ranging from the type of paper (handmade, parchment, standard wedding) to whether you'll have the announcements engraved, thermographed, or designed on a computer. On a separate sheet in your notebook, draw up a quick list of those you'd like to send announcements to so you have a "guesstimate" of the quantity and postage you'll need.

Picture the wedding invitations you'd like to send and the people you'd like to invite. Visualize the pre-wedding get-together (sometimes called a rehearsal dinner) as well as the wedding and reception venue, the rabbi who will perform the ceremony, the size of your guest list, and the type of transportation you'd like to have.

As the elements begin to unfold, continue to jot them down in as much detail as possible. Do you see yourself in a wedding gown of taffeta with a chapel train? A gauzy cotton dress and sandals? Or perhaps a dressy white suit? Do you picture a three-piece band, a boom box, a DJ, or a twelve-piece orchestra providing the music for your reception? Do you see your bridesmaids each carrying a single perfect long-stemmed rose or a full bouquet of exotic flowers? Or will you have no bridal party at all? Will the ceremony be followed by an afternoon reception at your parents' home, where dainty tea sandwiches and champagne will be served? A cookout on the beach? Or is a buffet cocktail hour followed by a five-course sit-down dinner at a fancy hotel more your style?

Then there's the photographer and videographer. And don't forget to plan the ultimate getaway—your honeymoon.

Once you have the broad basics as *you* see them, visualize your wedding and reception through the eyes of your arriving guests. Write down your vision in terms of the service and items that you'll need. Brainstorm with your bridal party and parents, in addition to your mate-to-be.

Start with your guests' arrival. Is there parking available for them? Do you want to offer valet parking? Don't forget to add in a spot for the tips.

Think of the season. Will your guests be bringing coats or jackets? Is a coat check available? Since you'll be covering tipping here as well, find out if the fee you're paying includes the tip for the coat-check person. If there's no coat check available, do you need to rent coat racks? If so, mark it down.

When your guests enter the ceremony site, will there be a staff member to greet them? If so, is his or her salary included with the fee you're paying the site? If you're having an outdoor ceremony in the park, what about licensing fees? Will you be paying for security? Someone to direct traffic at the location?

You may be using a room in the synagogue or hall as the bridal dressing room, rooms for the bridesmaids and ushers, for the *bedecken*, the *yichud*, to sign the *ketubah*, or for the groom and his party. Are they included in the rental fee for the synagogue or hall? As your guests arrive, will personalized *yarmulkas* be available to them? Who sets them out? And where? Do you need to have a table placed for that purpose? Does it require a tablecloth? Flowers? Will you need someone to place the flowers on the *bima*, around the *chuppah*, and the ribbons along the aisles? And if you'll be gliding down the white runner on the arms of your parents, is there an extra charge to provide it or for rolling it out?

What about those chair covers you want to rent for the reception? Does the cost include ironing them and actually putting them on the chairs? Are the place settings and silverware, champagne buckets, and barware included? Take nothing for granted. You don't want any last-minute surprises.

It's All in the Timing

Service can add up to big dollars. Think about the timing of the events of your wedding. Lisa[*] and Mark[*] were planning a Sunday-afternoon wedding. The day

[*]The names have been changed, because the pair have since dieted. We don't want to remind them of all the food they served at their wedding.

would include the ceremony, a grand buffet cocktail hour, and a formal dinner dance. They soon realized that the order of the segments of their wedding would make a difference in the overall costs.

Mark's parents suggested the festivities start with the buffet cocktail hour, continue with the ceremony, and then culminate in the dinner-dance celebration. This was so that guests driving a long distance to attend the wedding would be greeted with something to eat and drink before the ceremony. Also, should they be delayed in traffic, they wouldn't miss the all-important *chuppah*. And after the ceremony, guests would be ready to eat and drink once again.

Lisa's family believed differently. They envisioned the ceremony first, followed by the cocktail hour, during which time the newly married couple could take wedding pictures in the beautiful outdoor garden before losing the light. Then the couple could rejoin their guests for the dinner dance.

Both sides had valid points. But Mark's parents felt very strongly that if the ceremony comes first, guests, many driving a great distance on a hot summer day, should at least be offered a cool drink and a bite to eat before sitting through the ceremony. Thus coffee and mini pastries, or drinks and light snacks, should be available for arriving guests. It sounded good—until finances were considered.

This little extra, adding perhaps two to five dollars per head, can take a big bite out of your budget. So before setting up the order of your day, check with the vendors involved to see how their charges work.

The time of day, day of the week, and season you hold the wedding will affect your balance sheet. A band might charge less for an afternoon reception than for one held in the evening. The catering hall may be less expensive in the afternoon as well. A Sunday wedding will most likely be less expensive than one held on a Saturday night, and weekdays are better still. And the busier the season (May and June, for example), the higher the prices.

The Near, the Famous, and Your Connections

When choosing a ceremony site, the price can be affected by the proximity to a large city (where prices may go up) and your own connections (where costs can go down). If you want your wedding to be held in a public place, such as a famous museum, botanical garden, or historical mansion or house, you'll probably have to pay a rental fee, which can be nominal or up to thousands of dollars in addition to your catering costs. On the other hand, if you're planning your wedding in a house of worship and are a member of a synagogue or temple, you could get a lower rate than those who are unaffiliated. Planning to get married at your college's nondenominational chapel? An alumnus or student rental rate may be lower than the normal rentals, assuming the chapel is open to the public.

Does your cousin Joe's sister-in-law work for a catering hall? Perhaps she can get you a discount. Or maybe one of your clients is on the board of directors of the most perfect venue for your wedding and can make special arrangements for you.

If you're trying to find ways to stretch your budget, then, think about all the factors that your personal connections can help. But weigh the savings against future obligations for "the favor."

Adding It Up

Once you've decided on the elements, it's time to start filling in the dollars column. Go back over your elements list and get busy filling in any blanks. You can be as loose or specific as your personalities allow. You're not locking anything in at this point, but you'll start researching the costs so that you have an idea of where you stand.

Check with friends who have recently married in your area (and whose wedding basically reflects your style). Use the phone to do a quick survey of vendors, and call local unions and trade organizations for standard costs where they may apply. Of course, if you want the hottest band, the in-demand caterer, the most upscale florist, be prepared for charges above the standard rates.

Comparison-shop among vendors, whenever possible, and look into package deals that can offer more for your money than purchasing individual elements from different vendors. But don't take package deals blindly. Shop and compare both ways, and check on the quality of goods and services as you make the comparisons. And be sure to enter the results on your chart. Feel free to enter alternative elements that you may discover and their associated prices.

During this step, you may choose to consult with your parents. They, too, may have dreams for your wedding—probably dating from the day you were born. But if your parents are not taken to flights of the imagination, the sheer projected costs of your dream wedding might send them racing to the hospital's emergency room, or to a real estate broker to sell off the family farm. Make sure you let them know, in advance, that this is just your fantasy vision right now; you realize there will be lots of adjustments and compromises to come.

Step Two: Collecting the Cash

Just for now, set aside your dream. It's time to tally and determine how much money you'll actually have available to fuel your fantasy.

With the skyrocketing costs of throwing a wedding and the proliferation of mature, more self-sufficient brides and grooms, the age-old rule of "bride's parents pay for the wedding" has softened. It's not uncommon to have the bride's parents, the groom's parents, step-parents, and even grandparents or an aunt and uncle or two invest in the bridal production. And in some communities, friends, neighbors, and *shul*-mates may be willing to pitch in to help a young couple get off to a good start.

Only you and your fiancé can guess how the finances will fall within your own circumstances. Have your parents always told you that they've been saving for your wedding day, and that because you're their personal princess, it's their pleasure to make your every dream come true? Or perhaps your parents will offer you a set sum of money to do with as you please—you can spend it all on the wedding, spend part and keep the rest, or skip the big wedding and use it toward the start of your new life.

Should you and/or your fiancé be doing braggably better than your parents (hel-loooo, doctor!), you may be picking up all or the majority of your own wedding expenses. Indeed, some students hear their parents say, as tuition bills come due: "We're paying for your college education, so don't expect us to pay for your wedding, too." Other brides have listened to this mantra: "Your father and I paid for our own wedding twenty-five years ago, and if it's good enough for us . . ."

Then, too, even the best of intentions can go awry. An illness, divorce, or death in the family or a stock market decline can wipe out wedding dollar reserves. On the other hand, you may have a rich aunt who never married and (pinch your chubby little cheek) dotes on you to the full extent of her pocketbook.

If you're a mature couple or are remarrying, you'll most likely be assuming most or all of the wedding costs yourselves. In any event, may the treasure hunt begin.

Taking Inventory

The first thing you'll need to do as a couple is to check your own financial situation. Whether you're paying for your wedding or not, there are sure to be expenses. Have you been saving for your wedding day or is this a completely new venture? How much do you think you can afford to save between now and your projected wedding date? Remember that you or your "benefactors" will need money up front for deposits—so you can't rely on last-minute funding. Nor can you expect to pay wedding bills with cash gifts received as your reception comes to a close. Keep in mind that in addition to your wedding and honeymoon, you'll need money for announcements, invitations, and thank-you notes, for example. And most likely, you'll need to pay the first few months' rent and a security deposit on an apartment, dollars toward a co-op, or a down payment on a house, town house, or condo. Also to be considered: at least a minimal amount of furniture and household things. And don't forget to treat yourselves to a new "honeymoon" wardrobe as well. You might even need to buy some luggage.

After checking your own finances, you might want to approach your parents as contributors. (Or perhaps they'll be true angels and pick up the entire tab!) Don't go in with demands, but rather with a businesslike request for information about their financial plans for the wedding. There are many scenarios that can unfold. Here are just a few.

Bride's parents agree to pay for the entire wedding. For the traditionalists, the bride cuts the cake and her dad pays for it and just about everything else. Daddy Wedbucks (or Mommy Wedbucks, for that matter) completely holds the purse strings and can deliver the dollars based on a pay-as-you-go or a flat-rate approach. (See "Methods of Delivery," on page 23.) Caveat: you may have to assert your independence when it comes to style and substance. Would Dad really agree to fund a "skydiving" wedding, or something even less down to earth?

The traditional split. In this scenario, the bride's side and groom's side fund the wedding on the traditional split basis, heavily weighing in on the bride's side. Hopefully, the groom's side will also agree on its traditional share, like paying for the band and the honeymoon. Caveat: if the groom's invitation list is far larger than the bride's, splitting the costs so that the bride pays more might cause some friction.

Both the bride's and the groom's sides agree to fund the wedding as they decide, politically correct or not. Because of the high costs of weddings today, the parents of the bride and groom may decide to share the costs, rather than stick to the "she pays for this, he pays for that" formula. For this to work out, the wedding budget needs to be established up front and the dollars split equitably, if not necessarily evenly. Keep in mind that wedding costs usually spin higher than anticipated, so it's best to build a 10 or 15 percent buffer into the budget at the start.

A case in point: Reba,[*] an only child, was marrying Michael,[*] who had a sibling. When Reba and Michael became engaged, the bride's parents asked the groom's folks to contribute toward the wedding, requesting a set amount of money. Thrilled that "their kids" were getting married, the groom's parents readily agreed. That done, their wedding planning went full steam ahead with many ideas coming from other weddings the very social young couple were attending. The more weddings they attended, the more interesting "gotta-have" things Reba saw.

The cost of the wedding was escalating by leaps and bounds. But her parents loved her to pieces. She was, after all, their darling daughter and it was her wedding! They vowed that Reba would have whatever her heart desired on this special day. Cost would be no object, they said—until they ran short of wedding money. Since both sets of parents were sharing the cost of making the wedding, Reba's folks asked

[*]The names have been changed to protect the spendthrift.

Michael's dad for several thousand additional dollars to split the difference of the over-the-budget expenses. Needless to say, that put an immediate crimp on the so-far-amicable parental partnership. And when *machetenestas* start to squabble, things can get messy for all concerned.

Fortunately, the groom's family was able to scrape up the additional dollars, albeit reluctantly. The resulting wedding was indeed perfect. A dream come true, the groom's side admitted. But the underlying strain between families may yet take years to dissolve.

In addition to going over budget, the lopsided list may infiltrate this scenario as well. Even though both sets of parents may agree to split the costs, if the bride's list adds up to a hundred people while the groom's side is short-listed at thirty-five, trouble may ensue.

Best bet: parents should avoid the decision to "split the costs" or "go fifty-fifty" without qualifying it on a "percentage of use" basis. First decide what expenses fall outside the joint parameters: perhaps the expense of the bride's wedding gown or the cost of his tuxedo. Then, a look at each side's guest list would show who needs to pay more of the share. And when figuring the size of the lists, try to estimate the number of people who will actually *show up* as best as you can. Counting invited guests whom you feel fairly certain won't come is a false indicator of your costs. But allow a few in the count for pleasant surprises. It's a tricky dance, but if both sets of parents are up front from the get-go about sharing equitably rather than necessarily equally, things will go a lot smoother.

Groom's parents pay for the entire wedding. It's not unheard of for the father or parents of the groom to host the wedding and reception in its entirety. Perhaps the bride's family is unavailable or unable to afford a wedding. Then, too, the two families involved may have very different ideas about weddings. The bride's family may not believe in large (or even medium-sized) weddings. For them, an officiant, two witnesses, and city hall will do. Or let's face it: maybe they're just plain cheap and difficult. On the other hand, if the groom has always wanted a big wedding and his parents have been looking forward to "marrying off their son in style," they may decide to foot the bill. They may also want the wedding to double as a business/social event. Perhaps they simply love the bride and want to give her a memorable wedding. Bottom line: they agree to pay the bill—often, but not necessarily, with their son's financial contribution. Just remember this rule of thumb: the side that pays gets the say.

Cobbling dollars from divorced or separated parents. Family structures can include divorced or multiple divorced parents—some willing to contribute to a wedding, others hard-pressed or unwilling to do so. There's the doting step-parent who wants to be a major financial player; another who, sadly, wants no part of your wedding. When figuring the dollars and contributions, take into consideration that contributing step-parents or remarried parents may wish to invite their own guests to the wedding as well. They should be provided the opportunity to develop their own lists; you can then weed out those that duplicate guests you've already accounted for.

The grand connection. Oh what a joy! Your grandparents are *qvelling* with *nachos!* Their grandchild is getting married. And soon, they hope, they can be great-grandparents. Nothing would give them more pleasure than to dance at your wedding—and help pay for it, too.

Elder-dollars could be a wonderful blessing and even a save-the-day gift if the family is feeling cash-strapped. Tagging their gift to a particular "purchase" may make it more meaningful to them and less of a hassle when designing the wedding invitation verbiage. Would Grandma like to buy you your wedding gown? Or perhaps Gramps could host the rehearsal dinner.

Other contributors. Depending on family circumstances and the dynamics of today's intertwined relationships, there are no limits as to who can make or contribute to your wedding—with your approval, of course. The aunt or aunts of a bride can elect to fund the wedding or contribute to the affair. The biological parent of a child who was adopted may come forward and want to be a financial part of this event. And a loving foster parent may want to contribute. Even a group of close friends can get together and make a couple's dream come true.

It's not unusual, these days, to cobble together your wedding budget based on contributions from many sources. In this situation, the flat-rate approach works best—each contributor setting the dollar amount he or she is willing to invest. A gentle reminder to those who made promises but have yet to deliver in a timely fashion may be a necessary reality. Unfortunately, sometimes people get carried away when thinking of the wonderful things that they'd love to do for you lovebirds, and then find themselves hard-pressed to deliver. Others may be unaware of your timetable and the up-front deposits you'll be required to make. Still others may be thinking of offering their share as a check on your actual wedding day. So as you plan your wedding, do so with dollars already in hand.

Another way to handle the finances is the divide-and-conquer approach. Each contributing party claims responsibility for a particular segment or segments of the wedding—be it the flowers, the band, the transportation, or the catering. Their portion is billed directly to them by the vendor supplying that item. In this way, no one has to deal with the uncomfortable situation of asking others for money.

Bride and groom foot the bill themselves. With the average age of brides and grooms edging up, fewer and fewer couples are marrying "from their parents' house." Once established in their own careers and living accommodations (separately or together), a bride and groom may want to fund their own wedding. This is especially true if the bride has been married before. Whether simple or lavish, the planning, implementation, and financing of your wedding will just be between the two of you. Enjoy!

Methods of Delivery

Unless you're financing the wedding by yourselves, others may have a definite say in how they will deliver their dollars to you. Following are some suggestions for collecting contributions.

Pay-as-you-go plan. Depending on your family dynamics, this method can give your "benefactors" a little (okay, a *lot*) more control over the spending. Or, surprisingly, it can actually work to allow you to splurge on special touches. Since Dad and Mom (for example) will write out the checks or pass their plastic as payments are due, there's always the possibility that they may not agree with your choices and with-hold payment, or insist on having a major say about how you plan your special day. This may prove to be your biggest nightmare. After all, it's *your* wedding, and you might begin to feel that your parents' taste and control are compromising the things that are important to you. On the other hand, it could be a blessing. If you're relatively inexperienced at comparison-shopping and negotiating, Mom and Dad may be able to work wonders for you. Remember, most parents have been through their own wedding, and may have previously planned weddings for your siblings as well. And if your parents *don't* have a tight budget, the pay-as-you-go approach can allow room for upward adjustments when you spot something that simply *must* be included in your wedding.

The flat-rate approach. In this case, your parents let you know exactly how much they're going to contribute to your wedding. Perhaps it's the same amount they spent on a sibling's wedding—no more, no less. Or a sum they've saved over the years. They hand you the money and you're on your own. You can spend it all or scale down the wedding and keep the rest toward your new life together. Or you can even elope and stash the cash. You control your wedding, but the budget is usually strictly enforced.

Sweet Charity

Remembering the sick or poor on your day of joy is a Jewish custom that allows others to benefit from your good fortune. Giving *tzedakah* (charity) can take many forms. The groom's family, as well as the bride's, can donate *tzedakah* in honor of the newlyweds. The bride and groom themselves can make contributions to their favorite charities. Or guests can be directed to make charitable contributions in the bride and groom's names.

Since many caterers will not donate leftover food to the poor or homeless shelters for food safety reasons, a better way is to donate a certain percentage of your catering costs (suggestion: 3 percent) to Mazon. This national nonprofit agency allocates donations from the Jewish community to nonprofit organizations that provide food, help, and hope to hungry people of all faiths and backgrounds. Reach the national office by contacting Mazon: A Jewish Response to Hunger, 1990 South Bundy Drive, Suite 260, Los Angeles, California 90025-5232. Phone: (310) 442-0020; fax: (310) 442-0030. For further information, the Web site is www.mazon.org. You can also donate to local food banks and charities in your area.

Another opportunity to be charitable is to donate flowers. Instead of having guests take home the wedding flowers, with the administration's permission, donate them to a nearby hospital or nursing home. If that's your plan, inform the master of ceremonies at your reception to make the appropriate announcement so that guests won't unknowingly take them home.

Step Three: Zipping It Together

Once you know how much money you have available, you can draw up your budget. And yes, you do need one. Rather than being a restrictive concept, your wedding budget will help you make choices that mesh your dream with reality. It will also guide you in making creative choices that can best reflect and fulfill your fairy-tale dream.

Equipped with the dollar value in your wedding's "cash register" on the one hand, and the elements of your ultradream wedding on the other, you can begin to prioritize your plans and make compromises when necessary to fit into your budget.

Say you are planning a wedding with two hundred guests. Here's how everything's been turning out so far. You've been looking at wedding gowns in the fifteen-hundred-dollar price range. While meeting with the caterer, you discover that for an additional $2.50 per head, you can offer guests a third entrée choice. That comes to five hundred dollars more. The invitations you are seriously considering will require additional postage due to their weight. You plan to order 150 invitations, remembering that married couples or those living together usually share one invitation. So you figure you'll need about thirty-five dollars extra for the additional postage. Your second choice of invitations, while the same price, would eliminate the extra postage charge. You can have the envelopes addressed in hand calligraphy, or perhaps save about a hundred dollars by having them done by computerized ink jet. And finally, you've narrowed your choice down to two wedding favors. Although you're more partial to one, this choice would add a total cost of a hundred dollars to your tally.

The time has come for compromise.

You'd really like to add that third dinner choice because you know for a fact that Uncle Marty hates chicken and can't digest beef. And your future "dad," the politician, is tired of all those rubber chicken dinners but must watch his cholesterol. For them and others, a fish dish would be best. And you, yourself, fell in love with the idea of dining on sumptuous Salmon en Croute. Ding! There's an unexpected five hundred dollars out of your cash register. How can you make up the difference so you can remain within your budget?

Well, you did see another wedding gown that looked great on you, and it was only thirteen hundred dollars. You decide you don't need the one with the bustle at your butt after all. Bing! That'll save you two hundred bucks. And what about the invitations? You really, *really* love the ones you selected, despite the need for additional postage. It's a sacrifice you're not willing to make. But despite your mother's protest, you feel that computerized calligraphy instead of hand-crafted lettering would be just fine. Bing! You've "collected" another hundred dollars. Only two hundred left to go.

How about those wedding favors? You could go with your second choice, which are just as lovely. Bing! A hundred bucks saved, and only a hundred to go.

Yes, I know that those last hundred dollars (like those last five pounds) are always the hardest. But wait a second. Your old college roomie mentioned that she would be on her own honeymoon on the date of your wedding. You're horribly disappointed that she and her new husband won't be there to share your special day. But . . . at

$100 a plate for the catering (oops, now $102.50 with the added choice of a fish entrée), that will actually cut more than $200 from your total.

So now you can reinstate the hand calligraphy, make your mother happy, and keep the wedding budget on track. Or—you can forget the hand calligraphy, borrow your sister's headpiece, and order the original wedding bustle-back gown after all.

And there you go! With a little compromise and a clear view of what's really important to you, your real-life wedding can also turn out to be your dream come true.

Red Ink Removers

Are your expenses bloated? Is the red ink figuratively dripping from your bottom line? Fear not. Just explore some cost-cutting options:

- ❦ Get married on an off-peak day. Sunday-afternoon weddings are popular, yet may be less expensive then those held on a Saturday night. Thursday evening is a sophisticated choice, and Tuesday is an appropriate religious day on which to marry.

- ❦ Cut down your guest list. In addition to saving on the per-head catering costs, there will be fewer favors to buy, fewer invitations to order and mail, and, if you cut out a table or two, fewer floral centerpieces to order.

- ❦ Hold the wedding ceremony outdoors in a community park—with proper permissions from the town or city, of course. You may have to purchase a permit, but it will most likely be relatively inexpensive. Also, holding a wedding outdoors is a longtime Jewish tradition.

❦ Hold a craft gathering. Invite members of your wedding party to help create labor-intensive items that will reduce the cost of professional decorating expenses. Craft ideas to consider: making the *chuppah,* the ring pillow, the bride's gift bag, centerpieces, computer-generated place cards and "hold-the-date" announcements, and programs with explanations of Jewish ceremonial rituals and customs.

❦ Be creative with space decor. Fill large background spaces with rented or borrowed silk or live trees rather than fresh flowers. Save the flowers for areas that people more readily notice. And don't book a room that's too big for your crowd. It will be costly trying to fill large expanses of "nothingness."

❦ Planning a morning-after brunch for stay-over guests? Substitute breakfast instead.

❦ Determine how many musicians you *actually* need (it's usually determined by guest head count) and cut back on extras.

❦ Look for ways to eliminate hidden expenses: the design of the cake, the type of flowers in the centerpieces, the fabric of the wedding gown. Become a comparison-shopper for all wedding items.

You Shouldn't Know From It But . . .

You've been busy planning your wedding, putting down deposits on this, and deposits on that. The caterer required half the total amount way before your wedding. The band's contract insisted on one-third down upon signing.

Your wedding is all planned and set to go when the unthinkable happens. The reception hall goes bankrupt, the groom's dad gets rushed to the hospital, the dog eats your wedding gown, or the blizzard of the century strikes, closing all area airports and roadways.

Given the high cost of many weddings today, it's a good idea to insure it! You have collision and comprehensive insurance on your new car. Most people wouldn't think of owning a new (or semi-new) car without it. Today's weddings can cost about as much as that car—maybe even more.

Most contracts you sign with vendors hold you liable for payment for their services for a specific day and time, no matter what.

Wedding insurance, underwritten by the Fireman's Fund, is available at a nominal fee and, together with options, can cover you for a host of unexpected situations. Did your caterer forget to show? You can be covered up to the insured amount minus a deductible. Did your photographer fail to come, and you need to gather the wedding party for a reshoot? Were the groomsmen's tuxedos stolen? These and many other situations can be covered. Be sure to check the policy for details of actual coverage and complete information. What it won't insure you against, however, is a change of heart!

Traditional Financial Breakdown

Bride's Side

- Bride's dress, veil, and accessories

- Lingerie

- Honeymoon outfits

- Mother-of-the-bride dress and accessories

- Father-of-the-bride formalwear/suit and accessories

- ❦ Household items, bath and kitchen items, linens (not received as gifts)
- ❦ Paper, printing, addressing, and postage for invitations and announcements; other stationery (except for groom's personal stationery)
- ❦ Imprinted and specialty items such as napkins, ribbon, matchbooks
- ❦ *Tzedakah* (gift to charity)
- ❦ Engagement party
- ❦ Bridesmaids' party
- ❦ Cost of ceremony site
- ❦ Fees for setting up site, rental of *chuppah,* aisle carpet, seating, other rentals
- ❦ Flowers for the *chuppah,* ceremony site, gazebo, reception site, at-home parties
- ❦ Bouquets/corsages for maid or matron of honor, bridesmaids, flower girl's basket
- ❦ Music for ceremony and reception
- ❦ Groom's wedding ring
- ❦ Bride's gift to the groom
- ❦ Gifts for maid or matron of honor, bridesmaids, and flower girl
- ❦ Gifts for the bride's parents to give to the bride and groom
- ❦ Engagement and wedding photography and albums
- ❦ Videography
- ❦ Housing for female members of bridal party
- ❦ Extra help: valet parking, traffic control, wedding-time baby-sitting, and so on
- ❦ Transportation (limousines, et cetera) to ceremony and reception and back for bridal party

- Reception-related costs including rental of site, food, liquor, and decor
- Tipping

Groom's Side

- Bride's engagement ring or gift
- Bride's wedding ring
- *Ufruf* donation and any related expenses
- *Ufruf* reception and/or *kiddish*
- Groom's gift to bride
- Groom's formalwear/suite and accessories
- Groom's father's formalwear/suit and accessories
- Mother-of-the-groom's dress and accessories
- Bride's bouquet
- Bride's going-away corsage
- Boutonnières for groom
- Boutonnières for fathers, stepfathers (if appropriate), grandfathers, and great-grandfathers
- Boutonnières for best man, ushers/attendants, and ring boy
- Corsages for mothers, stepmothers (if appropriate), grandmothers, and great-grandmothers
- Marriage license
- Extra-guest catering per-head charges
- Officiants' fee—rabbi, cantor, and so on

- 🐚 *Tzedakah* (gift to charity)

- 🐚 Groom's personal stationery

- 🐚 Bachelor's dinner (groom's family—optional)

- 🐚 Second engagement party (optional)

- 🐚 Ushers', best man's, and ring boy's gifts

- 🐚 Ushers' and best man's housing, if necessary

- 🐚 Family/rehearsal dinner

- 🐚 Cigars and cigarettes (if politically correct in time and place)

- 🐚 Transportation to airport for honeymoon

- 🐚 Honeymoon

- 🐚 New home/furnishings (big pieces)

Bride's Attendants

- 🐚 Their part of the shower

- 🐚 A shower gift

- 🐚 Their dresses

- 🐚 Their accessories

- 🐚 Their part of a bachelorette party or girls' night on the town (if given)

- 🐚 Transportation to and from the wedding (if from out of town)

- 🐚 Wedding gift for the couple

- 🐚 If local, may offer to host out-of-town attendants (also see "Bride's Side")

- 🐚 Assorted errand running

Groom's Attendants

- Their tuxedos or suits

- The bachelor party

- If local, may offer to host out-of-town attendants (also see "Groom's Side")

- Transportation to and from the wedding (if from out of town)

- Wedding gift for the couple

- Decorate groom's car (if legal in the wedding's municipality) with JUST MARRIED sign, trail of shoes, tin cans, and so forth

- Assorted errand running

More Savvy Saving Solutions

- Buy a diamond that shows more face than depth. It might look bigger when set.

- Have talented friends design table centerpieces.

- Compare costs of a buffet reception versus a sit-down dinner.

- Serve open bar during the cocktail hour; switch to punch, wine, and beer during the reception.

- If your guests tend to be eaters instead of drinkers, consider a hosted bar (each drink put on your tab) instead of an open bar throughout the cocktail hour and dinner. Ask "per-drink" versus "open-bar" prices.

- Skip white-glove service.

- Don't have servers automatically refill empty glasses. Let guests ask or go up to the bar.

- Cut the Viennese table and serve petits four at each table along with wedding cake.

- Enlist a friend's cool car for transportation instead of hiring a car and driver.

- Rent just about anything you can instead of buying it. Check price differentials, first, however.

- Send beautiful thank-you notes without enclosing a wedding photo in each.

- Make up engagement party or shower invitations, wedding programs, and direction sheets on your home computer rather than having them engraved or thermographed.

- Choose a reception hall that already looks good, eliminating the need for massive decorating.

- Order standard wedding packages and upgrade selectively.

- All prices and quality being reasonably equal, consider the caterer who adds no-charge extras such as linens, dance floors, and decor.

- Consider plated dinner service in a restaurant's party room.

- Purchase your own liquor if the caterer allows.

- Elope!

Quiz: How Much Do You Know About Wedding Finances?

Does your concept of wedding dollars make sense? Before you ask your parents to dip into their retirement savings, and before you max out all your credit cards, see how much you really know about wedding costs and the reality of funding your dream. Choose the answer that best completes each statement by circling the corresponding letter.

1. Oh my goodness! Your dream of marrying the perfect prince is coming true. You have your wedding clearly in mind, so:

   a) with trusty charge card in hand, you quickly book and leave deposits with the caterer, band, photographer, and florist before someone else grabs them away.

   b) you ask Daddy to hand over a check for thirty thousand dollars within two days. You feel that if you pay for the wedding and reception in advance, there's no way it can be called off.

   c) considering your families' dynamics, you hold discussions to sort out who will be contributing and how much they can offer, thus arriving at a reality-based budget. You then make choices that mesh with the amount of money available for the wedding.

   d) You put financial considerations out of your mind. After all, the wedding is still three months away!

2. You know there isn't enough money available to fuel your Cinderella-like wedding dream, so you:

   a) mail out a letter with a pledge card to every friend and relative, asking them to circle the amount they will contribute toward your wedding.

   b) beg your banker for a loan, which you will pay back over a ten-year period. You offer your engagement ring as collateral.

c) call off your engagement. If you can't have the wedding of your dreams, you don't want to get married at all!

d) find creative ways to lower the wedding expenses. After all, marriage is about loving your partner, not about how much you spend on the party.

3. You're planning to get married in eighteen months and have eight thousand dollars saved toward the wedding. You'd like to keep what you have and get some more, so you:

a) withdraw the money in your individual retirement account and invest in pork bellies.

b) invest aggressively in the stock market.

c) buy a jumbo certificate of deposit with a two-year maturity date.

d) talk with several certified investment advisers before making any investment decisions.

4. All things being equal, the cost of a wedding and a reception tends to be:

a) the same all over the country.

b) less expensive if you take out a bank loan and pay for it all up front.

c) less expensive if held during off-peak times.

d) cheaper by the dozen. Invite everyone!

5. When preparing your wedding budget, you should:

a) toss your efforts into the shredder. It's boring and so unnecessary.

b) remember that guests under sixteen eat for free.

c) add 10 percent to the total budget for unexpected costs.

d) mimic your friend's wedding budget. She had the same type of wedding you're planning, although she lives in a different area of the country.

Answers: 1—c; 2—d; 3—d; 4—c; 5—c.

Scoring: Give yourself 5 points for each correct answer.

0–5 points: Stop right here. Don't touch a penny until you get some decent professional advice, darling. And while you're at it, find out about an investment plan that will work for you and your honey *after* you're married, too.

10–15 points: Okay, you win some and you lose some. But your goal is to win some and keep all—until you pay your wedding bills, that is. You and your honey should get together and talk to investment professionals. They can guide you toward the best place for your money right now. You'll need to consider the amount of money you have, the current investment climate, and your wedding date. Then set up a plan for your post-wedding investments, too.

20–25 points: Hey, are you a stockbroker or an investment banker or something? Be sure, however, to consider the date you'll need to start shelling out the dollars (deposits, you know) when making your plans. And it never hurts to talk to other knowledgeable people (read: *professionals*) for opinions, too. Use your smarts to set up a savings and investment plan for your successful financial future together.

3

With This Ring

YOU'RE STANDING UNDER THE *chuppah* on this magical day, a true queen as every Jewish bride is considered to be. And the long-awaited moment has come—you and your love are about to officially become husband and wife under Jewish law.

Your ring bearer has nervously walked down the aisle with your wedding band nestled atop a small white pillow. Or perhaps your honey's best man is fumbling in his jacket pocket to produce the simple gold ring that will help unite you and your *be-shert* as one.

After your groom specifies a witness who attests to the ring's minimal value, the rabbi accepts the ring—considered to be the monetary equivalent by which the groom "acquires" the bride. As you wait in joyous anticipation, the rabbi hands it to your groom as part of the betrothal ceremony. All eyes are focused on this plain metal ring. Along with your acceptance of it, it holds the power to change your life forever.

Mesmerized, you offer the index finger of your right hand to your groom, ready to accept the ring. And following prompted words (lest he forget in his nervous state), your groom repeats the ancient wedding formula both in Hebrew and English—or Hebrew and a language native to your country:

"Har'ey aht me'kudeshet le, b'taba'at zo, k'dat Mo'sheh v'Yisro'el."
"With this ring, you are consecrated unto me according to the law of
Moses and of Israel."

He then slips the ring onto your finger.

Although not practiced by many Orthodox Jews, these days, a double-ring ceremony is not unusual. The bride, in turn, can slip a ring onto her groom's finger. She
need not say a word, but if she chooses, she can repeat to him the *Har'ey aht* formula
adjusted for the female gender—changing the word *aht* to *ahtah*. She may also recite
this beautiful passage:

"Ah'nee l'dodi v'dodi le."
"I am for my beloved and my beloved is for me."

Engaged in Rings

But let's rewind for a bit. Back to your engagement. Unlike the marriage ceremony, where the ring is unadorned, there are no such restrictions on your engagement ring.

In fact, for many brides, receiving a diamond ring epitomizes the "official" beginning of the couple's path toward marital bliss. Of course, there are suitable substi-
tutes—anything from a cigar ring (how fun!), to a watch, to a family heirloom, to
other types of precious or semiprecious stones. And for those who like the sparkle of
diamonds but have limited funds, or would rather spend their dollars differently, there
are manufactured "diamonds" such as cubic zirconia (CZ for short), and the more expensive but far more brilliant moissanite.

But it's the natural diamond—that chunk of ice with the heart of fire—that has
long held the mystique that tantalizes man and woman alike. A symbol of enduring
love, diamonds have been around for millions of years.

Whether your honey surprises you with a ring or you pick one out together, buying, receiving, or giving a diamond is not an everyday ho-hum activity (unless you're in the diamond or jewelry business).

Before setting out to invest in a diamond, you need to arm yourself with some basic information. Knowledge is buying power. It's easy for the uninitiated to get overwhelmed—and ripped off.

Buying a diamond ring is so filled with emotion that it's difficult to keep a clear head. And although the majority of those selling diamonds are helpful, honest, and thrilled to share a slice of this fabulous time in your life, there are always some vultures seeking to take advantage of those with their heads in the clouds.

What you spend on an engagement ring is entirely up to you. But you want to make sure you get what you pay for!

Before you let emotions force your honey into buying what might be the wrong ring, put on your "wise consumer's hat," and look for the four C's that determine value: cut, color, clarity, and carats. You might want to add a fifth: cost!

Cut

A diamond's *cut* refers to the proportion, symmetry, and finish of the stone. The cut can make the difference between a stone that sparkles with fire and brilliance or one that just sits there—kind of flat and not doing very much. The cut is a combination of the stone's natural properties and the precision and talent of the diamond cutter to make the most of what the stone has to offer.

To maximize the brilliance of the stone, the diamond cutter must place each of the diamond's facets, which act as light-dispersing mirrors, in exact geometric relation to one another. Many finished diamonds have fifty-eight facets.

Color

The Gemological Institute of America (GIA) grades the color of diamonds using a scale of D through Z. Other organizations may grade diamonds on a different scale. According to the GIA in the normal color range, less is more! D, having no visible coloration, is their highest rating. Differences in color can affect the price of the diamond. True "colorless" diamonds are rare; diamonds in the normal color range are *nearly* colorless, with faint yellow or brown tints.

Now that you *think* you might have even a tiny handle on this color(less) thing, take a deep breath. We're going fancy! The GIA advises that naturally colored diamonds with a depth of body color are considered "fancies." Although a diamond in pink, blue, yellow, orange, black, brown, green, red, purple, or violet may tickle *your* fancy, don't get your hopes up. They are rare. And they can be pricey.

Clarity

Called quality in Europe, *clarity* is a measure of purity: how free the stone is from inclusions—spots of trapped carbon, crystals within the stone, and blemishes on the surface of the polished diamond. The fewer inclusions and blemishes, the better. Clarity has a major impact on the value of the stone.

A diamond can only be considered flawless if it has no visible surface cracks or other imperfections when viewed under 10X magnification by a skilled diamond grader:

GIA Clarity Scale

(Fl) | FLAWLESS
Shows no inclusions or blemishes of any sort under 10X magnification when observed by an experienced grader.

(IF) | INTERNALLY FLAWLESS
Has no inclusions when examined by an experienced grader using 10X magnification, but will have some minor blemishes.

(VVS1 and VVS2) | VERY VERY SLIGHTLY INCLUDED
Contains minute inclusions that are difficult even for experienced graders to see under 10X magnification.

(VS1 and VS2)	VERY SLIGHTLY INCLUDED Contains minute inclusions such as small crystals, clouds, or feathers when observed with effort under 10X magnification.
(SI1 and SI2)	SLIGHTLY INCLUDED Contains inclusions (clouds, included crystals, knots, cavities, and feathers) that are noticeable to an experienced grader under 10X magnification.
(I1, I2, I3)	INCLUDED Contains inclusions (possibly large feathers or large included crystals) that are obvious under 10X magnification and may affect transparency and brilliance.

© GIA. Reprinted by permission.

Carats

The weight of a diamond is stated in carats—described as a decimal or fraction of a carat. If the weight is given in decimal parts of a carat, the Federal Trade Commission (FTC) advises that the figure should be accurate to the last decimal place. For example, a "0.30 carat" diamond could represent one that weighs in between 0.295 and 0.304 carat. If your diamond merchant describes the diamond in fractions, such as "½ carat," it could actually weigh between 0.47 and 0.54 carat. If your retailer is describing the diamond by fractional parts of a carat, he or she should disclose the fact that the weight is *not* exact and also the reasonable range of weight for each fraction or the weight tolerance being used. A carat is *not* a determination of how large the diamond is.

Caveat

A little knowledge is not a substitute for the analytical or appraisal services of a credentialed jeweler or gemologist. Before purchasing a particular diamond or piece of jewelry, please consult with a credentialed jeweler or gemologist about the importance and interrelationship of cut, color, clarity, and carat weight.

Consider Certified

Most good jewelers will have certified diamonds available for sale. Before you buy a diamond, you'll want to see a copy of its certification, because this represents your guarantee of the value and quality of the stone. A certificate can also be called a diamond grading report, diamond dossier, or diamond quality report. It's developed by one or more gemologists who have analyzed it under a microscope to check out its dimensions, clarity, cut, color, finish, symmetry, and other factors.

There are various certifying laboratories, but the GIA and American Gem Society (AGS) are independent labs, and most respected in the industry. A certification from either of these two is "the gold standard."

In Europe, HRD in Antwerp, Belgium, is accredited to grade polished diamonds. If you're excited about a diamond that isn't certified, you can always send it out for certification.

The Band

Bands come in varying widths, metals, and embellishments. Of course, your wedding band will be plain, no-frills gold or made of another metal. But you can always give your honey a second band after the ceremony to wear on other occasions. It can be embellished with diamonds or other stones, and be composed of mixed metals. White and yellow gold can be mixed, as can the triple golds: white, pink, and yellow. There's also platinum, a very popular choice.

Inscribing Your Band

Inscribing the inside of your wedding band can add much more meaning to something so meaningful to begin with! The inscription might be your initials and those of your love and the date of your marriage. A tag line, such as "forever" or "with love," can be added.

Hebrew by Design

Some jewelers or catalogs carry *dodi* rings, available for both men and women. The wide band is intricately cut out to form the Hebrew words dear to your heart. Other rings can be embossed on the outside of the wide band.

Have It Appraised

You'll need to do this for insurance purposes, so don't be shy! Just as you may bring a used car to an independent appraiser before you buy it from a used-car dealership, so too should you get your potential purchase appraised. The appraiser you select should be a Graduate Gemologist, holding a G.G. degree from the Gemological Institute of America; holding an F.G.A. degree from the Gemological Association of Great Britain (there are U.S. offices as well); or be certified by the American Society of Appraisers. Be sure you ask for the fee in advance. It could be based on the carat weight of the stone or on an hourly rate.

The appraisal should include the value of the stone or ring, a detailed description, the dimensions, weight, quality, and an ID of each stone, with information about its tone, intensity, hue, transparency, and clarity. For diamonds, it must include the four C's, as well as identify the metal used to mount your stone.

Insure It

Talk to your insurance agent about adding your ring to your homeowner's or renter's insurance. Many policies allow you to itemize your jewelry separately. You'll need the appraisal as well as a photo of your ring. Don't forget to read the fine print: some companies may cap the amount you can claim if you experience a loss.

If you don't have a homeowner's or rental policy, or want to check out another option, look into Jewelers Mutual, a company that offers personal jewelry insurance.

Birthstones

If diamonds are not your forte, pretty birthstones can be lovely for engagement rings. And there's nothing to say you can't add little diamonds to the side of a birthstone.

January—garnet
February—amethyst
March—aquamarine
April—diamond
May—emerald
June—pearl
July—ruby
August—peridot
September—sapphire
October—opal
November—citrine topaz
December—turquoise

The Gold Standard

Before you "go for the gold," know your markings. The word *gold* by itself really means twenty-four karat (24K), which is all gold. Nothing added. But pure gold, as wonderful as it sounds, is actually very soft, so it's usually mixed with other metals to make it more durable.

The karat marking on the gold tells you what proportion of gold is mixed with other metals. Fourteen-karat gold (14K) is fourteen parts of gold mixed throughout with ten parts of base metal. Thus, the higher the karat rating, the more gold is in the ring or piece of jewelry. Following are some gold terms you should know.

Solid gold. No, it's not a vintage 45-rpm rock record or an old CD. When it comes to jewelry, *solid gold* refers to any karat gold, if the inside of the item is not hollow.

Gold plate.   Gold that is plated to a base metal. This can be accomplished by mechanical means, electroplate, or a few other ways. Eventually gold plating wears away; how soon depends on how thickly it was plated with gold and how often the gold is worn.

Gold electroplate.   This describes jewelry that has a layer (at least 17.3 microns thick) of a minimum of ten-karat gold placed on the base metal by an electrolytic process.

Gold-flashed or gold-washed.   These terms are used to describe products that have less than 0.175 micron of gold electroplated onto the base metal. Items so marked will wear away more quickly than gold plate, gold-filled, or gold electroplate.

Gold-filled.   Jewelry that has a layer of at least ten-karat gold mechanically bonded to a base metal. If the jewelry is marked as "gold-filled," it should include the karat quality of the gold used. If the layer of karat gold is less than one-twentieth of the total weight of the piece, the marking must state the actual percentage of karat gold, such as "$\frac{1}{40}$ 14K gold-filled."

Ring Facts

- A ring is not used in the marriage ceremony at all times. Sephardic brides may be given a gold coin instead.

- It's said that the first diamond engagement ring was given by the emperor of Austria in 1477.

- The ring is a symbol of eternity since it has no beginning and no end. Thus it can represent the unending happiness of your marriage.

- In the traditional Jewish ceremony, the wedding ring must be made of metal unembellished with stones so that its minimal value can be determined.

❧ Although gold is the "gold standard" for the wedding band, any metal, including platinum, can be used.

❧ For those who don't subscribe to the double-ring ceremony due to religious considerations, the bride can give the groom a ring during *yichud*, or sometime later.

❧ The wedding band must belong to the groom prior to his giving it to the bride.

4

The Invitations

THE NAMES HAVE BEEN rolling around in your head ever since you got engaged. Who will you invite to your wedding? And on the other side of that coin comes the troubling question: who can you *eliminate* from that growing list without causing permanent damage to those relationships?

You sit down with a pad and paper, or perhaps at your computer keyboard, and start drawing up "The List." And hardly just begun, you've already hit five major snags:

1. Your father and mother, divorced about five years ago, still refuse to be in the same room together. Yet you love them both dearly, and you want them by your side as you walk down the aisle.

2. You love your second cousin Ivy, and the two of you are very close. Of course, she's one of the first people you put on your list. But does that mean you have to invite twelve other second cousins—some you know and some you don't?

3. Your mother was invited to her childhood friend's daughter's wedding in Florida three years ago and now it's Mom's turn to reciprocate. But does a limited budget for guests mean you have to eliminate your fringe-friend Caroline?

4. You work with Mary, Sue, Brett, Joan, and Dan. But only you and Joan are "this-close." Must you invite the others?
5. Cousin Evelyn fully expects that her three rabble-rousing kids will be invited. At the last family wedding, her four-year-old twins set fire to a tablecloth and her infant wailed in full voice during the cantor's beautiful rendition of *"Erev Shel Shoshanim."* What should you do?

After careful consideration, you decide it's time to tell your parents to grow up and get over it. They both mean the world to you and they *have* to behave if only for this one special day. You decide that you are *not* inviting any second cousins whom you wouldn't recognize even if you were riding in the same elevator. And that's that, Mom! But you also feel that in the long run, helping to maintain your mom's thirty-five-year friendship with Molly is more important than inviting your fringe-friend Caroline—especially since she's not part of your close-knit coterie and you'll probably lose touch with each other anyway when she moves to Dallas. As for your team at work, you decide that you will not invite any of your colleagues. And as far as Cousin Evelyn goes, she has forced you to institute the "no kids under five" rule, with the exception of your flower girl, who is, after all, your sister's daughter.

It was hard, it was gut wrenching, and you feel slightly uncomfortable, but alas: mission accomplished. You at last have your list. End of round one.

Round two comes when you and your beloved compare lists and tally up the final damage. At this point, judging from the numbers on your individual lists, a decision may be made as to how you're going to split the bill. A major consideration you will have while you're making up your list is whether or not you should invite people you absolutely know will not be able to attend. Do you invite Tante Chana who lives in Israel? Or Uncle Max who lives across the country and is in ill health?

Some feel that sending an invitation to people in these circumstances is an imposition on them. They may feel compelled to send a gift or at least go through the trouble of sending their regrets. But in the Jewish tradition, you'll send the invitation anyway—it's a way of honoring the recipients and letting them know you love and care for them.

By Golly, You've Got It!

With your combined lists whittled into place, it's time to get "The List" charted. By doing so, you'll be able to keep track of your guests. Go high-tech with an interactive guest list online, or set up your list on a spreadsheet such as Microsoft's Excel or a database program like Microsoft's Access. If you're using the computer for your list, be sure to keep a backup copy! If you're not the computer type, devise a manual chart with all the information.

On your spreadsheet, database, or wide piece of paper, set up columns for the fields of data you'll need to keep track of. Column headings should include: the names of your guests as you would address them on an envelope (husband and wife together, for example); separate fields for the wife's and children's first names (to help when writing thank-you notes); address; number of people in the party; date the invitation was mailed; engagement or shower gift (date and item); date you mailed the thank-you note; date the wedding response came back; number of people actually coming in response to your invitation; wedding gift received and what it was; and when you mailed your wedding gift thank-you notes. Yes, it *is* a big chart with lots of columns, but keeping all the information in one place will be ever so helpful as you orchestrate the days and months to come.

You're Invited

With everything you have to do, don't forget the key element: actually inviting your guests. And be sure to send copies of your invitation to your parents, your officiant(s), and save one for the photographer, who may wish to photograph it as backdrop for one of the pictures in your wedding album. Last, but certainly not least, remember to save a few "keepsake" copies for yourselves!

When to Order

Getting or making invitations is a *process,* so start early—about five months before your wedding if possible. This will allow you enough time to develop your wording, select your invitations, get proofs, and have the invitations printed up and delivered to you for addressing or sent out to a calligrapher. Once they're ready, you still have to put them together, stamp them, and get them in the mail in time for your guests to respond. Be sure to allow extra time if you're having a destination wedding and people need to make travel plans.

When to Mail

For the "standard" wedding, invitations should be mailed six to eight weeks before the special day. If you know many of your guests live far away or have superbusy social schedules, mail closer to the eight-week date.

Perhaps you have a small family or want to invite just a few close family members and friends to join you on your wedding day. Or maybe you've impulsively decided to get married two weeks from today. For those types of affairs, you may decide to send out informal notes inviting your guests, or just make personal phone calls. Under most circumstances, informal invitations should go out within a month of the date. But if you're scrounging for time and the wedding is informal, you can (precariously) wait until two or three weeks before.

If you're having a destination wedding, allow at least three months between mailing out invitations and the wedding. But you probably need to keep guests in the loop for much longer so they can save dollars and schedule their vacation time.

Being Selective

You and your honey meet at the stationery shop or wherever you have chosen to get your invitations from. You settle down and make yourself comfortable before the table of huge scrapbook-like catalogs. It's time to pore over those fat, elegant volumes filled with sample wedding invitations of every kind. Perhaps you already discussed your wedding invitations when you ordered your engagement notices, and you may already have a certain "look" in mind. But still, you can't help but take another glance.

Along with the invitations themselves, there are many other enclosures available. And if that's not enough, there are the choices of paper and font color, font style (including Hebrew), and the quality, thickness, and smoothness of the paper. Shall the paper content be wood or cotton? How about handmade?

Shall the style be formal, semiformal, contemporary, or reflect a theme? Simple or ornate? With or without embellishment? What about translucent overlays? Embossing? Appliqués? Fabric? And do you want one envelope or two? Lined or unlined? Or how about something unique like parchment paper sent as a scroll? Engraved or thermographed? Suffice to say, choosing your wedding invitation is not as simple as one-two-three.

Paper Patter

Since your invitation sets the tone for your wedding, you'll want it to reflect the type of wedding you're having. Most likely you'll select the best paper you can afford. Paper made from 100 percent cotton in a 40-pound weight is very smooth and luxurious. Like your wedding gown, the paper can be either white or off-white (ecru). While ecru is most popular in the United States, Crane & Co., paper makers, reports that white is more popular in Europe.

For a classic look, you can select plain invitations or invitations with panels. Generally, if you're using a script font, it will flow better when splayed across the invitation and not restricted by a panel. Conversely, print styles look more attractive when contained within a border.

If you are a bride who prefers some embellishment on her invitations, there's plenty to choose from. Some papers include embossed images and even appliqué, which could be perfect for less formal affairs—a beach wedding, for example. Your invitations could include artistic renditions of Jewish themes as well as prayers and sayings in Hebrew alone, or in Hebrew and English. One way to combine both language texts is to have the front of the invitation embellished with an artistic drawing, and have both English and Hebrew texts on facing inside pages. Another form puts one text on the outside and the other within.

There are many ideas out there for hand-creating your invitations. Take Ditti and Uri for example. Both living in and marrying in Israel, they decided to make their own invitations. They selected fabulous paper and made duplicate copies of an attractive photograph they glued to the front. They used computer-generated fonts to present the text inside the invitation. With a guest list in the hundreds (not unusual for an Israeli or Orthodox wedding, where three hundred guests could be considered a "small affair"), their handmade personal invitations carried the warmth of the loving couple directly to the recipients. The crafting of their invitations was a wonderful pre-wedding project. "We had photos, paper, and glue all over the apartment," Ditti recalls with a laugh.

Unique Invitations

Here are some interesting suggestions for unusual wedding invitations.

Tree-planting Invitation

Plant trees in Israel in honor of your guests and the Jewish National Fund will provide colorful wedding invitations customized for you.

CD or Audio Invitations

Your great-aunt Becky may not know what to do with it, but if you're inviting folks who have a CD player or a cassette recorder, why not send them a personal audio invitation? With the proper equipment, you can burn your own CD or make a cassette inviting your guests to your wedding, spoken in your own voice. You can add music in the background, making sure the all-important date, time, and place can be clearly heard above the tune.

Or log on to www.Wedding-Grams.com or www.Partypop.com to order Wedding-Grams. The company—HDI, Inc.—will make up individual personalized CDs for you. Give them a list of your guests' names, select the words for your invitation script, the background music you'd like, and the label art (or you can provide your own—perhaps your pictures). HDI will, in turn, make CDs individualized for each guest with his or her name mentioned on the audio invitation and on the label. The company can provide packaging, but you can also package the CDs yourselves or slip each one into the printed invitation you'll send to help make a more personal and emotional connection.

Let Us Count the Guests

Your guest list should be pretty well sewn up before you order your invitations. But things change. Suddenly his (or her) mom might come up with five or ten "forgotten" guests. Or perhaps you've inadvertently left others off the list. Not to mention that some invitations might get lost in the mail. When you're ordering them, be sure to get extra invitations and all accompanying inserts. It's easier and probably less expensive to get them up front than to order more later.

When tallying up your guest list, consider some individuals as couples or as part of family units. You may have Aunt Rose, Uncle Billy, and preteen children Georgia and Jeffrey. That's four guests but only one invitation. If Georgia and Jeffrey are eighteen or older, however, you'll need to send out three invitations: one to Aunt Rose and Uncle Billy, and a separate one to each of the now-adult children, even if they're living at home.

The Envelope, Please

The envelope should, of course, match your invitation. Some come with attractive linings that may add a little cost but a lot of "statement." You can get the traditional lick-and-seal kind or the self-sticking variety. Inner envelopes (see following page) are not sealed. Always order extras at the time that you order your invitations. Even if you're *sure* that you'll never make an error, it's been known to happen. And you may need to resend an invitation that has been returned as "undeliverable" from the post office. Ask if you can get the envelopes in advance of the invitations so that you can get a head start on the addressing process.

The Lore of the Double Envelope

Many wedding invitations today come with a double envelope. One houses the actual invitation; the other, slightly larger, serves as an outer envelope. Why two? It's a tradition that started a long time ago.

Way back when, a wedding was a big deal, just as it is today. As Crane & Co. (www.crane.com) says in its *Wedding Blue Book,* "If you were a bride back in those days, your footman delivered your invitations to your guests' homes. Their servants received the invitations and removed them from their mailing envelope, an envelope much too pedestrian for your guests to handle themselves. The servants, then, presented the invitation to your guests in its pristine inside envelope."

The book points out that since the invitation was already at your guests' home, the inner envelopes did not need to be addressed. They simply had to indicate the names of the household members who were being invited, so that each invitation could be properly directed.

Although times have changed, the tradition of the double envelope remains. Using a single envelope is still an option, however, and some styles are available only as singles.

Tips for Addressing Envelopes

- ♥ Married couples who are living together are addressed on the same line: Mr. and Mrs., followed by their address on subsequent lines.

- ♥ Two unmarried people living together each get their own line for their names, no joining word.

- Two engaged or seriously together people, living apart, should each get their own invitation.

- If one guest has a title and the other does not, the titled name comes first whether male or female. If partners have different names and each has a title, list them alphabetically by name.

- If a single guest is invited to bring a guest, try to find out the guest's name beforehand. If not possible, it's all right to then address the envelope "and guest."

- If a married woman and her husband are living together but she maintains her maiden name, list both her name and her husband's on separate lines; or join them on the same line.

- Kids over eighteen living at home should get their own invitations. Or you can choose to make the break once a son or daughter has become a *bar* or *bat mitzvah*. If more than one adult child lives at home, one invitation can be addressed to both.

- To address kids under eighteen (or thirteen) who are living at home, use just their first names on the line after their parents' names. Do not use the term "and family."

- If a woman has been divorced and has not remarried, address her as Ms. (or Mrs.) followed by her first and last names. She does not take her former husband's first name.

- A widow who has not remarried can use her husband's first name.

- Always address a person by the name he or she chooses to use.

And if perchance you were inviting the president of the United States and the first lady to join your *simcha,* you'd address both the outer and inner envelopes to "The President and Mrs. [last name]"—or "The President and Mr. [last name]."

Transferring Your Words to Paper

Engraving

Engraving is very expensive but produces the most elegant and traditional types of wedding invitations. Usually, the cost per invitation comes down as the quantity increases. So if you're having "the superformal wedding of the century" and inviting a lot of guests, this might be the option for you. You'll need to go to an upscale or boutique-type stationer, since most likely those catering to mass production don't take orders for engraved work. Allow eight or more weeks for your invitations to be ready.

Thermography

Thermography, explains Crane's *Wedding Blue Book,* "is sometimes called 'raised printing,' although the printing is not raised at all. Unlike engraving where the paper is actually raised, the raise in thermography is created by a resinous powder that is melted over the flat-printed ink. Thermography is less expensive than engraving and can give your invitations a look similar to but not quite as nice as engraving." This is the most popular method used today, and can save you a considerable amount of money and time over engraving.

Embossing

Sometimes referred to blind embossing because it uses no ink, in embossing a raised impression is made on the paper. It's very expensive, and sometimes used to create a border on your invitation. It can also be used for the return addresses on envelopes.

In addition to having your envelopes embossed professionally, you can buy an embossing tool—a handheld device you press together on the flap of an envelope to add your return address. It needs to be made to order. Since using the embossing device for your return address takes time, careful placement, and hand power, if you have a lot of invitations to send, it's best to have the return address put on the envelopes professionally.

Handling Responses (or Lack Thereof)

Years ago when women of leisure sat about hand-writing letters and responses to wedding invitations in third person, all was well with the world. A simple R.S.V.P. on the lower left of the invitation was all that was needed. Not only did she have the time, but she also had the know-how to handcraft the letter in the third person, either accepting or sending regrets.

Fast-forward to today's lifestyle. Women are working, raising families, attending classes, and practicing Kung Fu. They're sending e-mail, faxes, and using the phone. Yes, this is your very special day, and everyone *should* take the time to "do the right thing" and respond in the proper way. But to be gracious and help those you invite manage their time, you'll probably enclose a response card along with a stamped, self-addressed envelope for their convenience.

There are several different formats you can use for the reply card, but all use spaces for the guests' names and their response. A second ingredient is a request for a response, followed by a date by which the guest needs to respond.

Some folks today are so harried that they return the cards while forgetting to fill in their names. A little trick some use to track the missing: they code the response cards to their master guest list. Unobtrusively, in light pencil, they place a number on the inside of the response envelope's flap, or on the back of the response card itself. In that way, if the name is missing, they can match the returned envelope to the guest lists.

Some cards include a line for the number of people attending. It's a nice stab at making things easier when you're working up a head count, but it's a bad move when Aunt Aviva feels it's an invitation to bring along her four children and a houseguest. You might want to leave it out.

The response set you provide will use the same font as your invitations, but in a smaller size, with the return envelope addressed to the host of your wedding, you and your honey, or another person who is accepting the replies.

The stamp on the envelope will ideally match the stamp on the invitation. Many bridal families choose one of the attractive LOVE stamps issued by the U.S. Post Office, which are perfect for the occasion.

As the responses come in, keep them together in one spot—whether it's in the carton they came in, a shoe box, or a plastic box you pick up at the 99-cent store. Check them off on your master list, marking acceptances and regrets. You'll then be able to see at a glance just who has responded, and how many acceptances you have.

The "Forgetful" Responder

Despite all your efforts, there are usually at least a few people who don't make the deadline on the response cards. You steam, you toss a hissy fit, and you vow never to invite them to anything ever again. Wait a few more days if time allows. Then call them. Perhaps the response card *did* get lost in the mail. And heaven forbid, maybe they never even received your invitation (even though it didn't come back to you). Your family or friendship history may reveal that the same people consistently have stuff "lost in the mail." Do yourself a favor and don't just assume that they are coming even if they haven't responded yet. You could find yourself throwing significant money away on plates for no-show guests. Call them. Yes, it's hard to chase after people who don't care enough about you to think of your wedding, but the alternative is to pay the caterer and have the food go to waste.

Inserts

In addition to the actual invitation to your wedding, and the response card and envelope, there may be more information you need to tell your guests. That's where inserts come in. Some possible inserts include the following:

- Reception cards

- Direction cards with maps to the ceremony and reception

- Evening before family dinner information

- Transportation cards asking people to respond if they need transportation from the ceremony to the reception

- Accommodation cards for out-of-towners, letting them know about the availability of blocked hotel rooms. It's a good idea to add the hotel's cutoff date so they can make arrangements with the hotel in time

- *Shabbat* dinner invitation card for out-of-town guests

- Invitations for other events such as teas, a walking tour of the town, a bowling party

- An announcement about the availability of baby-sitting or supervisory services for the young children invited

You may see some additional insert offerings in wedding invitation catalogs, which may include pew cards, within-the-ribbon cards, and ceremony cards. These are not generally used for the Jewish wedding. They, may, however, be used for an interfaith wedding, depending on the way it's planned.

Proofing It

Proofreading is definitely one of *the* most important aspects of making up your invitations. Ask your printer for proofs, even if you have to pay for them. If you're ordering your invitations online, you may be able to get instant proofs.

When the proofs are available, bring along a "second set of eyes." Since you're familiar with what you wrote, your eyes may automatically skip over errors that a friend might pick up. Read the wording aloud. Go over it carefully, line by line. With both your eyes and ears working for you, you may pick up errors that your eyes alone may have missed.

After you've proofed your invitations, make any necessary corrections and point them out immediately. Find out how long it will take for the actual invitations and envelopes to come in. If you haven't received them by the specified date, be proactive. Call or e-mail to find out where they are and why the delay. You don't want your order to slip under a pile, forgotten! There's a chance that you may even need to send them back once again for correction—so don't let the time slip by.

Once your invitations have arrived, you're ready to make the final check. Again, bring some extra people with you if possible, and go over the invitations again. First and foremost, you'll be checking the same information that appeared on your proof to ensure that the printer made any necessary corrections, but you'll also be looking at the paper stock, ink, and other factors that didn't come into play when you saw your proof.

That Little Piece of Tissue Paper

Another tradition from the past, but one that can serve the present, is the little piece of tissue. Crane's *Wedding Blue Book* relates that the tissue was used to separate the invitations when they came from the printer. It prevented the slow-drying ink from smudging the invitations. Unwittingly, many brides at the time included the tissue with their invitations when they mailed them, and it became accepted practice either way.

Today you can send your invitations with or without tissue placed over the invitation and enclosures if you like. Is it proper etiquette? Opinions vary. One modern-day practicality of the tissue paper is that it does serve to prevent the postmark from possibly coming through onto the invitation. If you want your invitation's outer envelope to be particularly nice, ask your postmaster to hand-cancel the stamps.

Weighing In

Once you've picked up your invitations, take one complete set with all inserts to the post office. Have it weighed to see how much postage is required. Purchase enough for all the invitations you propose to send out, as well as first-class postage for the response envelopes.

Buy the postage you'll need for any invitations going to foreign countries as well. Ask your postmaster about purchasing international reply coupons to slip in with the response card in lieu of American postage.

Other Stationery Selections

Wedding announcements. These will be sent to people who haven't been invited to your wedding, but whom you feel should be notified. They aren't mailed until *after* your wedding. You can prepare them in advance, address and stamp them, and leave them with one of your parents or your maid of honor to mail the day after your wedding. They will be worded very much like your invitation—but of course you won't be "requesting the honor of their presence." Instead you can say, "happily announce the marriage" or "have the pleasure of announcing the marriage."

Informals. Personalized stationery for thank-you notes. They fold over in half with your name(s) or monogram on the front. Order them with your maiden name for gifts received in honor of your engagement or at your bridal shower. The second set can have both your names on the front for thank-you notes you'll write after your marriage.

Save-the-date cards. Send from a year to three months before the wedding, especially for a destination wedding.

Seating cards (table cards). These cards have blank spaces to fill in the name of your guest(s) and the table they are assigned to sit at during the reception. The names and table numbers can be filled in by a calligrapher for an attractive look. They're usually placed on a table at the entrance door of the reception room.

Reception cards. These can be used in addition to the invitations if the reception is being held at a different location than the ceremony. They're ideal if including the reception information makes the invitation itself look overcrowded. They can also be used for those invited only to the reception; this is not the norm at Jewish weddings, however, as guests are invited to the ceremony and the reception.

Transportation cards. Informing guests that transportation will be available to them between the ceremony and reception or to other accompanying events. To make your transportation arrangements more accurate, ask guests to respond.

Wedding programs. These are particularly helpful if guests may be unfamiliar with the traditions of your Jewish or interfaith wedding. A program not only indicates the order of the ceremony but can also describe the history and tradition behind signing the *ketubah,* the Seven Blessings, circling, and the breaking of the glass. They are often kept as a keepsake, having your names, wedding date, and location on the front, as well as the names of your bridal party and officiant(s) within. An attractive addition: a ribbon insert, a bow, or a lace appliqué.

Menu cards. Placed on each table at the reception, they describe the food that will be served.

Place cards. If you assign exact seating at your reception, these are placed at the exact seat you have selected for your guest. At the majority of wedding receptions, however, the bride and groom assign guests to a particular table, allowing them to select their own seats.

Quiz: How Much Do You Know About Wedding Invitations?

For each statement, circle the letter that represents the best answer.

1. Formal invitations should be sent out:

    a) three days before the wedding so they will arrive right on time.
    b) by overnight carrier to ensure that guests have up-to-date directions.
    c) six to eight weeks before your wedding unless guests are required to travel out of town.
    d) by e-mail or posted on an online bulletin board.

2. When inviting guests to your Jewish wedding, your mailing *must* include:

    a) a response set, your registry information, and return postage.
    b) directions, room reservation notification, and a family dinner invitation.
    c) your rabbi's business card, an entrée selection card, and a valet parking voucher.
    d) your wedding invitation.

3. You're having an "adults-only" wedding reception, so you:

    a) have the printed invitations note "no children" on the lower left-hand corner.
    b) do not include the children's names on the invitation or inner envelope.
    c) add a handwritten note asking guests to get a baby-sitter for that day.
    d) enclose a listing of baby-sitting services near guests' homes.

4. Wedding invitations that include a double envelope do so because:

a) it's for a double wedding.
b) the weight of the second envelope will round off the postage charges to the nearest whole dollar.
c) one envelope is for the male guests, the second for females.
d) the outer envelope takes the beating along its way to your guests, and the inner remains pristine.

5. To ensure that you get an exact count of those guests who are coming to your formal, sit-down reception, it's wise to include the following statement(s) on your invitation:

a) regrets only
b) *Respondez, s'il vous plait;* R.S.V.P.; *RSVP; R.s.v.p.; r.s.v.p.;* the favour of a reply is requested; or kindly respond, along with an address for responses.
c) E-mail if you want: dk&x!Xz@mindpulse.com
d) Please pass the word, dude!

Answers: 1—c; 2—d; 3—b; 4—d; 5—b.

Scoring: Give yourself 5 points for each correct answer.

0–5 points: You're seriously expecting guests to show up? If so, you need to review your invitation protocol. For additional backup, why not spend some time with a knowledgeable wedding invitation specialist at a retailer near you? If you're having a Jewish wedding, bring along someone who has specific knowledge of how to word Jewish invitations, and what enclosures you will or won't need.

10–15 points: You know more than many when it comes to the topic of wedding invitations—but it won't hurt to spend some time with those who have had some personal experiences that worked out right.

20–25 points: Congratulations—either you've done this before, or you really pay attention! Be sure to double-check the steps to preparing your invitations along the way. *Mazel tov* on your forthcoming wedding!

Insider's Interview:
Invitation Manufacturer

Brian D. Lawrence, vice president, Encore Studios

www.weddinginvitations.com

Background: Encore Studios designs, manufactures, thermographs, and engraves personalized invitations and announcements.

"The invitations reflect the taste of the bride," says Lawrence. "The traditional invitation is made of 100 percent cotton, which is the best quality. There are also very rich-looking papers imported from all over the world. A very popular style is a thick paper stock with a vellum overlay. The overlay may have a monogram and the wording of the invitation appears on the stock, or the entire invitation can be printed on the vellum overlay.

"The beauty of the invitation starts with the envelope. Many contemporary invitations include just a single envelope. The recipient will open the lined envelope, and the contents will be inside.

"A modern trend on the response cards is to give the recipient the space to say what they would like to say. But a more efficient mechanism is to have the response card formatted so that you will have accurate information to offer the caterer.

"One of the challenges that the bride has is trying to discover who sent back a response card without a name. The strategy is to write a number on the card to identify the response. But a modern trend is to have the name of the recipient machine-calligraphied on each response card. Not only is it more personalized, but it's pretty much fail-safe.

"The font used for the invitation can be traditional or more contemporary in taste. The typography has a profound influence on the appearance of the invitation. You can use a traditional stock paper and you can make it look contemporary based on the typeface. A unique paper makes its own statement.

"A good formula for determining the quantity of invitations to order is to calculate the number of people on your guest list, then multiply it by 0.6, then round it to the next highest 25. That should give you enough extras for an A list and a B list and for people you may have forgotten.

"Before addressing the invitations, call people to make sure you have their current addresses. Also, take a completely stuffed invitation to the post office to have it weighed. Off-sized envelopes can create additional postage charges. But it's almost automatic that the invitation will require double postage by the time you get done.

"If so inclined, you can send out an engagement announcement. It's usually sent out by the couple themselves, although the parents can make the announcement. It precedes sending an invitation to an engagement party. The engagement announcement is smaller than an invitation—more of an informal size. It's very simple and usually says 'Engaged,' followed by the names of the two people and the date.

"People will sometimes get married on a holiday weekend, and sending out an invitation within the recommended time frame of six to eight weeks before often puts the guests in a precarious position—they want to go to the wedding but have already made plans. So you can send 'save-the-date cards.' Typically they are small-sized cards listing the bride and groom's name and the date. No location is mentioned but it can say, 'Details to follow.'

"If the reception is being held in a different location than the ceremony, it's equally important—sometimes more important—to give directions to the first location as well as the second. It's the tasteful thing to do. Sometimes the reception place will issue cards, or you can have the printer do it.

"If you have negotiated a block of rooms at a hotel for your guests, this information can go on the same direction card. The guests handle their arrangements directly with the hotel.

"Informals can be ordered at the same time. Since they can serve as your personal stationery on an ongoing basis, you can order extra. The informals can read 'Mr. and Mrs. [husband's name],' both last names, or just a monogram."

5

The Bridal Party

WITH ALL THE SEEMINGLY zillions of things that need to be done to prepare for your wedding, and with so many details to handle during the event, your heads are probably spinning out of control. It seems like there is just *no way* you can accomplish it all in time for the big day! And remember, your wedding responsibilities aren't over once you dance the last dance; there are vendors to pay, tips to give out, documents to get together for your honeymoon—not to mention that someone has to return the rented tuxedos, bring your bridal gown to the dry cleaners, and even deposit your wedding gifts in the bank. That's where your attendants come in. In addition to helping you plan for the big day, they are also there to help you coast through the wedding, and then to perform all the necessary post-wedding mop-up tasks.

Choosing Your Attendants

With a coterie of friends and relatives to help you, you *should* manage to get through the preparations, the wedding, and the mop-up with ease. Right? Not quite so easy. To make things run smoothly, you must choose your attendants wisely and let them know what you expect of them before they accept the honor.

It's totally unrealistic to ask your sister who lives two thousand miles away to join you while you shop around for your wedding gown, even if she *is* your matron of honor. Or for your fiancé to delegate his best man the job of returning all rentals the following day if he must fly back home directly after the wedding.

So as you select those who will be your maid or matron of honor, your brides-maids, the best man and ushers, think carefully before offering the honor (and work and expense) to your friends or family members.

Let's get this out right up front. You can't invite someone to be in your wedding party and then *disinvite* him or her later on. So be sure that the people you select will indeed help you, not hinder you. That is, unless they're token attendants (see page 73). Keep in mind, you are going to be asking these people to spend a lot of money and time on your behalf. Be sure to choose wisely. Following are the standard members of the bridal party.

Matron or Maid of Honor

Your very special honor attendant can be a matron of honor if she's married or a maid of honor if she's single. She can be your sister or your best friend. Your honor attendant is your "best girl," so to speak, helping you out throughout your wedding planning, the day of the wedding, and even afterward. She could help you select your wedding gown, organize the bridesmaids' gown fittings, welcome out-of-town guests, help write up announcements and invitations, help you dress for your wedding, and be useful in many other ways.

At the wedding, she walks down the aisle after the bridesmaids and right before the bride, unless there's a flower girl, who walks directly before the bride instead.

The honor attendant's duties continue as she helps arrange the bride's train under the *chuppah* and holds her bouquet while she says her vows. The maid or matron of honor is usually called upon to make a toast at the reception, too.

If you're hard-pressed to select just one honor attendant (perhaps you have two sisters), you *can* designate two people. Be sure they each know their specific "job" duties, however. You wouldn't want two people fussing with your train or reaching out to hold your bouquet at the same time.

Best Man

He's usually the brother or best friend of the groom and has a lot of runaround duties to perform. He may help pick up guests at the airport or train and bus stations, help make sure all the guys get their tuxedos on time, help the groom get dressed in his wedding attire, hand out the envelopes with tips after the ceremony and the reception, drive you to the hotel or airport after the wedding reception, and see that all the tuxedos and any leased equipment are returned to their various rental places.

During the ceremony, he'll stand next to the groom under the *chuppah* and hold the wedding ring. Hopefully, he won't have to hold up the groom! At the reception he'll make a toast to the new couple, too, and partake in the bridal party's dance.

Bridesmaids

In ancient times, the job of the bridesmaids was to protect the bride from evil spirits or old boyfriends. Today they help during the wedding planning, participating in "work parties" to address envelopes or make decorations and by being available for dress fittings. Together, with the maid or matron of honor, they may help throw and pay for a bridal shower or bachelorette party. They will handle special tasks you assign to them on your wedding day, and attend pre-wedding parties and a post-nuptial brunch or luncheon. Following your timetable for the wedding, they will be at the right place at the right time for pictures, the bridal party's dance, and other duties. They will also mingle with your guests and see that everyone is well taken care of, point the way to the rest rooms, or what have you. And most of all, they will be there to offer emotional support and act as sounding board for your problems, if any should arise!

Junior Bridesmaids

A young girl between the ages of nine and fourteen, a junior bridesmaid can be "bumped up" to bridesmaid at age twelve, after she's been *bat mitzvahed*. This will depend on whether the bride feels her young helper is mature enough to blend in with the other bridesmaids and can wear the same type of gown.

Ushers (Groomsmen)

They help the groom in many ways, from picking up guests at airports or train and bus terminals to helping to transport people from the hotel to the ceremony and on to the reception if rides are needed. They go for fittings and pick up their formalwear. Although a bachelor party isn't always the norm for Jewish weddings, the groomsmen are instrumental in planning and giving the party if there will be one. The ushers and groomsmen can be friends or relatives of the groom or the bride. Although they're called "ushers" in Jewish weddings, they don't actually seat guests at the ceremony. Guests select their own seating, knowing that the first one or two rows are reserved for grandparents, step-parents, and others who may sit after walking down the aisle.

Junior Usher

A young boy between the ages of nine and fourteen, the junior usher can be "bumped up" to usher at age thirteen, after he's been *bar mitzvahed*. This depends on whether the bride and groom feel he's mature enough to blend in with the other groomsmen and can participate in their activities without restriction.

Flower Girl

Symbolizing fertility, a young girl between the ages of four and eight carries a basket of flower petals and scatters them along the carpet ahead of the bride. In place of a basket, she can walk carrying a loose collection of ribbon-tied flowers in her arms.

Pages (Train Bearers)

Two little boys between the ages of four and five, they walk down the aisle behind the bride—one on the left, the other on the right—holding her train. Suitable for cathedral-length trains.

Ring Boy

A young boy between the ages of four and eight, he walks down the aisle holding the ring(s) on a pillow. The rings can be tied down with ribbon from the pillow to keep them from slipping off. Nervous ring boys can carry a "dummy"—and the best man can hold the actual ring.

Tokens

You know who they are: the friends or family members whom you *must* ask to be a part of your wedding party. How could you not ask your only sister to be your maid of honor? How could your honey choose someone other than his brother to act as best man? But if you know that circumstances will not allow them to actually carry out the necessary duties, you should try to ensure that the other bridal party members you select can indeed carry the load. If the person your honey wants to be his best man historically gets loaded at weddings, will he be able to make a speech and distribute the tips? And you definitely don't want him driving you to the airport right after the reception! But if family unity forever depends on his being the best man, a more responsible person should be asked to handle these important duties.

Likewise, if your sister is your maid of honor and you *know* she has horrible taste in clothes—or at least not *your* taste—why would you have her help you select your wedding gown? Although under most circumstances, the person holding her honor would be the one to go shopping with you, maybe your mom or someone else with great fashion sense can quietly be asked to accompany you instead.

Are Twenty Too Many?

How many attendants do you want? Need? A lot has to do with the size and formality of the wedding. Usually, the more guests you're inviting and the more formal the event, the bigger the bridal party can be. At a large formal wedding with more than two hundred guests, six bridesmaids, six ushers, a maid or matron of honor, best man, ring boy, flower girl(s), and train bearers make for a full house of attendants. The number dwindles as the wedding gets smaller and/or less formal. You should try to have an equal number of bridesmaids and ushers. But if not, then two ushers for every bridesmaid is a nice way to go; one man can escort the girl on each side. For a small, informal wedding, parents, a maid or matron of honor, and a best man will do.

Although your attendants are there to help you, you have a responsibility to them as well. And the more people involved in a project, the greater the likelihood that something will go wrong or that disagreements will arise. Someone won't like the dresses you've selected; another won't like the menu. Try to balance things so that you can get the help you need without having everyone tripping over each other and giving you grief!

The Plump and the Pregnant

You really want Joanie* to be one of your bridesmaids. You've been friends forever, she's the "pitch-in" type and really a great organizer. She's perfect . . . but pregnant.

Of course, her belly won't deter you, but what you do have to consider is when the baby is due, the type of dresses you'll be selecting for your bridesmaids, and her general well-being.

If Joanie's due date is within a few weeks of your wedding, it might be uncomfortable for the both of you if she were to be in your bridal party. You'd be worried about her going into labor during the wedding, or having the baby right before! And if you have your heart set on your bridesmaids all wearing matching gowns with cinched-in waists, this might pose another problem. You'll have to be flexible and let her wear a modified version, if one is available. Or you'll need to select a style that looks good on her (Empire, perhaps), and then have the rest of the bridesmaids wear the same style. And most important, as a member of your wedding party (even a token one) she'll be standing for a relatively long length of time. Will she be physically up to it? Remember, it's not how she feels now, but how she'll feel at the time of your wedding. If Joanie is very pregnant now and your wedding is quite a distance away, that shouldn't pose a problem—as long as she can get a baby-sitter!

*The names in this chapter are fictitious and do not represent real people.

Then there's Marcy. You love her dearly. She's always there for you, and is the perfect person to keep you calm, put out the fires, and generally support you in every way. But you envision your bridesmaids, lean and long-legged, lined up like beautiful statuettes along the aisle. Everything is picture-perfect—with one exception. Dear Marcy is rather short and a size twenty-two. Well, you know what? Get over it. You're honoring your friend for who she is, not what size she wears.

High-Strung Me-is-kite

You're also considering Bekki to be one of your bridesmaids. She could be helpful, but she's given to histrionics. Everything she does takes on a whole new dimension—and it's always about her. As you envision it, you'll need the mirror for a quick touch-up as you prepare to walk down the aisle. She'll be there hogging the space, putting on yet another coat of lipstick. You'll be trying to be so careful so as not to wrinkle your wedding gown, and she'll be ranting and raving about a pucker in her pantyhose. She's not a "token" who must be asked, so should you? Think hard. This is *your* day. If anyone has the right to rant, shouldn't it be you?

Kvetch *and* Fetch

What about Rozie? Can you really rely on her? Sure, she'll be there when asked, she'll get you anything you need, and she'll take care of her duties hour after hour—while complaining a mile a minute. "Sure, I'll get you the needle and thread, but *oy!*—let me take my shoes off first. My feet are *killing* me!" Do you have the patience for this?

Swell and Qvell

Oh yes, you must include Sophie. She's one of your biggest supporters. She's always so proud of you, and is totally thrilled that you're getting married to the guy of your dreams. She'll go the extra mile with a smile and help make your day run smoothly.

Maiden Fair

She's twelve years old and so grown up, full of energy, and so *totally* wanting to be your bridesmaid. After all, you're marrying her favorite uncle! *"Please, please, pretty please?"* How can you resist? So April becomes your junior bridesmaid.

Petal Pusher

She's cute as a button with rosy cheeks and a shy disposition. Five-year-old Felicia is the epitome of the flower girl you've always wanted. But can she make it down the aisle without withering? You check with her mom, who assures you that this would be her second flower-girl experience—she's a real pro! And Felicia promises you that *this* time she'll toss the rose petals on the white carpet, not directly into the faces of the "audience."

Let's Hear It for the Boys

Between you and your honey's side you have three little Musketeers; Alex, Bradley, and Chuckie. Chuckie is four, while the twins are five. Perfect! With a little rehearsal and some time to practice, you hope everything will work out fine. Their moms have agreed to help out—why, it's almost like preparing them for their first school play. Chuckie is a little nervous with his responsibility of bearing the all-important ring, but you'll coach him and with ample encouragement, he'll gain the confidence to do the job in style. And working with a long white sheet, Alex and Bradley will practice holding your train as you walk down the aisle.

Parent Power

Add your parents to your list because they, too, will have some duties to perform for you. If your mother is the stereotypical Jewish mother, one of *your* jobs will be to hold her at bay. And to let her annoy you. She has probably been dreaming of your wedding day since you were born, and will be everywhere and into everything! With the two of you in a highly charged emotional state, lean on her, ask her advice, and let her have the joy of helping you. When you run into those snags that just seem overwhelming, simply cry out, *Maaaaa!* She'll solve the problem. That's what moms are for.

If you have the stereotypical dad, expect him to be somewhat dazed. His little baby girl is getting married, and somehow the years have just crept up on him. As did the wedding's sticker shock! Rely on him for the million and one things you'll need, as well, and let him know that you'll be just fine. He'll also be one of the men to take over any "best-man duties" that your honey's choice may not be able to do. Although Dad may not initiate activities on your behalf, give him an assignment and he'll do his darndest to carry it through.

His Team

While you're assembling your team, your honey is doing the same. He's hoping that his choice of best man is up for the job. He, too, is choosing his ushers with care, knowing that each will be instrumental in making the wedding and reception a total success.

Consider the Expense

You're honoring your family or friends by asking them to be in your wedding party. But at the same time, you're asking a lot of them. In addition to the actual "jobs" they'll be doing for you, they will be incurring expenses—some of them hefty. To begin with, the bride's attendants will be buying their own gowns, headpieces, shoes, and underwear (if something special is needed). They may be chipping in to throw you a shower and will be buying you gifts. And if they're going to be shopping with you, driving your out-of-town guests, and running errands, they will be absorbing carfare, gas, and related expenses. They probably will be paying professionals for their hair, nails, and makeup, too. Then they'll be giving you a wedding gift, to boot!

The male attendants will, likewise, be incurring expenses. They will be renting formalwear, including shoes, buying silk socks, perhaps hosting or chipping in for a bachelor party or guys' night out, running errands, and doing "guest detail" as well.

Of course, your wedding is unique, but if you hang with a crowd who are "of marrying age," they may be making the rounds as attendants at several weddings, and that means coughing up the cash and time for each.

If your friend is a poverty-stricken grad student, living off boxed macaroni and cheese, accepting your honor may be a financial imposition. If you truly want your chosen attendant to serve, or know that he or she will be angry or feel slighted if *not* asked, then by all means ask, acknowledging that you'll understand if he or she is "too busy" (with school, life, exams, work) to serve at this time. That should provide your relative or friend with a gracious way out.

Gifts, Glorious Gifts

They've given you their time, showered you with their attention, and expended their dollars. They've helped you get through the trials and tribulations of wedding planning (and hopefully did not contribute to any of them!). Now it's time to say thank you by getting each of the members of your wedding party a gift. The ideal time to present them with their gifts would be at a luncheon held in their honor, or at the pre-nup dinner the night before the wedding.

Now the question arises: what in the world can I get them? Ideally, it would be something meaningful that they can use or treasure as a keepsake. And normally, you would get identical or similar gifts for all. In addition to the "serious stuff," you may want to toss in a fun gift, casually distributed at the beginning of your wedding process.

Serious Stuff for Her

A piece of jewelry is always appropriate, but make sure it's tasteful. For the girls, think pearls. Cultured pearls are always appropriate, unless your attendant is a biker chick. A necklace of floating pearls on nearly invisible filaments makes for a nice look. A set of stud earrings or a simple gold or silver bracelet is also appropriate. If you try to match jewelry to the bridesmaids' and honor attendants' gowns, they can wear your gift at the wedding. Watches are nice, too. You can even select ones with Hebrew faces if you like.

Other choices for your ladies include small jewelry boxes (with or without music), hand-painted Limoges porcelain boxes, really good pens, crystal table clocks, sterling-silver engraved picture frames, heart-shaped trays, bud vases, or boxed sets of exquisite soaps.

Serious Stuff for Him

For the men, fourteen-karat gold cufflinks are always appropriate, as are good watches (and like those for the ladies, they can have Hebrew faces), sterling-silver key rings, crystal paperweights, sterling-silver or fourteen-karat gold money clips, sterling-silver letter openers, fine pens, wallets, and I.D. bracelets engraved with the attendant's name.

Junior Gifts

Your junior attendants may enjoy a porcelain or fine china set consisting of a plate, bowl, and cup in age-appropriate motifs; a fine comb and brush set; and for the girls, a simple gold or pearl necklace, or a birthstone bracelet is always nice.

Parent Gifts

For your parents, step-parents, or others who may be sponsoring your wedding, a beautiful silver, gold, or crystal picture frame they can fill with your wedding picture makes a wonderful gift. So, too, does a silver tray engraved with their names and your names and wedding date, or a beautiful decanter. A pair of silver or crystal candlesticks along with a note saying "You light up my life" would be a heartwarming gesture.

Fun, Fun, Fun

For fun motifs for any of your attendants, how about a collection of CDs or DVDs, chosen to match their individual tastes? This would go well for the younger attendants, too. Or a pair of tickets to the theater, a comedy club, or the big game, depending on your attendants' individual preferences, would be a welcome gift.

Don't forget to write a short note of thanks to each attendant to give along with the gift. No e-mails or photocopy paper for this one!

In addition to the gifts that you give for their service, you might want to indulge in something whimsical at the beginning of the wedding planning. Once you've asked and they've accepted the offer to be in your wedding party, how about giving each of your attendants a baseball cap announcing his or her part: bridesmaid, maid of honor, groomsman, mother of the bride, and so on, or a T-shirt printed with the name of the bride and groom, the date of the wedding, and the names of all the members of the bridal party?

Wedding Toasts

Toasts are traditionally given at the reception by the best man and the maid or matron of honor, in coordination with the caterer, the band or DJ, and the photographer and videographer. Many a best man has agonized over the speech he is going to make before the communal clink of champagne glasses. But actually, a prepared speech from the heart, with a touch of humor, always does the trick. Parents may also propose toasts to their children, as can the bride and groom not only to each other, but to their parents as well.

A lovely way parents have offered toasts is for both parents to get up together and alternate paragraphs of a prepared speech toasting the bride and groom.

The perfect time to toast is after the salad has been served and before the main course arrives. An alternative time is right after the first dances. Before embarking on the toast, however, the best man needs to speak with the maître d' to make sure that all the guests' glasses have been filled with champagne, wine, or a nonalcoholic beverage. He also has to notify the band or DJ that things are getting ready to rock 'n' roll, and alert the photographer and videographer.

Often the bandleader or DJ takes the lead in arranging toast time—and if so, he or she must make sure the bride and groom, best man, and matron or maid of honor and parents are in the room, ready and available. Nothing can be more embarrassing to call out to them only to discover that the bride is in the bathroom!

6

Wedding Attire

UNLIKE BIBLICAL EVE, WHO didn't have much of a selection when trying to clothe herself, you have far more than a variety of leaves from which to choose for yourself and for other featured participants on your wedding day. There are literally thousands of wedding dresses out there awaiting your perusal. And there are dressmakers and designers who will cater to your every whim. Coupled with your attendants' outfits, accessories, foundations, the men's clothes, and those of the parents, there'll be a whole lot of shopping going on!

Choosing Your Bridal Gown

For many, this is the first time out for buying wedding clothes, and it can be daunting indeed—even for the most avid shopaholic. The wedding clothes industry is a big business, and everyone would like to have yours. So before you leave the starting gate, arm yourself with some background information. Yes, you'll need help from salespeople (also called bridal consultants in some shops) or from dressmakers or designers, but you should be able to meet them at least halfway. You don't want to walk into a shop or warehouse full of expansive white and find yourself like a deer caught in headlights. Nor do you want to be intimidated as the consultant tosses out terms only a fashion designer would understand.

So before you step into the first bridal store, stop at the magazine stand.

Research

There you will find hefty volumes of bridal magazines filled with advertisements for wedding gowns exquisite and plain. Do yourself a favor and purchase some of these magazines so you can take them home and leisurely peruse them over coffee, tea, and your favorite snack.

Flip through the pages with a critical eye. "Hmm, this gown looks like it can walk on its own," or "If the top of *this* gown gets any lower," or "This one is simply too plain." And finally: "Ohhh! *This* one is absolutely perfect!" Tear out the page and begin a folder for dresses you especially like. Keep looking and keep tearing out those pages depicting those perfect-for-you gowns. Don't worry if your tear sheets prove to be eclectic. You may find you've selected gowns that differ quite a bit—a sleek sheath that stole your affection, a big ball gown that begs to be danced in, or a fishtail frock in a perfect fabric. Your final choice might encompass elements from several of your selections.

The Internet is another wonderful tool for checking out styles. There are many sites that offer thousands of possibilities. Do an Internet search for "Bridal Gowns" and you're all set to go.

Deciding on Style

Now that you have an idea of what you like, you want to be sure that the dress will "like" you. Different strokes for different folks, and all that. Here's where your fantasy must take a reality check.

Take a few unhurried moments to stand alone before a full-length mirror. You can be in the privacy of your home or in a department store dressing room, but be alone! You're going to be brutally honest with yourself, and no one needs to know.

Keep a tape measure and pad and pencil with you. In either your birthday suit or your underwear, take a realistic look at your figure and shape. Release your sucked-in stomach muscles that may make you look thinner or more buxom. Unless you intend to walk around in isometric torture the entire day of your wedding, just be natural and comfortable. You'll be wearing a dress that will make the most of the way you really look, so be totally realistic.

Really look at yourself. Are you plump in certain areas? Do you have a long swan-like neck or a shorter version accompanied by a double chin? Are your shoulders broad or narrow? Are you small- or big-busted? Are you short- or long-waisted? Are your arms full or thin, and are they long or short? Are you long-legged or short? Check out your derrière. Is it flat or full?

Now, with your trusty tape measure, take your bust, waist, and hip measurements and jot them down. Take realistic notes. The whole idea of this frankness is to then find a dress that will play up your best points and camouflage others. (And trust me, everyone has those "others.")

At home, take the face-shape test. This will be important as you select a neckline for your dress and choose the design of your headpiece. Pull your hair back from your face and secure it with bobby pins, clips, or a headband if necessary. Look straight ahead into the mirror. Using the corner of a slightly dampened cake of soap, or a lipstick (with glass cleaner on hand), draw the outline of your face on the mirror. Step back and look. You will now be able to clearly tell your face shape. Is it round? Is your forehead wider than your chin? Is the shape oval? Do you have a square jaw?

Once you learn these things about your face and body, you will be able to select a gown that best accentuates your unique features. Following are the elements of gowns, from overall shape, to neckline, to sleeves, and more.

Silhouette

The *silhouette* is the shape of the gown. Do yourself a favor: Pick the one that's most flattering to *your* body shape. You may love the dress that sleekly slides over the form of the stick-thin model in the magazine, but if your hips tend to stick out, this might not be the style for you. Following are some of the most popular styles.

Sheath. This silhouette follows the body's natural lines and is formfitting in nature. It's a good pick if you're slender and have a well-proportioned figure. It helps elongate the body, so if you're short, it will also work well for you.

Ball gown. Ideal for people with narrow hips since it fills you out, this classic Cinderella look has a fitted bodice and usually a natural waist. If you're top-heavy or short-waisted, this may not be a good style for you. And be careful if you are petite: it can overpower you and make you look like a walking powder puff!

A-line. Also known as a princess silhouette, this is a comfortable style that has no seams at the waist. Instead it has a distinctive set of seams running down the length of the gown from the shoulders to a slightly flared-out skirt. Rather than hugging the body tightly, it skims your figure, widening into a triangular shape toward the bottom. Flattering to almost anyone, it's ideal for those with large hips. Ditto for the short-waisted. The seams help make your torso look longer.

Empire. A beautiful look that has a small, high bodice with the fabric falling from under the bustline to form a slender skirt. Since it has no waist, it's ideal for those heavy around the center, and can work well for the pregnant bride. Those with big chests should beware of this style, however, as it does tend to accentuate the bust.

Mermaid. Like the sheath, this gown is tight and formfitting, but the mermaid splays out at the bottom. The contrast between the two silhouettes plays up your figure big time. That classic 34–22–34 (give or take an inch here and there) figure works best for this one.

Slip dress. Minimalism at its height. Elegant on the slender individual with nice shoulders, it resembles a sleeveless full-length slip. The beauty of the fabric prevails.

Necklines

The neckline you select works with your face shape, neck, and upper body. It should accentuate the positive and downplay less flattering areas. Some necklines work better with various types of gowns, so you'll also have to consider the big picture.

Jewel.   Classic round neckline that sits right at the base of your neck. Avoid if you have a full, round face, as it duplicates the moon effect.

Scoop.   Rounded U-shape that sits lower than the jewel. This works well for those with full figures.

Sweetheart.   One of the most popular looks today. Covered on the shoulders and open-necked in front, it dips down to a point at the cleavage line. It can show off your curves in a most delightful way.

Bateau.   Similar to the boat neck often seen in sweaters, it follows your collarbones. Avoid if you're strongly square-jawed or if you have a broad face or chest.

Portrait.   Frames the face with a shawl-like effect. It can be worn off the shoulder. Avoid this if you're wide across the top.

Collar band.   Ideal for the long, swanlike neck. This tight-fitting collar comes up high on the neck.

Halter top.   The bodice is built up with straps that tie around the back of the dress. Shoulders are bare, the back is low, and the front is revealing. It can be worn with an over-jacket or other cover-up in *shul*.

V-neck.   An ideal neckline for the round, full face, or one with a double chin or short neck. It pulls the eye downward, elongating the face and neck. Avoid this neckline if you have a long neck and/or a long face.

Square.   Lines form the bottom part of a square.

Sleeves

The sleeves of your gown can be chosen to hide imperfect arms or show off arms you've been working out at the gym. Sleeves can also be a major consideration of the time of year in which you marry. Here are a few of the main types.

Cap sleeve.   More cover-up than sleeveless, but it's barely a sleeve.

Fitted point. Long and tight sleeve that comes to a point over the hand. Lengthens the arms.

Three-quarter. Flattering and modest. Can work well with the heavier arm.

Sleeveless. Flattering as long as upper arms are flab-free.

Spaghetti strap. A sleeveless dress held up by two thin straps from the bodice over the shoulders.

Juliet. Fitted on the arm and puffing up high (not wide) at the shoulder. Lovely on the slender of arm and narrow of chest. Avoid if you're top-heavy.

Gauntlet, balloon, and leg o' mutton. All have poofs of various lengths. Can be attractive, but can make you look top-heavy.

Poet. Gathered at the shoulders and loose and puffy to the wrist.

Bell. Widens slightly as it progresses down the upper arm, forming a slightly flared bottom.

Back

Don't forget about your back. You are a real, live, three-dimensional bride, and you'll be seen from all sides. In fact, your back may get more attention than your front as you swirl around the dance floor.

If you have a nice back, you may want to show it off with a strapless gown or one with an illusion (the cutaway area filled with transparent tulle, net, or lace). Other options for backs include cowl, lace-up, keyhole, halter, heart-shaped, or a V-back set off with some embellishment. If you're bottom-heavy, try to avoid any styles or embellishments—bustles, bows, or silk flowers, for example—that will lead your audience's eye to your derrière.

A long row of covered buttons down the back adds a touch of elegance while elongating the look. They can actually be used to close the gown or simply stand as a decorative addition over the zipper. Be sure that the buttons exactly match the fabric of your gown.

Hemlines

The main determiner of your hemline is what time of day you will be having your wedding and what type of wedding you are having. A floor-length gown screams formality, while a tea-length dress is perfect for an afternoon garden wedding. Here are the various dress lengths.

Floor. Falls about an inch or so from the floor. The tips of your shoes will be showing.

Ankle. Stops a little higher than the floor length, just showing the lovely turn of your ankle.

Tea. Stops at the shin.

Street–length. Just at or slightly under the knee.

Mini. Stops halfway up the thigh.

Trains

A train can be a permanent part of your dress, or it can be a piece of added fabric. Some attach at the shoulder, while others are detachable to let you dance up a storm at your reception.

Different manufacturers and designers attribute different lengths to each type of train, and the amount of fabric that falls behind you on the carpet depends on how tall you actually are. But here's a general guideline:

Sweep or brush. Just touches the top of your shoes or sweeps less than a foot on the floor. Good for the shorter bride.

Chapel. Starting at the waist, it extends between three and a half and six feet from your waist. A popular choice, it offers drama without inconvenience.

Watteau. Starting at the shoulders, this forms into box pleats from the neckline, gracing into a short train.

Semicathedral. Extends approximately six to seven feet from your waist.

Cathedral. Long and dramatic, it extends eight or more feet from your waist. In most cases it's too overwhelming for the petite bride. If you want to go the entire Princess Diana look, think nine or more feet from your waistline.

Bustles

Unless you opt for a trainless gown, a sweep that doesn't extend very much along the floor, or a detachable train, you'll have to have your train made to bustle up after the ceremony. Your dress and train will be designed with nearly invisible hooks (sometimes snaps or buttons) that hold the train up off the floor and keep it attached to the back of your gown. The draping can be attached under a bow at your waist, or as a French bustle, which hooks up under your ball-gown-type skirt with a series of loops and ribbons.

Sometime after you've made your debut bridal walk down the "runway" and after your portrait-type photos have been taken, you'll slip into your dressing room with your "bustler" (the person you have enlisted to bustle your gown) and quickly get to work with the hooks, buttons, or snaps. Once you're all hooked up, your bustle is well placed, your hemline is even, and you're picture-perfect, you'll make your entrance once again.

If you'd rather hold on to your train and have the grace to make it look attractive, have a loop sewn in that you can slip over your hand. Bear in mind: it can get very tiring carrying a heavy train around all night.

Gloves

Gloves can nicely complete your bridal outfit. The general rule is that you should wear short gloves with long sleeves and long gloves with short-sleeved or sleeveless gowns. But do take your arms and the design of your gown into consideration. If you're wearing a long-sleeved dress, you can skip the gloves or wear "one-button gloves"—short, wrist-length gloves. If your arms are pleasingly plump, avoid long opera-length gloves. Stop them at the elbow. Ditto if you're petite.

But what do you do with your gloves when you're under the *chuppah* and about to accept your wedding band?

One solution is to wear Mousquetaire gloves, which are elbow- or above-elbow-length. They have buttons at the inside wrist. When it's time to receive your ring, you gracefully unbutton the right glove, remove your hand, and tuck the glove into itself on your inside wrist. You may want to practice this a bit so that you don't fumble at this important moment in your life. Why the right glove? In the Jewish wedding ceremony, the groom places the ring on the right index finger of his bride, a custom that has prevailed for many centuries.

You may also slit the seam of your glove's right index finger before the day of your wedding. In that way, you can release your finger when it's time to accept the ring. But if you don't like the idea of poking your hands or fingers out of gloves while under the *chuppah,* you can always wear shortie gloves that you easily pull off and hand to your attendant along with your bouquet. Or you can wear fingerless gloves, also known as sleeves. These gloves, preferably made of your gown's fabric, are elbow-length. They come down over the hand, forming a **V**-shaped point, and attach to your thumb or third finger with an elastic band.

And what about after the ceremony? Etiquette dictates that you wear your gloves when you're in the receiving line shaking hands with well-wishers. And nothing looks lovelier than a gloved hand and arm resting on a gentleman's shoulder during a slow dance. Be sure to remove your gloves while dining, however.

Veils

The bridal veil holds a special place in the Jewish wedding, and plays a pivotal role in the premarriage ceremony called the *bedecken*. In Genesis, Jacob mistakenly married Leah instead of his love Rachael because he didn't see his bride's face before they wed. So now, Jewish grooms and their male celebrants come to the bride, ensconced in her own area and sitting on a throne-like chair decorated with flowers. She is flanked by both mothers and often surrounded by other female guests. The groom looks at his bride—often the first time he's seen her in a week—to ensure that she is indeed "the one." He then places the veil over her face, and the wedding procession begins.

Veils are made of a fabric called "illusion." Although it resembles netting, it's actually silk or nylon and softer to the touch. They come in many different lengths and styles.

Blusher. Often attached to a longer train, the blusher is worn forward over your face and can be pushed back over your headpiece for that all-important kiss.

Birdcage. Short, covering the face to the chin, attached to a hat. Dramatic when worn with a wedding suit or a fitted gown. Ideal for informal weddings.

Fingertip. Falling down across your shoulders, it's wide enough to touch the fingertips of your hands. Multiple layers.

Flyaway. Brushes the shoulders and has several layers. Complements ankle-length gowns.

Elbow-length. Perfect for the petite bride.

Angel wings. Wide sides, with a long, straight cut.

Mantilla. Spanish influence. A large circular veil usually made of lace or lace-trimmed tulle. It attaches with a comb and frames the face.

Chapel. Falls about seven feet from your headpiece. Looks good with a floor-length gown with a train or with a short sweep train.

Waltz- or ballet-length. Falls to your ankles.

Cathedral. Cascades ten or more feet to complement a cathedral train. For formal weddings.

Vintage veils. No matter what length or shape, a vintage veil may be just the perfect emotional touch for you. Perhaps your mother wore this veil at her own wedding, or you unearthed it from a trunk in your parents' attic. The color does not need to match your gown. Don't try to dye it. And for the adage, "Something old . . ." It will certainly fit the bill!

Headpieces

Headpieces or hats add the crowning glory to your bridal look. Often they hold the veil in place. The type of headpiece you select depends on your hairstyle, the type of gown you'll be wearing, and the way it complements your overall look.

If you're custom-making your gown, the headpiece can also be custom-made, with scraps saved from your wedding gown, if you like. Here are some common types of headpieces.

Headband. A popular choice. The headband can be covered in fabric that matches your gown, encrusted with pearls and other embellishments, or wrapped with flowers. It can be worn alone or as a base for veiling. Works well with long or short hair.

Tiara or crown. The Jewish bride is considered to be a queen, so the popular tiara or crown can be an appropriate choice. The tiara works well with either a ball gown or a Miss America–like sheath. Rhinestones catch the light and add extra sparkle to your eyes. For the more reserved, it can be fashioned out of metal, sans the stones. Works with hair worn up or down and veiling as well. The crown, with crystal or pearl detailing, works nicely with pulled-up hair.

Profile. A highly embellished comb that can be worn at the nape of your neck, or worked in multiples into your hair. Does not work well with cropped hair. Attractive with long hair and hair pulled back.

Kippah. A fashionable version of a skullcap, it can be handcrafted with glass and metal beads and wire to twinkle in the light. Or it can be a more substantial hatlike circle covered in fabric and trimming. It is attached with a comb. Your female attendants and mothers can also wear them. If you want to splurge, wire and beaded *kippot* can be ordered in quantity to replace the little lace head coverings offered to female guests entering the sanctuary on your wedding weekend or for the *aufruth* held the Saturday before.

Hats. Ideal for short-haired brides and especially effective for outdoor weddings or informal weddings, depending on the style. Can range from pillbox to large brim hats ideal for garden party weddings.

Snood. Fabric that encases a low bun at the nape of the neck.

Back pieces. Attaching at the back or crown of your head, these usually hold a veil. They work for long hair, or a low chignon. Can be used for second marriage where you would not have a veil covering your face.

Bun wrap. Narrow garland of flowers, circle of rhinestones, or other material, the bun wrap is worn when hair is styled in an upswept bun, pulled through the wrap.

Where to Shop

It's is somewhere between a year to six months before your wedding, and the clock is ticking. Armed with information, the time has come to venture forth and find the gown of your dreams. Where can you find your perfect dress? May the hunt begin!

Bridal Salons

Call ahead and make an appointment before you enter the realm of the bridal salon. Like the wedding gowns they sell, salons come in all sizes and varieties—ranging from the small shop on Main Street, to the salons in department stores, to those of a specific designer. Many offer "one-stop shopping" for just about every bridal accessory you can think of, including shoes.

Don't expect to walk in, try on a few gowns, and walk out with your gown in tow. The salon may have one dress in each style it carries—in a sample size. Your consultant at the store will work with you to help envision how it will look on you. Expect to spend an hour on your initial appointment.

Depending on the manufacturer of the gown you select, it could take from three to eight months for your gown to come in. Since it's made especially for you, you may have some options in changing necklines or sleeves, for example. Once your gown has arrived, you'll need more time for fittings and alterations, which are done at the salon by an experienced staff specializing in wedding gowns. Since many of the gowns have designer names, they will most likely be pricey.

Warehouses

A no-frills approach to shopping for your wedding gown, a warehouse has a vast number of gowns in a variety of sizes. They can be collected from various sources—such as manufacturer's overstock, samples, or designer names you may be unfamiliar with. If bargain hunting turns you on and you're an avid shopper, you may be able to walk away with a good buy.

Top-Name Designers

You've drooled over their gowns in bridal magazines, heard their names bandied about on pop-culture and bridal television shows, and seen their work on the red carpet at the Oscars, Emmys, and other Hollywood spectaculars—or perhaps even on friends who've gotten married before you. And you, dear princess, want a one-of-a-kind dress designed by your favorite designer expressly for you. Some designers *will* work with you to make your dream come true. Of course, you'll be spending big dollars, but, in turn, you'll get a personally designed gown and hand sewing, fabulous fabric, and attention to detail—and it will most likely be fitted on you by the designer him- or herself. But more than likely, you'll buy the designer's gown through a bridal salon or at a sample sale.

Samples

Every so often you can find a sample sale being offered by a designer or a salon, often with deep discounts from the original prices. Gowns offered directly from designers may be last season's, and are usually limited to several sizes. Salons and other bridal outlets also sell off their floor samples. These may be shopworn or have stains. You buy at your own risk. Although you may be told they can be cleaned up, some stains may not be removable.

Dressmakers and Tailors

A good dressmaker or tailor can look at a picture of a gown in a magazine and make a similar one—or suggest design changes that will work especially well for you. Fitting the gown right to your body, first with a muslin pattern, a talented dressmaker or tailor can have the lines and seams of your dress fall in just the perfect place to complement a graceful collarbone or to hide a blemish. Some dressmakers specialize in wedding gowns only. If you haven't seen your prospective dressmaker in action (other gowns he or she's made), request a custom-made outfit for yourself first, so you can judge the results. Depending on your dressmaker's schedule, you will probably have your custom-made gown in less time than one ordered from a bridal salon, and for less money as well.

Trunk Shows

Trunk shows are advertised either in the newspaper or on signs posted in bridal salons. At these shows, the designer actually comes in person, along with some models who show off his or her creations. You can buy your gown at the show, and if you're lucky, the designer can even help you directly.

Dress Rental Shops

For the nonsentimental and eminently practical, renting a dress might sound like the ideal solution. After all, you'll only wear it once, right? And then you won't have to worry about cleaning it, preserving it, and locking it away, never to be seen again. Need another incentive? If men can rent their wedding outfits, why not you? Check in your yellow pages for bridal rental shops, or inquire at a men's tuxedo rental shop. They may have a recommendation.

Other Gown Options

Buying your wedding gown is only one option you have in finding the perfect dress. If you are good with your hands, or very sentimental, the following options may give you more satisfaction.

Do-It-Yourself

If you (or a good friend or a family member) are talented and can wield a mean sewing machine, fabric shops have pattern books that include bridal gowns. Making your own gown is a toughie—and the best of friends can begin to lose their cool. But then again, you can have a very special gown without incurring the cost of the designer's fee.

The Heritage Gown

Your mother carefully preserved her wedding gown, dreaming of the day her very own daughter would wear it. And now the time has come. With a strong sense of family history, you'd like nothing more than to walk down the aisle in the very dress you've seen in her wedding pictures over the years. Or perhaps you've discovered your grandmother's trunk in the attic—and there, carefully wrapped, is her wedding gown. You gasp at its beauty and you're hooked!

If the gown fits you, miracle of miracles! You can walk in the footsteps of the family matriarch before you. Beware of dry-cleaning the gown or attempting to alter it: the fabric may be too fragile. If some work is absolutely necessary, try to locate a fabric restoration service that specializes in antique fabric.

Secondhand Gowns

An unfortunate bride's misfortune can be your stroke of good luck. She bought her wedding gown but the wedding was called off. And here she is, all dressed up and nowhere to go. Make arrangements to see the dress, and find out if it fits or can be altered with ease. She will be happy and you will be happy. And finally, the beautiful gown will have the moment it was created for—a fabulous wedding to attend!

Or perhaps, the seller wore her gown to her wedding and decided she has no room or desire to store it forever. She's offering it for sale at a fraction of the cost, and you may have hit it just right. But be careful when buying a secondhand gown, either new or worn. Check carefully for stains, tears, and discoloration. They may be hard or impossible to repair. Make sure the zipper, if it has one, operates freely. And even though you may be getting a bargain, consider the cost of cleaning and alterations.

Attendants' Attire

However you visualize your wedding, if you're the queen, your attendants are the princesses. But don't let your fantasy of a picture-perfect wedding cloud the various realities of people's* lives. Your sister Barbara, who is your matron of honor, recently gave birth to her second child. As such, she's still a little—how could you put it politely?—rounded! She's a tad more buxom than usual, too.

Your best friend Mandy just lost her job and is frantically trying to make ends meet on her unemployment check. She desperately needs a new interview suit, but has been making due with her trusty old skirt and twin sweater set.

Susie, now living halfway across the country in Chicago, is delighted to be your attendant. She can't wait to fly in for your wedding. She has yet to discover the price of her airfare and hotel. Can she afford a bridesmaid's gown, too?

And then there's Julie, who called you excitedly just the other night to tell you the

---

*The names in this chapter are fictitious.

good news. She and her husband just found out she's pregnant! Do you still want her to be your bridesmaid? Of course you said yes. What's a bride to do?

And let's not forget about Marisa. Dear, dramatic Marisa. "There's no way in the world I'd ever be caught dead in *burgundy!*" she shrieked as you told her of your beautiful vision.

Welcome to the wonderful world of the bridal party.

Before your bridesmaids decide to hold a mutiny, consider some compromises and win–win situations:

- ❦ **Create a shaded wedding party look.** Pick a basic color and have your bridesmaids select gowns along the color range. This gives each attendant the opportunity to select a shade that most flatters her coloring—and the overall look will be lovely.

- ❦ **Same color, same length, but different style.** No, you don't want Lisa wearing a ball gown with puffy sleeves while Julie stands next to her in a sexy sheath with a cowl neck and a side slit up to the kazoodle. But gentle variations, such as a scoop versus a jewel neckline, a cap sleeve versus a three-quarter one, or an Empire silhouette instead of a slip dress, can allow each bridesmaid to pick a style that looks most flattering on her.

- ❦ **The reusable gown.** Forget the purple powder puff: think practical. Although black has traditionally been a wedding no-no, the black bridesmaid's gown is a sophisticated way in which to create a black-and-white wedding. And here's the bonus: a basic black evening gown can be worn again and again, or even cut down into a cocktail dress for future use. Don't like black? Try navy, cream, or another neutral color.

- ❦ **The snow-white wedding.** Going against original tradition, confident brides don't mind sharing the spotlight with attendants who also wear white. The key here is that the silhouette is dramatically different, and more low-key than the bride's. Perhaps you march down the aisle in your dramatic ball gown and they flank the aisle in narrow-profile gowns.

❦ **The eclectic wedding.** You've been there, done that, and can fully understand your bridesmaids' plight. As a generous bride, you decide to let them wear whatever they choose. You can give them some *guidance* if they want it—for example, "Anything you like, as long as it's full length and in a jewel tone." Your bridesmaids will love you! And believe it or not, your photos may be more interesting than having look-alike clones surrounding you.

In selecting the gowns for your bridesmaids or guiding them in their own selections, consider the modesty level of the dresses. If you're having a religious ceremony, the décolleté look is inappropriate. A dress with a matching jacket or shawl top will help make their dresses *shul*-appropriate. Removed for the reception, the dresses transform into party wear.

Your maid or matron of honor should wear a dress that's similar to, but differentiated from, the bridesmaids' outfits. If the bridesmaids are wearing a solid color, her dress can be a print, picking up the same color. If they are all wearing the same neckline, hers can be cut differently. But all the lengths should match.

Your bridesmaids can buy their dresses in the same place you buy yours. This will make fittings much less taxing. Or, if their dresses are custom-made, hire the same seamstress or tailor to make theirs as you did for your gown.

Junior Miss

If you have junior bridesmaids in your wedding party, they can get the same dresses or choices as your other bridesmaids. If the look is too mature for a young girl, however, a more modest version in matching color and/or fabric is appropriate.

Flower Girl

Your flower girl's dress should reflect the general style of your other honor attendants. Or her dress can be similar to yours. Mary Jane–style shoes are appropriate with ankle-length socks, with or without frills or lace cuffs.

Dressing Moms

Since in the Jewish ceremony, both mothers walk down the aisle with their respective children, the moms' dresses should coordinate in length and level of formality to the overall wedding.

Since Jewish mothers may normally cover their heads in *shul* (unless they're attending a Reform ceremony), they can wear hats or attractive female *kippot* designed to match or coordinate with their outfits. Those made of wire and beads are lightweight and attractive as well.

As a general rule, mothers should *not* wear white. This is the bride's day to shine, no matter how much a mom might feel it's her long-awaited day. Wearing white may look as if the mother is trying to steal her daughter or brand-new daughter-in-law's glory. Although this would never happen in a million years, others, or even the bride herself, might perceive it that way. As far as wearing black goes—these days, it's perfectly acceptable, especially to a formal evening wedding. Moms tend to love it—it's sophisticated, attractive, and flattering to most. But some older family members may disapprove, because black is the color of mourning.

So have the mothers talk to each other and to you about their outfits. You want to get your signals straight on this one. Styles popular for mothers of the bride or groom include long gowns with jackets of varying lengths, and those with slender profiles.

The Boys

When Stan was getting married, he envisioned himself, as well as his ushers, in top hats and tails. Although his ushers said they wouldn't mind going "black tie," they refused to look like Fred Astaire. So Stan compromised: he wore tails and his ushers wore tuxedos, and everyone looked great!

Most guys rent their formalwear for weddings, so matching is much easier once the basic style has been selected. Even those who already own a tux should rent for this occasion so that the look among the groomsmen will be uniform.

For sticklers, there are standard formalwear rules. The type of tux worn depends on the time of day, the formality of the wedding, and whether it's a contemporary or traditional affair.

The time of day usually breaks down to "before six" or "after six." The level of formality of your wedding and reception can include very formal evening, semiformal evening, very formal daytime, and semiformal daytime. A dinner jacket (or tuxedo) can be worn for a late-afternoon wedding that stretches well into the evening.

A traditional, very formal evening affair, calls for a black full-dress tailcoat, for example. According to the International Formalwear Association, this outfit should be worn with a white, wing-collar, piqué formal shirt, and a white piqué vest and bowtie. (Hence the term *white tie*.) The black trousers have a formal satin stripe, and the tailcoat just covers the vest. Black patent leather shoes complete the look.

For a semiformal contemporary evening wedding, the choice is yours: tuxedo or tailcoat, in white or a range of season-appropriate colors. The shirt can be white or coordinate with the color of the tuxedo, with a pleated or flat front.

A traditional, very formal daytime affair usually calls for a cutaway coat, gray striped trousers, a gray vest, and ascot or striped four-in-hand tie. An optional top hat, spats, walking stick, and gray gloves can be added, the organization notes.

For a complete set of guidelines, you can log on to the formalwear Web page of the International Formalwear Association at www.formalwear.org. Also, a visit to a local tuxedo rental outlet will also be informative. Tell the salesperson there the date and time of day of the wedding, and explain some of the arrangements so he or she can determine the level of formality.

Fathers' Formalwear

The fathers of the bride and groom should wear the same outfits as the ushers or one very similar. If the groomsmen are wearing something rather flamboyant (like multicolored vests) and Dad's more conservative, he can be harmonized, but toned down. After all, he'll probably have to face the important business clients he invited to the wedding.

The Little Guys

Ring bearers and pages *can* mimic the style of the groom or ushers. But they also look totally *adorable* in short pants with tall white socks and dressy shoes.

Men's Formalwear

Tuxedo jackets. These come in various styles: with notched or peaked lapels, or a shawl collar. They also come in different button styles—double-breasted or single-breasted. They can be vented (slit) or nonvented.

Dinner jacket. Worn in warmer climates or during the summer. Can be worn in place of the tuxedo jacket and, yes, over black tuxedo-type pants with a satin stripe.

Cutaway (also known as morning coat). Traditionally black or gray. Has a button at the waist, and cuts away to a wide tail in the back. Worn with striped trousers. For a very formal daytime wedding.

Stroller. A hip-length variation on the cutaway.

Vest (waistcoat). Worn in place of cummerbund. Come in high-neck and regular-neck styles and can be full-back or backless. (Backless may *feel* cooler, but full back is *really* cool looking if guys remove their jackets.)

Ties. Bowtie either premade or not. Premade are easier and look uniform. Making your own bow is the only way for traditionalists, and can look more charming.

Four-in-hand. A regular tie in a formal fabric.

Euro-ties. Look like regular long ties but the knot sits lower and is fluffier. Usually worn with a pocket square, it's more formal than the four-in-hand.

Ascot. A wide scarf, often printed, sort of looped under the chin. Hold it in place with a tie tack or stickpin. For formal morning weddings.

Studs. They replace buttons on the shirt and usually match the cufflinks. Some shirts have removable buttons on a strip—so you can pull them away and replace them with attractive studs.

Cufflinks. Replace the buttons on the cuffs. Usually match the studs.

Button covers. For shirts with banded collars that you wear without a tie. These cover the top button at the neckline. Studs can be worn the rest of the way down.

Pocket square. Worn in the breast pocket. Optional but attractive.

Suspenders (also known as braces). Since belts aren't worn with formalwear trousers, these come in handy to hold up pants.

Spats. A cloth leg covering from the instep to the ankle.

The kittel *and the* kippa. The Orthodox Jewish groom may wear a *kittel,* a white ceremonial robe, to his wedding. Guests can wear business-type suits or formalwear as appropriate. All Orthodox and Conservative males, whether in the wedding party or not, will wear a *kippah,* also known as a *yarmulka* or skullcap, during the ceremony. They can be kept on during the reception as well. They can match the color of the formalwear and can be as simple or ornate as desired. This can include embroidered (silver or gold thread is nice), knitted with an attractive pattern, or made from satin or silk. The groom can wear a higher, more formal *kippah* than his groomsmen if he likes.

Formalwear Tips

- ❧ Begin your formalwear process four months before the wedding.
- ❧ Wear silk socks with formalwear outfits.
- ❧ Black or navy-blue suits can be worn for nonformal occasions.

- For totally casual weddings, anything can go, including print shirts. Just make sure the men's outfits coordinate colorwise with the ladies' clothes.

- Tuxedos can be worn with vests or cummerbunds.

- Cummerbunds are worn with the pleats facing upward.

- A long solid tie, in a formal fabric, can replace the bowtie. It can also be worn by the groom only to distinguish him from the groomsmen, or vice versa.

- The "wings" or points of a winged collar fold down *under* the bowtie.

- The groom can distinguish himself from his attendants by wearing a different kind of boutonnière or different tie.

- The bride takes the lead as to the formality of the clothes. The men's clothes follow the same level of formality.

- Keep in touch with your tuxedo rental shop every few weeks, especially if you're involved with a destination wedding. You don't want to place your order and then show up two to four months later for your wedding to find that your order never got processed.

- When picking up your formalwear the day before the wedding, take off the plastic covering and carefully try on your outfit. You want to ensure that all alterations are correct and that you indeed are handed *your* tux and not someone else's in error.

7

Beauty and the Bride

ALL EYES WILL BE on you as you walk down the aisle to take your place under the *chuppah*. Your blush, your glow, your inner shine is something so special that it radiates to all those around you. But that's not to say that you won't do everything you can to enhance your natural sparkle.

Your Hair

Whether you've worn your hair the same way as long as you can remember, or you're the type known for the trendiest tresses in town, you'll be giving careful consideration to how you will wear your hair on your wedding day. In fact, you probably started thinking about it when you started to shop for your wedding gown, veil, and hair accessories. So don't wait until the last minute to begin some serious planning with your hairdresser-to-be. The type of veil and headpiece you have selected may dictate the type of hairstyle you'll be wearing. For example, if you ordered a bun-wrap type of headpiece, you naturally need to have a bun, and so forth.

The type of wedding dress you've selected may also have an impact on your hairstyle. Certain necklines call for hair worn either up or down. And if you're taking in your entire image (as everyone will be), you'll want to balance your hair with the shape of the dress. A big poofy gown may look unbalanced when worn with a close-cropped hairstyle, and big, teased-up tresses may overpower a sleek, slim column gown.

Six months ahead of your wedding isn't too early to start working on your hair. Many brides-to-be who have short hair decide to let their hair grow out before their wedding. In that way, they will have many more options open to them. But a word to the wise: do not drastically change your hairstyle or color at the last minute. You want to be comfortable with yourself and not feel that you're dressed up in someone else's hair!

If you color your hair, you'll need to consider the timing of your color work. Ditto with a perm or relaxer. If you're trying out something new, start your experimentation at least six months in advance.

The time of day your wedding will be held can affect your choice of hairstyles, as can the type of reception you're having. The more formal the affair, the more formal you can wear your hair. But that's not to say a simple, understated style won't work perfectly.

So, when selecting a hairstyle, take the following into consideration:

- The length of your hair

- The type of hair accessories and veil you've selected

- The shape of your face

- Your natural neck

- The neckline and overall proportion of your wedding gown

- The type of hair you have naturally—thick, thin, curly, straight

- Whether you color your hair

❦ Whether you perm or relax your hair

❦ The time of day of the wedding

❦ Your hairdresser's expertise and advice

Dress Rehearsal

If you're holding your wedding in your local area and your regular hairdresser is sharing your joy and his or her creativity with you, you're in luck. He or she will know your hair and how best to work with it. But you'll still want to rehearse!

About a month or so before your wedding day, arrange a meeting with your stylist. Discuss your wedding vision. Tell your hairdresser about your gown, its shape, neckline, and other salient information. Bring in your headpiece and veil (or, if it's not ready, at least a photo cut out of a magazine or a sketch). Replicate the neckline of your gown with an old white sheet. With all of these elements in place, together you can decide on a hairstyle to try.

Have your hair done in that style and wear it for a "comfort fit." Ask opinions of friends and family members. Take some photos in your hairstyle so that you can judge how it looks for yourself. Have the photos taken from the back, front, and sides, so you can get a full look at how others will see you.

Steer clear of the trendy if possible. Classic styles will always look nice—the day of your wedding and years after as you browse through your album.

It's also a good time to "book" your date with your hairdresser. He or she may have to make special concessions for you in terms of the time of your appointment and whether he or she can come to you or you need to come to the salon. Your best bet for your wedding day: have your hair and makeup done after you put on your undergarments. That way, you won't have to worry about messing up your hair or smudging your mascara when you pull your slip over your head.

Emergency Hair Supply Kit

- ♡ **Slippery scarf.** Keep a smooth-type silk or polyester scarf on hand for emergencies. Tie it lightly over your head so that clothes you may need to put over will glide over, rather than tug at your hair.

- ♡ **Rat-tail comb or pick.** This is useful to lift hair that may have flattened.

- ♡ **Hairbrushes.** Have a big one and a small, narrow one on hand.

- ♡ **Headband.** If you have hair that went flat on you and needs a lift in the front or sides, slip on a headband and spritz on some volumizing spray until your hair is slightly damp. Let it dry, and carefully remove the headband.

- ♡ **Curling iron.** To repair any last-minute droops.

- ♡ **Hair spray.** Good to have around, but use with a light hand, if necessary. You don't want it weighing down your hair.

- ♡ **Assorted hair clips, bobby pins, hairpins, and a beautiful barrette.** Just in case!

Shaved Heads

Not everyone has the problem of how to handle her hairstyle on her wedding day. There is a custom among some Jewish brides to shave off their hair before the wedding and before attending the *mikvah,* where they will immerse themselves in water as a pre-wedding purification ritual. Since every hair has to be immersed at the same time, it's easier to do so when the hair is shaven short. Another explanation is that by shaving and then covering her head, the woman makes herself unattractive to other men. And, in biblical times, covering the head was considered an act of modesty.

Once an ultra-Orthodox lady is married, she will keep her head covered at all times by wearing a *tichl* (a large kerchief). Other Orthodox women do wear a *shaytl* (wig) as their headcovering, with their own hair shaven or cut short.

Your Face

You certainly want your skin to look flawless for your wedding day, so start pampering it weeks before. You don't want your skin to be shiny, or dry and flaky. Photography flashes tend to reflect the shine if your skin is oily. And nervous tension may make your skin erupt.

Giving yourself a facial once a week or so will help unmask the beauty beneath the surface of dead skin cells and workaday grime. Cleanse and exfoliate. A cosmetologist can help you select the best products to use, depending on your skin type: oily, dry, or combination. Your selection will probably include a cleanser, a toner to help reduce oil, and a moisturizer to condition your skin.

And it's important to drink at least eight glasses of water a day. This will keep your skin hydrated and flush out any possible toxins.

For real pampering, why not get a professional facial? Not only will it make you feel good, relax you, and help drain that pre-wedding stress, but it will help you look your radiant best as well. A facial can include a hand and shoulder massage, paraffin wax treatment, steam to open your pores, pore cleansing, moisturizing, and sometimes a seaweed treatment to add extra moisture to the skin. If you're wearing a gown that will expose your back, you can have a back "facial" as well.

As tempting as it may be, think twice about undergoing any special skin "jobs" such as chemical peels or laser repair very close to the time of your wedding. Since you don't know how you will react, you don't want to worry about being caught red-faced as you walk down the aisle.

Makeup

A radiant bridal glow is a good foundation, and you also *know* that inner beauty always shines through. But if you don't want your face shining away more than it should, or don't want to pale under photo lights, some makeup is in order.

Keep your makeup subtle—but that doesn't mean nonexistent. A makeup artist will have an arsenal of products at his or her disposal for the express purpose of making you look "natural." If you want to use color on your eyes, it should be done lightly, picking up the colors of your bridal party's gowns or matching your eyes.

If you don't normally have someone doing your makeup for you on a regular basis, you'll want to "audition" several makeup artists. Have them make you up for a pre-wedding event, or for your engagement photo shoot. Again, start early. Talk to your makeup artist about your vision. Hear what he or she has to say and come to a meeting of the minds.

When meeting your makeup artist, try to bring a color swatch of your gown (there are so many different shades of white) with you, if possible. It will help fine-tune your makeup so that the shades of foundation will correct any color drain created by the fabric closest to your face.

After you've had your makeup done, show it off! Ask several people what they think. Take some close-up photos and get the opinion of friends and family members. Have your makeup done by several different people during the course of your "selection process."

If you'll be doing your own makeup, keep in mind that less is more. Match your makeup to the overall look of your gown. You don't want overly dramatic makeup with an Empire-type gown accented by a wreath of spring flowers in your hair.

Swinging to the minimum, you'll want some foundation that you'll apply with a makeup sponge. Natural sponges are good, as are those fine-grained white triangle wedge sponges. When selecting a foundation color, lean away from those that are much lighter or darker than your skin tone. And when applying, go for a light touch. You want to even out your skin tone, but you don't want to hide your skin under a mask! As you apply the foundation, carry it down below the chin onto the neck and blend it carefully so there will be no line of demarcation. Don't forget to do your ear lobes as well.

When doing your eyes, make sure that you separate each lash after applying waterproof mascara. You don't want an artificial clump or "strip" look. Fill in your eyebrows, if necessary, and tweeze any stray hairs.

When applying blush, do so with a light touch and blend carefully. You don't want to look like you're wearing war paint!

Lipstick is best applied with a brush, but if you've never used one before, spend some time practicing. Blot, apply some powder or lip set stick, and apply another coat. Blot again.

And wouldn't you know it? All of a sudden, just when you want to look your best—out come the zits! It's probably your skin's reaction to the nervous tension that is usually associated with weddings.

In an emergency, concealer stick can be helpful, as can some green-tinted base to help neutralize the red. But professionals realize that zits, bruises, and other markings come in multiple colors, and they can address them like an artist—with different-colored makeup to blend it together.

When applying makeup, use water-resistant products—you'll probably be shedding many a happy tear! With all of the activity, you very well may get overheated, causing makeup to run. Use matte products—no glimmer, shimmer, or shine, which may show up weird in photography.

> ## *Emergency Makeup Kit*
>
>
>
> ❦ Oil-blotting sheets
>
> ❦ Small compact of powder
>
> ❦ Mirror (if not in the compact)
>
> ❦ A paper or cloth wraparound to shield your gown if you need to apply powder or makeup

Henna

Henna and gold are choices that *Sephardic* brides may invoke, giving a nod toward their heritage. In fact, some Middle Eastern brides have been known to wear all-gold bridal outfits, and all-gold jewelry as well.

Some *Sephardic* women enjoy the Middle Eastern bridal custom called *mehendi*. It's the ancient art of painting intricate designs on the skin with a paste made from the dried leaves of the henna plant and other ingredients such as oils, lemon juice, tea, or coffee. The artwork, which looks very much like tattoos, is usually applied to the palms, arms, ankles, and feet of the bride-to-be.

Designs can be drawn freehand with a toothpick or a tube similar to the kind used to put icing designs on a cake. You can also purchase ready-made stencils. The henna is left on until it dries on the skin and turns black. The longer the henna paste remains on, the darker the skin stain becomes, with the drier areas of skin absorbing the deepest colors. The paste should be kept warm and moist while on your skin. The usual wait time is between seven and twenty-four hours before it is scraped—not washed—off. Thus the color of the staining can range from light orange to deep brown.

This henna custom is believed to promote fertility and a happy marriage. Often the bride-to-be gets together with her friends, her mom, and the groom's mothers for a henna party. They can even hire an artist to come and do the painting, or take turns painting each other. The bride, however, gets the most intricate designs: florals, vines, geometrics, or teardrops, often running along the line of the legs or arms or covering the palms. While the painting is going on, there's lots of talk, fun-filled wedding and sex advice, tea drinking and food nibbling, and the general bonding and fun of a bachelorette-type party.

Grooming the Groom

Mention physical pampering and most of us think of women. Today, however, men also participate in getting groomed and pampered. They go to hairstylists, get facials, and have their hair permed and colored. Men blow-dry their hair, shape it with product, and otherwise take good care of themselves, too.

Beauty Quiz

Wedding day beauty is a little different than your everyday variety. There are lots of special little tricks you'll need to know to ensure that you look your best, feel your best, and photograph in a way that will provide you with wonderful memories forever. Discover how much you know about wedding day beauty by taking this quiz. For each statement, circle the letter that represents the best answer.

1. I'm getting married in my mom's hometown, and my hairdresser won't come along. I'm all thumbs when it comes to hairstyling. So I'll:

   a) switch the wedding locale back to my home base so that my trusted hairdresser can do my hair.
   b) shave off my hair and get a wig, even though I won't be doing it for religious or modesty reasons.
   c) tell the photographer there will be no pictures of the bride. It's bad enough my guests have to see me in person at the wedding!
   d) Make an appointment to visit my mom's hairdresser when I'm in town making other arrangements for the wedding. We can discuss my vision for the wedding, and have my hair done in a practice session long before the wedding day.

2. I'll be doing my own makeup for the wedding and want to look special, so I'll:

a) brush glittery powder over my foundation to add sparkle.

b) put on extra-heavy blue eye shadow. After all, it has to last the whole night through.

c) apply foundation, plain powder, natural-looking eye makeup, and a touch of blush, then blend, blend, blend.

d) apply makeup to match my wedding gown: extra-pale foundation, white eye shadow over my entire lid, and top off the look with powdered-down eyelashes and white lipstick.

3. Oh my goodness—my wedding is only three days away, and I must do *something* about my skin! So I:

a) quickly call up and make an appointment for a dermabrasion procedure. As luck would have it, they have a cancellation and can fit me in tomorrow afternoon. I didn't tell the receptionist about my upcoming wedding, however. Who has time to *talk?*

b) rush to my local day spa and request a medium-deep chemical peel. That should do it!

c) go to my day spa and splurge, once again, on the full-facial package that includes a steam treatment, paraffin wax treatment, pore cleansing, moisturizing, a shoulder massage, and a seaweed wrap. Ahh!

d) rush to the discount beauty supply, grab an armful of alphahydroxy products, and try them all. One of them will do the trick!

4. I've been so busy at my desk job and then making the rounds of the wonderful pre-wedding parties being held in my honor, I need to lose five pounds fast. My wedding is only three weeks away. So I'll:

a) go on a self-designed liquid diet, despite my doctor's warning. What could be so bad about a mix of cola, strong black coffee, and chocolate syrup?

b) fast for two days, eat anything I want for two, fast for two more days, and so on.

c) eat small portions of a well-balanced diet, drink lots of water, and skip desserts. And I'll take the stairs to and from my fourth-floor office rather than the elevator. Not particularly drastic, so will it work?

d) forget about joining a diet group just for five pounds and three weeks. But I *will* supplement each fast-food burger order with those frozen diet meals that I can buy at the supermarket. One should balance out the other.

5. Okay, I admit it. I'm a longtime couch potato. But the pre-wedding stress is getting to me, and friends say exercise and sports can help. So I'll:

a) climb aboard my dusty stationary bike and start by pedaling to nowhere five minutes a day.

b) decide it would be *fun* to go bungee jumping with my daredevil friend who does this all the time.

c) pack my bags and sign up for a downhill skiing competition in Gstaad.

d) turn on the television and watch the fly-fishing shows.

Answers: 1—d; 2—c; 3—c; 4—c; 5—a.

Scoring: Give yourself 5 points for each correct answer.

0–5 points: Make-over candidate. Beauty may be in the eyes of the beholder, but you owe it to yourself to take better care of your "temple." Whether you ignore your body or overdo in an attempt to play catch-up, learn that steady maintenance and a little knowledge can go a long way toward letting your natural beauty shine. Go for it!

10–15 points: Pretty pretty. You are generally concerned with how you look and feel, and for the most part make the right decisions about what's best for you. Sometimes, however, you leap into beauty or fitness issues before you think things through. Take the time to analyze your choices and pick the healthiest and wisest ways to achieve your beauty goal. Patience pays!

20–25 points: Beauty queen. Whether by instinct or through experience, you always seem to know the right thing to do when it comes to beauty and caring for your body. Don't worry: you'll come through your wedding looking absolutely smashing, no matter what obstacles are thrown in your path.

Insider's Interview:
Your Wedding Makeup

Sara Seidman-Vance, Makeup artist
Member of I.A.T.S.E., New York Local 798

Background: Virginia-based Sara Seidman-Vance has been doing makeup and hair for weddings, as well as for television and film production, for the past thirteen years. Her credits include *Dawson's Creek, The Young Indiana Jones Chronicles, Matlock,* and *Patch Adams,* among others.

"It's not about beauty, it's about the illusion of reality," says Seidman-Vance. "This is your show. It's a performance and affirmation at the same time. This is the time to be the fairy princess you used to play as a little girl.

"For weddings, you don't want to go overboard. If you're wearing white, unless you're into heavy, full coverage, I like the natural look that doesn't look made up but that brings out every bit of beauty in the face. Instead of 'gaudy,' you want 'beautiful.'

"The secret to really good makeup is blending. You don't want light color here and dark there. No paint-by-number eyes.

"You have to select makeup that won't reflect light back in the photographs. If powder has mica in it, it reflects back and you'll look like a ghost. Use colors that are as close to natural skin colors as possible.

"When doing makeup for a wedding, I'll first have a consultation with the bride to see what she's looking for and what I see. It has to be a joint effort. Don't let anyone bulldoze you. Corrective makeup is my specialty. If someone is broken out, I can cover it. I attack each one of the blemishes by itself, since they're not all the same color.

"If your skin is oily, cleanse and then use astringent mixed with water, and a light layer of moisturizer. If you use astringent only, the skin overproduces oil and actually becomes oilier. If you use moisturizer, the body gets tricked and you have a longer period before the oil comes out.

"I apply the highlighting, base, and then contouring is done. Everyone needs highlighting under the eyes. Very few over twelve years old have milky skin. Putting lighter makeup under the eyes makes you look awake, and makes your skin look fresh and flawless. If you are wearing a color, you can use a minute amount of the color in the eye shadow. You'll want to use natural earth tones, with a hint of the dress's color in the eyelid crease to pull it all together.

"To contour your face, use the base color but two shades darker, usually applied under the jawbone and under the cheekbone. It has to be in the right position and blended in so people don't see that the contouring is there. It takes skill. Don't do contouring if you're not experienced at it!

"After I apply the base, and the highlighting and contouring is done, I seal it all with powder. Then I apply blush and eye makeup on top of the powder. If applying false eyelashes, I use individual lashes in twos and threes. Three sets of threes on the outside edge of the upper lid give eyes a fairy-tale look. Get light brown ones. They are easier to put mascara on. Don't buy black unless you have really black natural eyelashes. And always use waterproof mascara. If you are going to use eyeliner, use pencil eyeliner, which holds up better than the liquid. Lipstick is always last. What I like to do if I'm doing a natural beauty look is a natural but enhanced lip look. I'll put on color in earth tones. It's okay to put pink on a young bride, but you don't want to put pink on an older woman.

"Some tricks of the trade: Should you have soft bags under your eyes, you can put a tiny line of eyelash glue under your bottom lashes and gently push up the skin under the eye and hold it until it dries. To correct a double chin, you can buy adhesive lifts at a makeup supply house. The lifts are attached under the ear and go up around the back of the neck with elastic, pulling the chin up. You can then comb your hair over it.

"If you are flying, drink a lot of water because airplanes will dehydrate the skin. Avoid soft drinks and alcohol.

"Finding a qualified makeup artist can be difficult unless someone has a reputation and huge résumé. Some may be good at hair but not at makeup. Check credentials. Ask for references and phone numbers to verify the information. Don't rely on photographs of work they claim to have done. Some salons have resident makeup artists, or you can find someone by word of mouth or you may have seen their work at someone else's wedding. Some states have film offices with directories that may list makeup artists, but the offices may not check credentials. You still have to do your research. Interview the person and have yourself made up first. If you don't like the results, you don't want this person doing your wedding.

"On the wedding day, the makeup can be done two hours before the actual wedding. I usually do it at the bride's home, or sometimes I go to the salon after the bride's hair is done. The bride should have her undergarments on before doing hair and makeup. I prefer doing makeup when the bride is in her slip, so she doesn't have to put too many things over her head. The bride usually steps into the dress. Or she can wear a loose-fitting button-down shirt, so she doesn't have to take anything back over her head.

"Makeup is designed to stay on for several hours. To remove makeup, use soap and water or a gentle cleanser, cleansing twice, and then lightly moisturize."

8

It's Party Time!

EVERYONE LOVES TO CELEBRATE love! And as such, your decision to marry may set off a whole round of partying that may culminate in your wedding—the biggest celebration of them all. The operative word is *may,* because in some Jewish sectors, the parties continue for a week after the wedding, and if you're having a destination wedding, your guests may continue to celebrate with you in a vacation locale even as you honeymoon.

There are so many opportunities to celebrate that if you attend them all, you may be too tired to show up at your wedding! You may be able to pick and choose your pre-wedding parties, but don't be surprised if you end up getting surprised. Many a bridal party has planned showers for the bride-to-be at times she would least expect it. So a word of warning, girls: if your best friend invites you to the corner coffee shop for some girl talk, change out of your junk clothes and put on a dab of lipstick. Sure, you might end up having a snack and a chat, but then again . . . you could be walking into your bridal shower!

The *Machetenestas* Meet

Perhaps they've known each other for years, but chances are, your parents will be meeting each other for the first time shortly after you've become engaged.

If the groom's mom doesn't take the first step (maybe she doesn't realize it's her move to make), there's nothing wrong with the bride's mom getting the ball rolling. Or you and your fiancé can set up the deal. Gather a few dates and offer to make restaurant reservations. Once your parents have met, chances are they will be inviting each other to many family functions for years to come.

If your parents don't live near each other, they can meet at a restaurant halfway between them. But if even that's not possible, a friendly call or lovely letter of welcome will do. They will probably meet at another time—perhaps at the family dinner before the wedding. But in the meantime, they will have touched base.

If you have step-parents, there's yet another occasion to celebrate. You and your honey can be instrumental in arranging a dinner party to meet the other members of the family. Under most circumstances, it's not a good idea to throw all the exes together for that first meeting. One at a time will do it—all the more reason to celebrate.

The "getting to know you" celebrations can continue. Perhaps you have a favorite aunt who would like to invite you over for lunch or tea. And Grandma and Gramps may host a gathering.

The Engagement Party

The engagement party can be as simple as an at-home gathering, a fun-time event at a bowling alley, a backyard cookout, or an afternoon tea, or it can be as elaborate as a fancy dinner in a restaurant or hotel. It can also take the form of an announcement during *Shabbat* services, after which parents can host a *kiddish* (meal or snack).

Today engagement parties can be hosted by the groom's family, if they wish; the bride's and groom's family together; or anyone else who cares to do the honors—including the couple themselves, if they'd like to announce their engagement to family and friends in person. And with people spread out in various locations, parties can be held in different locales so that everyone has a chance to celebrate. A bride's mom can set up an engagement party in her hometown for all her friends and relatives, while the groom's mom can host a party in her town, as well.

The dual-party concept also works well when family dynamics dictate separate but equal parental treatment, so long as the guest list is not duplicated. Dad and step-mom can host one party, attended by Dad's side of the family, while Mom and step-dad toss a to-do for her side of the family.

The Bridal Shower

Note to the bride: close your eyes, turn the page, put on a blindfold, or do whatever it is you have to do to pass this section on bridal showers along to your maid of honor unread.

"Legally," this is the time gifts are actually requested! The idea of a shower started several hundred years ago (so the story goes), when a father did not like the groom his daughter had selected and refused to give her a dowry. Her friends got together and planned a way for her to have all the stuff she would need in order to make up her new home with her husband.

Sometimes "specific" showers are given. For example, a linen shower requests gifts that will outfit the bride and groom's bedroom, bath, and dining room. Appropriate gifts are sheets, pillowcases, duvet covers, blankets, towels, tablecloths, and other items. Other showers may provide the bride with her trousseau—nighties, robes, and under-things suitable for the honeymoon.

And with the advent of egalitarian showers, guests can bring gifts that include hardware. Tools, workshop items, and gardening supplies are some examples. The "wishing-well" items could include packages of nails, screws, lightbulbs, hooks, and similar stuff.

Often gifts are selected from the bride and groom's bridal registry, if the couple is registered. Since money is the standard gift at Jewish weddings, here's a chance for guests to buy the newlyweds an actual item they can use in their life together.

The Bridal Luncheon

Some brides will host a bridal luncheon for their wedding party and close female relatives (moms, grandmoms) a few days before the wedding. This is the bride's way of saying thank you to those who worked, and will continue to work, so diligently on her behalf throughout the wedding process. It's a time for last-minute warmth and camaraderie before the excitement of the big event. During this time, the bride may give out the gifts to her attendants.

The Bachelor Party

Traditionally, the guys in the wedding party take the groom out for a whopping good time on the night before the wedding—a last-minute fling of "freedom." But today's American Jewish groom will most likely find himself at a rather tame family dinner party the night before his wedding, so he'll be well rested for the big event the next day.

Still, boys will be boys—and many *do* go out together for some last-minute bonding. In ancient times, the bachelor party lasted for three days! Nowadays the let-loose rowdy behavior is, at best, limited to one night within a week or so of the wedding.

Other cultures celebrate the bachelor party in different ways. In Morocco, for example, the groom is treated as a sultan or king, and his wedding party or male friends become his "royal court." A typical bachelor party includes a ritual cleaning of the bridegroom's home, references to casting spells for fertility and riches, and chasing away evil spirits. They enjoy an evening spent in celebration with musicians, singers, and great food. The party takes to the streets in the wee hours, with the groom and his men parading around, followed by the musicians and singers. Once back at the house, the henna ritual begins. After lighting candles and preparing the henna mixture in a bowl (all of which are provided by the bridegroom's mother), the best man applies henna to the groom's hands and then to his own. During the prep time, everyone is singing. After applying the henna, the candles are placed in the bowl, which is passed to all the guys who dance with it on their heads before the groom-to-be. After everyone has had his turn, the bowl is shattered to ward off evil spirits.

The Bachelorette Party

Why should the guys have all the fun? Today more and more girls are going for the gusto with a bachelorette party. During the week before her wedding, the bridesmaids and friends will take the bride-to-be out for an evening of entertainment. Girls only! No dainty tea party, this. Or the party can take a totally different turn—one of beautification and bonding. The girls can all go to a day spa and get facials, makeovers, manicures, and pedicures. They can go to the country club and play golf or tennis. No matter which type of event is chosen, the idea is for the bride and her friends to have a tension-relieving, fun-filled time.

The *Mikvah* Gathering

Traditionally, if you're an Orthodox Jew or have converted to Judaism, before your wedding you'll be going to the *mikvah*—a ritual bathhouse affiliated with a synagogue or group of synagogues and housed in a permanent structure. Today more and more liberal Jews are also discovering the *mikvah*, which has been part of the Jewish practice for thousands of years. You'll ceremoniously immerse yourself in a pool of rainwater, or water that has run off from snow, sometimes mixed with filtered chlorinated water. Immersing in the water is a means of ritual purification: water symbolizes the source of life.

Before entering the *mikvah*, you'll bathe, wash your hair, and cut your nails and toenails. You'll remove your nail polish and all jewelry and makeup. A "*mikvah* lady" will oversee your actual immersion into the *mikvah* pool and check to make sure you follow the ritual correctly. You will need to submerge completely in the pool, which is usually filled up to about shoulder level. Once in the pool, you'll lift your feet completely off the floor, open your eyes, and make sure that every single hair on your head is submerged. After the first dunk, a blessing is said, and the bride-to-be dunks several more times.

Attending the *mikvah* before your marriage is considered to be a joyous occasion, often followed by a females-only party for family members. In *Sephardic* cultures, female friends accompany the bride-to-be to the *mikvah* and also join the party afterward to celebrate her upcoming wedding.

Men, too, can attend the *mikvah* before their marriage. And some men also have males-only parties after the occasion.

The *Ufruf Kiddish*

In some Jewish communities, the groom is called up to the Torah on the Saturday before, or if *Sephardic,* the Saturday after, his wedding. Sometimes the bride and groom are called up together. Called an *Ufruf,* in this ceremony the groom or couple are honored and recite the *brochot* (blessings) before and after the Torah segment is read. The congregation then tosses little wrapped packs of nuts or candy at the bride and groom. The parents of the groom will host a *kiddish* for the congregation and invite guests after services. It can be as elaborate as a buffet with smoked fish, herring, salads, bagels, *challah,* coffee and cake, wine and some whiskey, or as simple as some wine and *challah* and perhaps a little cake.

The Family Party or Rehearsal Dinner

Traditionally, the Jewish wedding does not include a rehearsal or rehearsal dinner. Right before the ceremony, the members of the wedding party gather outside the ceremony room or sanctuary room and, with the help of the rabbi or caterer, are guided into lining up in the proper order. When the music starts, they go down the aisle. Simple, easy, end of story.

But today, with complicated family structures, planning who walks down with whom can become complicated indeed. So often families will get together to plan it out. But whether there is a rehearsal or not, the pre-wedding dinner the evening before the wedding is fast becoming a Jewish tradition as well.

The dinner, hosted by the groom's family, can be as simple as a home-cooked meal or barbecue at the groom's parents' home, or an all-out affair at a hotel, restaurant, or country inn that can rival the wedding to come. Usually, it's something in between. An aunt, cousin, or other relative can host the party as well.

All of the wedding party is invited with their respective spouses or significant others, as are the clergy, the parents, grandparents, great-grandparents, and often close aunts and uncles. Out-of-town guests who have come in for the wedding are generally invited, too.

Holding the dinner at the hotel where most of the out-of-town guests are staying is not only a convenience for them, but can eliminate transportation problems to and from their hotel to the party site. And as a bonus, some hotels may offer greater room discounts to guests if the rehearsal dinner is booked there.

During the dinner, the guests toast the bride and groom, everyone catches up with each other, and the bride and groom can exchange gifts. The bride and groom can also give gifts to their attendants at this time.

The After-Wedding Brunch or Breakfast

If the wedding is an evening affair and out-of-town guests are staying over, the family of the bride, groom, or both combined can host a breakfast or brunch the next day. The bride and groom, if still in town, can reunite with their guests in the morning, but everyone will understand if they've already taken off for their honeymoon.

The breakfast or brunch can be held at the hotel where the guests are staying or at the home of the parents of the bride or groom. If many guests are spending the night at the homes of your parents or nearby neighbors rather than in a hotel, the brunch can be held at home. But it might be easier to gather everyone up and go to a nearby restaurant than to try to organize a meal with sleep-over guests packing bags, showering, stripping beds, talking, and dashing about. And you *know* there will always be at least one aunt who will follow your mom around, demanding her full attention as she tries in vain to measure the coffee and arrange the lox.

Making the Rounds

In some of the more religious Jewish communities, the newly married couples continue to party for a week before leaving on their honeymoon. They are honored at dinner parties each evening.

Home Sweet Home

Once you settle into your new home and have your things organized, it's time to throw housewarming parties for friends and relatives. Usually you host several different parties for various small family groups—his aunts and uncles, yours and so on. As newlyweds you can proudly show off your home.

FROM OY VEY TO OLÉ

Malka spent a lot of time and effort searching for just the perfect favors to give out to the approximately thirty-five guests who would be attending Goldie's bridal shower, being held in a beautiful restaurant in New Jersey.

Malka nixed the idea of buying favors from the 99-cent store—little picture frames and other things. She also thought about getting little potted flowers but decided against that because she didn't want them to wither and die after the party.

"I was looking and looking and didn't see anything that I would like to buy," she said. Although she was told that favors weren't *really* necessary, she was determined to send every guest home with something lovely to help remember the event.

While shopping with the bride-to-be on Long Island, many miles from home, she spotted several eight-inch bonsai trees in beautiful ceramic pots in a nearby store. "A lightbulb lit up in my head, but I didn't say anything," Malka explained. "They cost much more than I was planning to spend, but I couldn't stop thinking about them."

The next day, she called the store and asked how many bonsai trees they had. As luck would have it, they told her they had forty. So Malka said she'd take them all, and asked them to please set them aside for her. The next day, together with the bride's fiancé, she drove all the way back to Long Island and picked up the boxes loaded with miniature trees. "I figured these little trees would last for a long time, and they were something different," she said.

When Malka and her sister-in-law went to the restaurant to decorate the room for the shower, Malka decided against placing all the trees out on the tables at the individual place settings. Instead, she arranged one tree on each table for eight people as a centerpiece. "Since no two bonsai trees were alike, I was afraid people would start picking and changing them," she said.

The owner of the restaurant agreed that putting them out on the tables would not be a good idea. "You can't put them out because some people are going to grab two and some will have none and you'll have a fight," he told Malka. His advice was to leave all the trees in the boxes, and as each guest took leave, she would get the favor. Malka agreed, and they placed the boxes of trees in a convenient location. Halfway through the party, however, Malka glanced over to the spot and was shocked to find that the boxes were gone! With her heart thumping, she raced over to her sister-in-law.

"Someone stole all the bonsai trees," she exclaimed in anguish, while the party swirled happily around her. It was not an unreasonable thought given that some guests had already helped themselves to a large supply of shower party favors that were in a basket nearby.

Happily, her sister-in-law was able to reassure her. The restaurant owner had moved the trees over to the far side of the large room so that they would remain out of harm's way. "Would you believe that some people go into the boxes and help themselves?" he said, ever watchful of the beautiful living gifts.

So as the fun-filled shower came to a close and each guest was about to leave, Malka and Goldie handed out a surprise: a beautiful living reminder of the wonderful day they spent showering Goldie with gifts for her wedding.

9

Ceremoniously Speaking

ONE OF THE FIRST things almost everyone will ask you after congratulating you on your engagement is, "So, when is the wedding?" Romantically, you gaze into the future and pick a date for your wedding. Maybe you always wanted to be a June bride. Or a winter groom. Maybe you're both starting school in September and need to marry before then so you'll have time for a honeymoon. Others may select a date that has special meaning for them, like the exact day of the month they met.

But not so fast: there are other considerations that play into the decision of when you can marry. These include Jewish marriage restrictions, ceremony site availability, your rabbi's availability, the schedules of important people in your lives, and the rules of the state or country in which you plan to marry.

No, No, Not Today!

In planning a traditional Jewish wedding, one of your most important considerations will be Jewish marriage date restrictions. Although some blackout dates apply to all streams of Judaism, others vary from denomination to denomination, community to community. Check with your rabbi before locking in your wedding date.

For all streams of Judaism, marriage is restricted on the following days.

Shabbat

This falls from sundown on Friday evening to nightfall on Saturday. A Hebrew calendar should provide exact times for your area.

Reasons. Marriage entails legal considerations, including signing the wedding contract. You don't perform business on the *Shabbat,* a day of rest, nor should you diminish the celebration of *Shabbat* by overlaying it with another celebration.

Special considerations. A Saturday-night wedding can be a dream come true—a time you can go all out to celebrate. And an exuberant celebration of a wedding is considered a grand *mitzvah.* But since Saturday-night weddings must start after sundown, this could cause a summertime wedding to start as late as 9:30 P.M., with food service starting after 10 P.M. Would this mean overtime charges for the staff, musicians, or photographer?

Additionally, before planning that Saturday-night wedding in the summer, consider your guests—they may need to start traveling home after two in the morning or make arrangements to sleep over. And don't forget to think about your own body clocks. When one early-to-bed-early-to-rise bride started thinking about holding her wedding on a Saturday night in June, her mom lovingly nixed the idea. "You'll probably fall asleep walking down the aisle," she teased.

The High Holy Days of Rosh Ha'Shannah *and* Yom Kippur, *As Well As the Major Holidays of* Pesach *(Passover),* Shavout, *and* Sukkot

The festivals of *Chanukah* and *Purim* are exceptions, since they are not considered major festivals. Check with your rabbi, however.

Reasons. Like the *Shabbat,* you don't want to mix one celebration with another; each should be celebrated in its own right. The solemnity of the High Holy Days may infringe on the joy of a wedding.

Exceptions. The intermediate days of *Pesach* and *Sukkot* could be exceptions. Although tradition holds that these days are included in the blackout, some Reform and Reconstructionist rabbis may permit you to marry on these days.

Orthodox and most Conservative denominations also add the following restricted dates.

"The Three Weeks," Also Known As Bein Ha'Metzarim

This is the period starting with the summertime fast of the seventeenth day of the month of *Tammuz* and extending through the fast of the ninth day of *Av,* known as *Tisha B'Av.*

Reason. This is a time of public mourning commemorating the destruction of our Holy Temple. During this time in 69 C.E., the Romans breached the walls of Jerusalem, and three weeks later, on the ninth of *Av,* the Temple was destroyed. It is also the date that the first Temple was destroyed by the Babylonians in 423 B.C.E.

Exception. Reform and other liberal practices vary, but usually allow marriages during the "Three Weeks," with the exception of the ninth of *Av.*

The "Seven Weeks," Also Known As the Sefirah *Period, or 49 Days, or the Counting of the* Omer

This is the period between the second night of Passover, in the month of *Nisan,* and *Shavout,* in the month of *Sivan,* with an "oasis" on the thirty-third day, known as *Lag B'Omer.*

Reason. This is a period in which, historically, many tragedies occurred, including the death of twenty-four thousand of Rabbi Akiva's students during the time of the revolt against Rome around 134–135 C.E. The deaths stopped on the thirty-third day, which is one of the reasons why weddings can be celebrated then. In fact, it's a very popular wedding day, especially in Israel. Planning a *Lag B'Omer* wedding? Check the calendar for the year of your wedding and time of day. Make sure it doesn't fall on *Shabbat,* which would make it restricted anyway.

Depending on your community, and whether you are *Ashkenazik* or *Sephardic,* there are many other variations of dates that restrict or allow weddings during this period.

Orthodox Practice

In addition to the fast days that fall during the "Three Weeks" period, the tenth day of the month *Tevet,* the Fast of *Gediliah* (the third of *Tisrei*), and the Fast of Esther (the thirteenth of *Adar*) are also wedding blackout dates.

Period of Personal Mourning

Here you are, filled with joy as you plan your upcoming wedding. Then the unthinkable happens. You lose a loved one.

If the wedding date has already been set and the plans made, the wedding should *not* be canceled due to the death of a family member. The reception should be toned down, however, and music and dance eliminated.

If either you or your honey are already in mourning when you decide to marry, or if definite plans have not been put into effect, you must hold off setting the date until after you've observed the appropriate mourning time. For traditionalists, this would mean you would wait until after you've completed the eleven months of mourning for a parent, or thirty days for a sibling. Reformed practice usually maintains the thirty-day period for parents and siblings.

After careful consideration, you've come up with a list of "allowable" dates on which you can hold your wedding. And if you'd like a spring or summer wedding, you've got your work cut out for you! Between Jewish brides trying to grab up June dates (the most readily available considering all the blackouts) and the secular popularity of June weddings, you might find it difficult to get the ceremony site of your dreams.

The Marriage License

This state-issued document proves that you meet the requirements to marry in the United States. It will document that you are not already married to someone else, and that you are of the legal age to marry in the state where you'll be holding the ceremony. Despite this age of e-mails, faxes, videophones, and electronic conferencing, and your busy schedules, you will both have to appear *together,* live and in person, at the appropriate government office. The "appropriate office" could be the county clerk, county auditor, or the marriage license bureau of the town in which you live, in which one of you lives, or in which you'll be married.

Each state has different regulations and provides different windows of opportunity. Most states have a waiting period between the time you get your license and the time you can actually get married. Some have residency requirements. And usually there's an expiration date after which the license is no longer valid. Some offices will require different paperwork, and some may require blood tests and/or physical exams.

If you're getting married outside the United States, call your destination country's embassy, tourist office, or consulate for information. Will they marry noncitizens? How long is the residency requirement and waiting period? Some hotels or cruise ships have wedding planners who can provide this information for you and smooth the way. Perhaps the embassy or consulate or tourist department maintains a list of recommended people. Also, make sure the appropriate licensing office will be open when you arrive. Different countries have local holidays and may maintain different workday schedules. (See chapter 16 for more information on "destination weddings.")

Once you obtain your civil marriage license, you will give it to your rabbi or officiant before the wedding.

The *Ketubah*

It may be read aloud during your wedding ceremony , and will later likely become a beautifully illuminated piece of art that hangs in your home. Unlike a civil marriage license or the *ketubah* of the recent past, today's *ketubah,* or Jewish marriage document, can be one of the most profound elements of your wedding.

Written documents outlining a Jewish man's financial obligations to his wife were around for hundreds of years before the Common Era. But divorcing her if she displeased him or if he found evidence of sexual misconduct was fairly easy. He wrote up a document of divorce, put it in her hand, and basically sent her packing.

But toward the end of the first century C.E., things began to change. Rabbis decided that it was important to offer a wife financial protection, as well as legal status and "alimony," if her husband decided to divorce her. And so the *ketubah,* a premarital legal document, was instituted. It was quite a social statement for the times!

The traditional *ketubah,* written in Aramaic, provided for witnesses to testify that the husband "acquired" his bride in the proper manner and that she agreed to marry him. It spelled out the amount of the dowry she brought, the money the groom contributed up front, his financial obligations to her during their marriage (providing her with food and clothing), and his sexual responsibility to her. It stated his financial obligation to his bride in the event of divorce, as well as her inheritance rights from his estate upon his death. The document also contained the names of the bride and groom, and the date and location of the wedding. Traditionally, two nonrelated males who were observant Jews witnessed the *ketubah.* It was then handed to the bride for safekeeping—forever.

In the not-too-distant past, signing of the *ketubah* became a perfunctory act for many. The rabbi handed the groom a preprinted, often mimeographed piece of paper with blanks filled with the Hebrew names of the bride and groom and their respective fathers and the date and the location of the wedding ceremony. The groom, rabbi, and two witnesses quickly signed it without any pomp. The groom accepted legal obligation by grasping and lifting a cloth napkin or handkerchief held by the rabbi. The *ketubah* was usually read during the ceremony and given to the bride. After the wedding, it was usually clipped to the secular marriage license and tucked away forever in some "important paper" file.

The traditional Orthodox wording of the *ketubah* has changed little over the centuries. This version is still used in Orthodox and some Conservative ceremonies, and it's considered to be the "kosher" (legal) version. Newer, varied *ketubot* are now being written, however, to reflect more liberal points of view held by some Conservative and Reform brides and grooms, as well as for same-sex and interfaith marriages. In some circles, the traditional words are maintained in Aramaic to maintain the legality, and a more modern and currently meaningful version follows in English.

The text of your *ketubah* can be written in the traditional Aramaic; Aramaic with the addition of an English translation; a Conservative text with English; a text that includes new references to the Jewish divorce; an egalitarian document with Hebrew and English; a Reform text; a gender-neutral egalitarian text; or one representing commitment vows and an interfaith document; among other variations.

The groom, rabbi, and two male witnesses can sign the document. The bride also signs egalitarian versions. She may include two witnesses of her own if she likes.

Decorative Ketubot

Recently the "art" of the *ketubah* has made a big-time comeback. As it has been for centuries past, the text, rendered in calligraphy, is embellished with fine art and can be illuminated as well. You can commission an artist or calligrapher to custom design a *ketubah* just for you, or you can have one hand-designed or reproduced from an existing collection. Some artists will offer you the opportunity to mix and match texts and artistic elements as they design your marriage document. Computer calligraphy for invitations and announcements has carried over to the *ketubah* as well.

Your choice of artistic renderings coupled with various versions of the text means a *ketubah* that will be particularly meaningful to you. Before commissioning or purchasing a *ketubah,* be sure to check the text you are planning to use with your rabbi, who needs to approve it.

You may need to provide artists with anywhere from six weeks to four months notice, and prices can range from several hundred to more than a thousand dollars for original work.

The Marriage Ceremony

In the Old Days

The Talmud indicates three ways that a man can "acquire" a woman as his wife: with money, through a contract, or by having sexual intercourse with her. The woman was not "bought" as one would buy a slave. She had to *agree* to be married to the particular man, even if her family had arranged the marriage. The amount of money was symbolic—sort of like the dollar we might exchange today to make a transaction legally binding. In fact, the lowest denomination of coin could be used, but usually the "money" was represented by a plain, unadorned gold ring that was property of the groom and given to the bride to keep. Since the ring had to be un-adorned, the bride could tell its value and could not be tricked. The woman's acceptance of the ring or coin was her way of showing that she agreed to the marriage. A woman could also agree to a contract or to having sexual relations. At all times, the decision was up to the woman.

The engagement, as a matter of fact, was a lot more binding than our present ones. Known as *Kiddushin,* the engagement was sanctified and as binding as a marriage, without the benefits of the couple living together. Usually initiated as much as a year in advance of the actual marriage ceremony, this period provided the groom with time to establish a home for his bride. The only way the relationship could be dissolved after this point was by divorce or death.

If all went well, the next step would be the *Nisuin,* which elevated the marriage to a higher plateau, so to speak. With the home now ready, the couple set up house-keeping and started their lives as a truly married couple.

The Present

Today both the *Kiddushin* and the *Nisuin* ceremonies are performed together on the couple's wedding day. There are many elements that make up a Jewish wedding, but most are a matter of custom. In fact, the Torah has very little to say about it. Since it is a private agreement between the man and woman, a rabbi need not actually be present, and an officiant does not *marry* the couple: they marry each other with guidance from their officiant. In the United States, a couple must have their marriage solemnized by either a civil or accepted religious official, however.

In this day and age, the couple typically become engaged, and then the wedding plans begin. Many couples have decided to live together before or as soon as they become engaged, much to the chagrin of their more old-fashioned grandparents (and sometimes parents). Whether living separately or together, the couple now prepare to marry and make it legal under civil law and Jewish law. In the United States, the age of consent varies from state to state, but usually falls around eighteen years of age. (Under Jewish law, a couple can marry early: thirteen for a boy, twelve for a girl—*bar* and *bat mitzvah* age—although the recommended age is around eighteen. Secular regulations prevail.)

Since the marriage is a "collection of customs," brides and grooms can choose from among a variety of elements that make up their wedding. Some are dictated by the stream of Judaism to which they subscribe, or are shaped by the directions of their rabbi and their community. Still others are a choice made by the bride and groom that infuses their personalities, style, and beliefs into the ceremony. However the wedding is shaped, it must include the signing of the *ketubah,* the *Kiddushin* ceremony, including the groom's vow said while giving a plain gold ring (or coin) to his bride, the *Nisuin* ceremony, and the pronouncement that the couple are husband and wife.

Both the *Kiddushin* and the *Nisuin* segments of the wedding ceremony are introduced with blessings over wine. The first blessing sanctifies the personal relationship of the couple, and both the bride and groom take a sip of wine.

After the *kiddushin,* the *ketubah* marriage contract is read, separating the two parts of the wedding.

The marriage ceremony concludes with the *Sheva Brochot,* or Seven Blessings. The rabbi or cantor can sing or recite the blessings, or seven people can be called up and each given the honor to recite one. The first blessing is recited over the second cup of wine.

At the end of the blessings, the couple drinks from the second cup, and they are pronounced husband and wife.

Customs You Can Use and Infuse

Since a majority of the wedding is a matter of custom, Jewish weddings do differ from denomination to denomination, family to family, and country to country. Many elements are left to the bride and groom and their families to work out. Talk them over with your spiritual leader and decide which ones are best for you to use.

Ta'na'eem

A new interpretation on the *Ashkenazik* custom in which the conditions of an arranged marriage were spelled out. Today it can be an engagement party where the couple make and publicly read a covenant they have written. Perhaps they agree to certain terms such as where they will live, who will follow whom if one's job requires relocation, how they will raise their children, how they will share responsibility within the household, or anything appropriate they would like to set in writing.

Separation

The couple does not see each other for a week before the wedding. This can be reduced to three days, two days, one day . . . whatever! Actually, the groom will see the bride just before the wedding when he places the veil over her face.

The Ufruf

On the *Shabbat* before the wedding, the groom has an *ufruf* at the synagogue. At this time, he gets an *aliyah*. He is called up and given the honor of saying a blessing over the Torah. Traditionally, folks toss candy, nuts, and/or raisins at him for fertility. It's a time of great celebration, and the groom's family usually hosts a festive *kiddish* for the congregation at this time. In egalitarian practices, the bride can have an *ufruf* as well. The *Sephardic* custom is to hold the *ufruf* the week after the wedding.

The Fast

The bride and groom fast the day of the wedding. The fast is broken by drinking from the first glass of wine. After the ceremony, at the *yichud,* they share something to eat together in private before joining their guests at the festive meal.

Reciting of the Memorial Prayer

If any of the bride or groom's parents have died, memorial prayers can be recited in the rabbi's study before the start of the wedding.

The Groom's Tish

The table where the groom, surrounded by a circle of close male friends and relatives, holds court before the wedding ceremony. He attempts to deliver a speech on a Torah topic, but is stopped by those present. There is lots of merriment and some drink and food. The groom and witnesses and rabbi sign the *ketubah,* the groom accepts it by holding the end of the handkerchief, and they make their way to the bride's "holding area."

Bride's Sitting

The bride sits in a separate area, surrounded by female family and friends, who talk and reflect with her.

The Bedecken, *or Veiling of the Bride*

The groom, together with his father and father-in-law-to-be, head to the bride's area. The groom looks at the bride (to make sure she's the right woman!) and places the wedding veil over her face. This represents modesty and dignity on part of the bride.

Signing of the Ketubah

Most grooms (or brides and grooms) sign the *ketubah* "backstage." Some actually sign it under the *chuppah* during the marriage ceremony.

Marrying Under the Chuppah

The canopy under which the bride and groom marry can be traced back to the sixteenth century, some say. Since weddings were held outdoors, the *chuppah* afforded some intimate space. Symbolic of the home the couple will be sharing together, it is open on the sides—as was Abraham's tent so that he could easily greet guests, the story goes. When weddings were sometimes brought indoors, the *chuppah* followed.

Bride Circles the Groom Seven Times (or Three Times)

There are many interpretations of this practice. One is that it wards off evil spirits; another that it represents the Seven Blessings.

Yichud

The bride and groom seclude themselves in a private room for about ten to fifteen minutes, where they share a bite to eat. It's symbolic of marital intimacy. In practice, it's a way to eliminate the receiving line!

Mezinka

The joyous dance at the reception where the mothers or parents who "married off their last child" are honored.

Candles

If not disallowed by fire codes, bridesmaids or *unterfuhrers* can carry candles as they walk down the aisle.

Breaking the Glass

The tradition that epitomizes a Jewish wedding: the breaking of the glass. The glass is wrapped in a cloth napkin or a specially prepared cloth bag and placed on the floor. With bated breath, the guests watch as the groom stamps on the glass with his right foot—smashing it. In egalitarian ceremonies, the bride joins the groom in breaking the glass. This custom symbolizes the destruction of the Holy Temple, or the fact that marriage is fragile and must be carefully nurtured. It's a fitting conclusion to the wedding ceremony, after which all present call out, *"Mazel tov!"*

10

Choosing a Location and a Rabbi

NOW THAT YOU'RE ENGAGED, you'll be busy planning your wedding. You have plenty of time, right? Think again! Many a bride has called a catering hall even six months or more before her planned wedding day to ask if the site is available for that date. Perhaps it's a special day—the anniversary of the date the couple met, or the only time they have to get away together for a honeymoon. Or it might be one of the limited numbers of days an observant Jewish couple can marry during certain times of the year. Without a moment's hesitation, the voice on the other end of the phone asks: "What year are we talking about? Next year or the year after that?" Depending on the season and location you choose, you might have to book your location one year to eighteen months in advance! Don't be surprised if it's the catering hall that decides when you will be celebrating your anniversary from this day forward, till death do you part.

Two Ways to Approach It

Despite the difficulty you may encounter securing a wedding venue, it may be more important to you to have a particular rabbi or cantor officiate at your wedding.

Jewish brides and grooms marry each other in front of two Jewish witnesses, and don't actually *need* to have a rabbi or cantor officiate at the ceremony. A Jewish community leader or Hebrew scholar can guide the ceremony as well. Most Jewish couples who are marrying in a religious (rather than civil) ceremony do engage a rabbi and/or cantor, however.

The rabbi can be the spiritual leader of the bride's or groom's synagogue. If you each dreamed of the day that *your* rabbi would officiate at your wedding, perhaps you can arrange to have the two rabbis share the honors. If you both are unaffiliated with a synagogue, or if your rabbis are unavailable, you'll need to find another officiant. You'll find that many rabbis will want to get to know you as a couple before they solemnize a marriage ceremony, and they may provide pre-wedding counseling sessions. It proves to be a richer and more rewarding experience when the officiant has developed a personal relationship with you. Contact your officiant or begin your search for one as soon as you have a date, or know that you'll be marrying.

A bride or groom who plans to marry someone of another faith may have a harder time finding a rabbi to officiate. Often the couple would like to incorporate traditions of both religions, and may have both a rabbi and a non-Jewish cleric co-officiate. Neither Orthodox nor Conservative movements authorize the performance of an intermarriage ceremony, but other denominations or postdenominational streams of Judaism may allow intermarriage, or leave the choice up to the individual rabbi.

Some Reform, Reconstructionist, and Humanistic rabbis will perform same-sex weddings or unions offering gay/lesbian couples an opportunity to unite in marriage. As of this writing, only the state of Vermont offers gay/lesbian couples from all areas of the country the opportunity to come together in a civil union under Vermont law.

The Coming Together of Rabbi and Venue

If you're planning to be married by your own (or your honey's) rabbi or cantor, the dates he or she is available will kick off your search for a wedding venue that can match availability. Your own synagogue is a likely choice, particularly if it has suitable catering facilities. But your rabbi or cantor may also agree to guide your wedding ceremony at a different location.

If you're holding your wedding ceremony at a location other than at your synagogue or temple, check with your officiant about the feasibility of his or her conducting an off-premise wedding. Expecting a rabbi who may be frail to perform your wedding at the end of a footpath on top of a mountain, for example, may pose some difficulty. So, too, if you are having a destination wedding. Perhaps your rabbi would enjoy a few days in the Caribbean, but then again, he or she may have obligations that prevent travel.

Here are some tips for finding a rabbi or cantor:

- Seek out the rabbi who *bar mitzvahed* your honey, or who "raised" you before you moved away from your hometown. You may want to marry at his or her pulpit (which could be your hometown) or ask that he or she come to the venue you've chosen.

- Some catering halls maintain a list of rabbis who perform weddings at their site, and can put you in touch or make the arrangements.

- Check with friends and relatives for referrals.

- Call up (or e-mail) a synagogue in your denomination (or a nondenominational synagogue) and speak to the rabbi or cantor. Some rabbis will want to be assured that you will indeed be maintaining a Jewish lifestyle as a couple, and that you're not just seeking a quick stamp of approval, before they'll agree to officiate.

- The United Jewish Communities, www.ujc.org, maintains a contact listing for 189 Jewish federations and more than four hundred independent Jewish communities in the United States, Canada, and the U.S. territories. Once you're at the UJC Web site, click on "Jewish Finder." From there, you can contact your community of choice, which may be able to put you in touch with a rabbi or cantor.

- The Union of American Hebrew Congregations can lead you to Reform congregations in the area in which you plan to marry. Contact the organization at www.uahc.org or UAHC, 633 Third Avenue, New York, NY 10017.

- The United Synagogue of America represents the Conservative movement. Contact them at www.uscj.org or United Synagogue of America, 155 Fifth Avenue, New York, NY 10010.

- Jewish Reconstructionist Federation offers leads to Reconstructionist congregations and *Havurot*. Contact the organization at www.jrf.org or Jewish Reconstructionist Federation, Beit Devora, 7804 Montgomery Avenue, Suite 9, Elkins Park, PA 19027-2649.

- If you contact rabbis or cantors who are unable to officiate at your wedding, they may be able to suggest a colleague who can. Don't forget to ask.

- If you're a college student or live in or near a college town, Jewish organizations such as Hillel on campus or the campus chaplain's office may be able to point you in the right direction. If fact, a nondenominational chapel on campus may serve as your ideal venue.

- If you're affiliated with or employed by a hospital, a correctional facility, or are in the military, contacting the chaplain's office may be a helpful way to get a lead.

- There are also rabbis who are unaffiliated with a pulpit who may be available. Some may be located through classified ads in wedding-related publications, or listed in telephone books.

If possible, visit with and talk to several rabbis before making a decision on who will guide you into marriage. You may want to attend a service officiated by the rabbi and speak with the rabbi to see if your "styles" match. You'll want to know if the rabbi will be available on the date you'd like to marry, and if he or she will be willing to co-officiate with another rabbi (or non-Jewish clergyperson if appropriate to your circumstance).

Once a rabbi has agreed to officiate at your wedding, he or she will most likely want to know about you and your intended, and your families, religious backgrounds, and beliefs. Were either of you previously married? If so, are your civil divorce papers in order? Do you have a *get*—the Jewish divorce decree? Orthodox and most Conservative rabbis will insist on a Jewish divorce even if you have a civil divorce. Do you have any children? He or she may ask you about your education, secular and religious, and about your jobs.

You will want to know about the rabbi and how he or she conducts the service. What Jewish rituals does the rabbi employ? Do you need to attend a *mikvah* before the rabbi will marry you? How much of the service will be performed in Hebrew or English?

Together you may discuss the making of a Jewish home, which can include discussions on keeping kosher, Jewish holidays and rituals, the Jewish education of your children, and placing the *mizzuzot* on the doorposts of your home. The rabbi may suggest readings as well. He or she may also discuss secular topics applicable to marriage such as money management, sexuality, sharing and compromise, and blended families if appropriate.

Don't be afraid to let the rabbi know if you're living together. Since it's so common today, the rabbi will not be shocked. You may want to discuss the pros and cons of a pre-wedding separation, ranging from a few days to a week. On the one hand it's a sure way to offer some time to privately reflect on your last days as a single person, to have sort of a "time-out" before the big day arrives, and to be with your family and close personal friends. On the other hand, it would prevent you from attending a rehearsal/family dinner or making any last-minute arrangements you need to do together.

Securing Your Site

If you've always dreamed of marrying at a particular site, contact it immediately. Perhaps you'll be lucky and acceptable dates will be open. Or maybe it's had a cancellation and you're just in time to fill the slot! But keep in mind that your wedding doesn't *have* to be on a Saturday night, or even on a Sunday afternoon—another popular choice for Jewish brides.

Tuesdays are often the day of choice for religious weddings, and Thursday evenings are considered a sophisticated choice these days. Weekday evening weddings may be ideal if your guests are local, but they're more difficult if people have to take time off from work to travel. But if you insist on *the* place and *the* date (especially if it's a holiday weekend or during high season for weddings), be prepared to wait. On the upside, you'll be able to plan your wedding at a more leisurely pace and have time, perhaps, to save up some more dollars for the event or for your new life together.

Compromising Position

As you search for the perfect trilogy of officiant, ceremony, and reception venue, you may have to make some compromises. You may find, for instance, that one venue offers everything you want, has the date available, but doesn't have a room large enough to accommodate your guest list. Chop. Chop. Maybe second cousins once removed will have to go.

Or perhaps you've found the caterer you want. The food and presentation are beyond belief. But so is the waiting list for the catering hall. Why not inquire if the caterer also does off-premise catering and can serve you at a different venue?

Work calmly, diligently, and creatively toward your goal and chances are everything will work out just fine—if you're willing to bend just a little!

Finding Your Venues

With so many choices available, how will you ever decide where you'll get married? If you don't have your heart set on a particular place, it's a matter of taking some time to decide what you're actually looking for in a venue, your own personal style, and a host of other factors. Once you've narrowed it down to perhaps a manageable five or six locations that spark your interest, you'll want to personally go down and check them out.

But to begin, take some time to explore your feelings about the place where you'd like to get married. Decide what's important to you. Since you can marry in one location and celebrate in another, or hold your wedding ceremony and celebration at the same place, your options are vast. Here are just a few:

- Ceremony in the rabbi's study; small luncheon or dinner reception in a restaurant

- Ceremony in the sanctuary; luncheon or *kiddish* at the synagogue

- Ceremony in the sanctuary; big-time dinner dance in the synagogue's catering facility

- Ceremony and reception at a catering hall

- Ceremony and reception at an off-premise, unique site

- Ceremony on a cruise ship; guests leave, and the bride and groom continue on

- Private ceremony at a honeymoon destination

- Ceremony and reception in a small inn or bed-and-breakfast

- Ceremony in a large, upscale hotel

- Private ceremony, then large reception in a catering hall, restaurant, or hotel at another time

- Ceremony and reception in the hometown of one partner, then a second reception in the hometown of the other

- Ceremony and reception in the rented facility of a local fraternal organization, firehouse, or like venue

- Ceremony and reception at home
- Ceremony and reception at parents' home

Synagogue Wedding

Since a Jewish wedding is most often a religious as well as civil event, your ceremony and reception can be held at a synagogue that offers catering services. The advantage is that the spirituality of your joining together is heightened as you walk down the aisle of the sanctuary. Perhaps the rabbi who "raised" you will have the pleasure of marrying you in the very synagogue where you had your *bar* or *bat mitzvah*. The rabbi may personally know you and your family and may share his or her thoughts about you with your guests. It's a warm and loving way to celebrate your special day.

At-Home Wedding

The warmth and personalized feelings of an at-home wedding are very special. But it can be a lot of work! You can have a caterer or wedding planner come in or handle the plans with your family or friends. You may even be tempted to redecorate the house and do some special gardening.

Renting a Community Hall

This alternative is usually more modest than a catering hall and easier to do than an at-home wedding, but—depending on the available facilities—it may lack charm.

Outdoor Wedding

It can range from a black-tie affair to a down-home country cookout. Lots of special preparation may be necessary, but the results may be well worth it!

How to Locate a Venue

The two most popular spots for Jewish weddings in the United States seem to be at a synagogue and at a catering hall. In Israel, the most likely choice is a catering-hall reception, since Israeli wedding receptions tend to be *huge*, with many hundreds of guests.

If you're planning to marry in your synagogue, you don't have far to look. But you may want a sanctuary wedding at another synagogue. You don't necessarily have to be locked into yours. The decision to marry in the "synagogue next door" may affect your choice of officiant, however.

If you'd like to marry in a full-service catering hall, check your local newspapers, regional magazines, and regional wedding magazines; ask friends in town for recommendations, too. Think about venues where you've attended other weddings and see if they would be appropriate for your own wedding.

Jump onto the Internet. Catering halls, synagogue catering facilities, and restaurants with banquet rooms have Web pages and listings.

Get opinions from off-site caterers. Perhaps they've worked weddings at a particular facility that they can recommend.

Search for a specific venue to match a theme—a castle for a medieval wedding, for example. Again, Internet sites are helpful. Just plug a theme into your browser. You might unearth a wonderful treasure.

Now that you've gathered more information than you'll probably need, it's time to start making some phone calls to set up appointments to visit locations. Go prepared with the following twenty-one questions, so that you can thoroughly check it out.

1. Is your venue available on the date and time I need?
2. Can your hall hold the number of guests I plan to have?
3. What is the general per-head price range?
4. Are you located conveniently near transportation hubs?
5. Can I hold both the ceremony and the reception here?
6. How many rooms do I get to use? How do you work out the logistics of the cocktail reception, the ceremony, and the dinner reception?

7. Do I have to guarantee a minimum number of people? If so, is it more than the size of my guest list?

8. Can you show me proof of licensing and insurance?

9. May I see recommendations and references?

10. How long have you been in business?

11. Do you have indoor and outdoor facilities?

12. How many weddings do you hold at one time?

13. Will we be sharing rest room facilities with any other weddings or social functions?

14. How large is the dance floor?

15. Do you have a bridal room where the wedding party can get ready?

16. Do you offer shuttle transportation to and from the airport? From the ceremony site to your facility? How many people can you shuttle? Is the service complimentary? If not, what are the charges?

17. Will there be another wedding directly before or after mine in the same space?

18. Do you serve kosher food? Who provides the rabbinical supervision?

19. When can we arrange for a food tasting?

20. Do you provide all-inclusive, full-service catering, including chairs, tables, place settings, *chuppah*—and if not, what portion of my wedding and reception can you handle?

21. Is there adequate parking on site? Valet parking? Coat check? Are they part of the deal or billed separately?

Ask if you can take a look around the facility. Check out the bathrooms to see the condition and the appointments within. Poorly maintained bathrooms can be indicative of a poorly maintained kitchen and generally lax management style. If you can, check out the kitchen as well. Look at the linens offered. Are they in good repair? Do the china and plates sparkle or do you see chips and worn spots? How are the steps and flooring in the lobby, the rooms, and the outside areas? Are they safe, or do they show cracks, upheavals, or buckled or torn carpeting? Where are the rest rooms in relation to the rooms you'll be using for your reception? Do you have to go upstairs or downstairs? Is there an elevator or lift for the elderly or handicapped? Likewise, if your reception is not on the main floor, is there an elevator?

Going the Extra Mile

In light of the rash of tragedies at catering halls around the world, be sure to double-check the insurance and licensing of any hall you are considering. If they wave a piece of paper in front of you, read it carefully. Are the inspections and licensing up to date or have they expired? When was the building inspected last? You might want to talk to building inspectors and fire inspectors of the town in which the hall is located. When was it last checked out for safety? Do they suspect any problems? Have the owners or managers made any necessary repairs or corrections in a timely manner? Have they ever been brought up on charges? Are there fire and smoke alarms and extinguishers in place? Is the building solidly constructed and approved to hold the number of people you'll be expecting there at the time of your wedding? (If they have multiple parties held simultaneously, you'll need to take that into consideration as well.) Is the building designed for the use you intend?

You may come off as a pain in the neck, but it literally could be a matter of life and death. Don't be intimidated—check it out!

All in the Community

If you're renting a hall from an organization such as a fraternal order, firehouse, community group, or the clubhouse of your housing complex, they may not provide full service. Be sure to ask them the following:

1. Does the hall provide food service?

2. Can I bring in my own? If so, are there any restrictions? Can I use any caterer I want?

3. Are there cooking and serving facilities? May I see them? Are the appliances adequate to prepare or warm my reception meal? Is there a bar?

4. Do you provide tables and chairs? If so, do I rent them from you or are they part of the hall rental fee? (If they're provided, check out their condition.)

5. Is the facility heated? Air-conditioned?

6. Do you have a sound system? Can a band or DJ be brought in? Do you have a microphone, amplifiers?

7. Can we decorate the facility?

8. Does the price include setup before and the breakdown and cleanup after?

9. Does the hall provide a wait service staff?

10. Does the hall provide china dinnerware, silver or stainless flatware, crystal or glass beverage and barware, cloth tablecloths and napkins, or only paper and plastic? Or none?

11. Will there be someone to oversee the affair or to be on hand for questions and problems during the party?

12. Are there adequate bathroom facilities? (Check them out!)

13. Is there a dressing area for the bridal party if needed?

And don't forget to do the following:

> 1. Check licensing, insurance, and the maximum number of people the hall is authorized to hold.
>
> 2. Check the condition of the walkways, steps, and other areas to ensure they are in good condition.
>
> 3. Check the list of twenty-one questions for full-service caterers and ask any of the questions that apply.

Under the Chuppah and Under the Sky

So you've decided to have your wedding outdoors—*mazel tov!* You'll be joining brides and grooms throughout the years who have married under the *chuppah* and under the sky. *Chassidic* and ultra-Orthodox brides and grooms have traditionally married outside, particularly at night under a blanket of stars. If you decide to marry outdoors, you're in good company.

Whether for traditional reasons, because the indoor space is a tad too small, or just because it's so beautiful, you may opt for an outdoor wedding. You can hold the ceremony outdoors and the reception inside, the cocktail party and ceremony outside and the dinner dance inside, or the entire wedding ceremony and reception under the sun or the stars.

Some catering facilities have a terrace or gazebo that can make a perfect setting for an outdoor wedding. Or you can choose to marry by a lake, on the beach, at a botanical garden, on the grounds of a public building, at poolside, in a vineyard, in your own or your parents' backyard, in a park, at a theme or amusement park, on a mountaintop, in an open field—you name it!

Holding an outdoor ceremony comes with some special considerations, however. Let's take a look at some of them.

Getting there. It may be your dream location, but can your guests, your food service, and your clergy get there? Would they want to stay there? The mountaintop may be a romantic fantasy, but can frail old Aunt Martha really don hiking boots and climb to the top? Would she be holding on for dear life and turning shades of wedding gown white if you whisk her up in a helicopter or plop her on a ski-lift chair?

Climate. The time of year and the weather are key. What will it be like at the date and time of your wedding? The location may be beautiful when you check it out three months before your wedding day, but you need to look ahead. If it's normally hot and humid at the time of year you've selected, your guests will be wilting by the time you walk down the aisle. So will your hair! And can you imagine how *you'll* feel in your wedding gown?

If it's normally cold and windy, you'll have to think about how you'll look in a wedding gown and ski jacket. And pity your guests, sitting there with ice-blue fingers politely shivering on your behalf. But if the weather is normally appropriate for an outdoor wedding, go for it. Do prepare an indoor backup in case of rain or unexpected weather surprises, however.

Permissions and permits. Just because you want to marry outdoors in the park, it doesn't mean you can simply arrive and start the ceremony. Most likely, you'll need a permit to hold the gathering, obtainable well in advance from the town or city hall. This could entail filing for the permit weeks before the event, and even paying a fee. The grounds of private places may charge quite a hefty usage fee—ranging from less than a hundred to several thousands of dollars. So be sure to check it out.

The "blow-away" chuppah. Brides have been horrified to see their *chuppah* start to fall over or blow away before or during their ceremony. You'd like your ceremony to be memorable, but this probably is *not* what you had in mind! Unless your *chuppah* will be held by four people you honor in this fashion, find out who will be setting it up—the caterer or the florist—and inform the person appropriately in advance. (He or she will need to bring the necessary materials to secure it.)

Seating. Who will be providing the seating for your guests? Do you need to rent outdoor chairs? Folding chairs probably won't do the trick unless your outdoor venue has solid surface flooring. Resin outdoor seats really work—they're available in white and green. If you do need to rent, can you find a supplier that has the appropriate number of seats plus a few extras? Will the company deliver and pick up? If not, who will be doing this for you, and does he or she have a U-Haul or truck to transport them? Who will be setting them out and collecting and stacking them for their return?

Secure walking area.   If your location doesn't have a secure walking area, consider renting flooring, if possible. Do you really want to get your beautiful wedding shoes colored with grass stains? What about your guests' attire? Their walking safety?

Flowers.   Do you need floral displays, or are the flowers on the *chuppah*, strung around a gazebo, and in the natural setting enough?

Lighting.   If the wedding is at night or at twilight, is there outdoor lighting? Is it sufficient?

Yichud.   Are you planning to have this secluded time together? Is there a separate spot you can be alone? One rabbi and his wife cleverly handled this situation when they married by covering themselves under his supersized *tallit*.

The Outdoor Reception

Alfresco dining—what a delight! But with it comes a host of additional things to think about, unless you have a full-service, off-premise caterer handling the whole shebang.

Your outdoor reception can range from an afternoon cookout to an all-out formal affair, either during the day or under the stars. It can have a garden party feel, a western motif, or rival a five-star hotel ballroom dinner dance. Here are some things to think about, in addition to the ceremony considerations:

- Is there running water at the site? If not, how will it be brought in?

- Is there access for caterers to come in and set up? Is it feasible?

- Can a band or DJ set up and have the electricity necessary for amps and equipment?

🐝 What about tables, seating, buffet and serving tables, head tables, a dance floor, bandstand, and general flooring? Can they be delivered? Who will be in charge? Who will set up and who will do the breakdown?

🐝 What about table linens, china, silverware, glassware, table skirting, and the like?

🐝 What will you do in case of inclement weather? Do you have an indoor alternative? How about a tent?

Enter the Tent

A wonderful solution for outdoor receptions, a tent can turn an outdoor location into a perfect site. True, you may have chosen an outdoor spot specifically for the stars and the night air, or the sun and the natural beauty of wildflowers, or the dramatic view. But perhaps you "went outdoors" to increase the available space: you're having 350 guests and your indoor space only holds 150. Or you've held your ceremony outside and this would be the perfect accompaniment for the dinner dance.

A far cry from pitching a tent around the campfire, the tent you can rent for your wedding can be glorious indeed. It can be a festive striped affair, or a sophisticated white billow of attractive fabric complete with hanging chandeliers!

There are various types of tents to choose from, depending on how they are set up and the look they achieve. Prices may vary according to type—be it a push pole, frame, or tension model.

Talk to several tent suppliers for suggestions so that you'll get a true idea of what will serve you best, not just what one supplier happens to carry or can get. Tell them what you'll be using the tent for—a cocktail party, or a full-out five course sit-down dinner dance, for example. Discuss the number of people you'll be having, along with the number of tables—including head tables, serving tables, buffet tables, gift and place card tables, and their size and shapes. Don't forget the chairs! Most likely, they will be indoor-reception-type chairs or folding chairs, as opposed to the resin outdoor chairs. Also don't forget to mention a bar, a dance floor, and a bandstand.

Speak to your supplier about allocating enough space for your musicians and their instruments, including a piano (spinet or grand), and a drum set, if applicable. You'll need to not only rent the tent but also the bandstand, bar, dance floor, tables, chairs, and maybe the piano and the lighting fixtures as well.

In addition to space requirements and rental items, talk about delivery date, times, fees, setup, and breakdown. Discuss feeding electricity, heating, or cooling into the tent, if necessary. You'll also want to discuss flooring for under the tent. Check with party rental shops and the Internet for suppliers. And find out about insurance on the tent and any items you rent.

11

Food and Spirits

IT MAY BE A generalization, but most Jewish people love to eat. Food and meals are tied in with holidays, the *Shabbat*, and of course other *simchas*. In fact, probably more than half of the money you'll be spending for your wedding will be on food service. It's a big-ticket item that requires lots of thought and careful planning.

That said, people have very different ideas about the type and quantity of food they'd like to serve at their wedding. It can range from a few platters of cold cuts to a full-out buffet, followed by a sit-down dinner. Since Jews may marry at almost any site, the food service can be provided by an on-site caterer, an off-premise caterer, or a host of other options.

About Caterers

On-site caterers have their established kitchen in a certain facility, whether it be a synagogue, country club, catering hall, or what have you. Love the food? Love the space? It's a match made in gastronomical heaven. Off-premise caterers, on the other hand, come out of their kitchen to provide food service at locations such as parks, museums, botanical gardens, and even your home.

Some on-premise caterers have off-premise divisions, and vice versa. So if you love the caterer at your synagogue, for example, but want to hold your reception at the boathouse by the lake, they may be able to accommodate you. Likewise, the company that catered your friend Dory's kosher wedding dinner at the museum may be able to handle your wedding at their own catering facility if you like.

Certain venues have a catering panel, also called "an approved catering list." If you want to use this venue, you must select a caterer from the group. Other places will allow you to bring in caterers of choice, but they (and you) must adhere to the regulations of the facility. There may be an extra fee to bring in an off-the-panel caterer. The caterer will also have to show proof of insurance coverage.

Your Synagogue Reception

Many congregations have their own catering facilities. Some may have an exclusive contract with an on-premise caterer, while others may have a panel of caterers authorized to work at their synagogue. Still others may allow you to bring in your own food, as long as you follow the regulations set forth by the congregation and they grant approval.

The Hotel or Country Club Reception

If you're planning your wedding and/or reception in a hotel or country club, you may need to use its exclusive caterer or select one from a panel. If you'll be having kosher food service, you'll need to check whether this can be provided for you, if you can bring in your own caterer, and whether the facility can support kosher catering.

Restaurant Reception

Some restaurants have one menu for their regular patrons and another for their banquets—and they may have separate chefs for each. If you've eaten in the restaurant before and simply *love* the food, you may find that the actual meal you get for your wedding might not taste quite the same. Be sure you have a food tasting prepared by the chef who'll be handling your wedding, not the chef who handles the restaurant fare.

The Local Delicatessen or Take-Out

If you're having a rather informal reception and live in an area that has take-out food services, this provides yet another option for you. Be sure to inquire whether the establishment can handle the job based on the timing, the menu, the number of guests, and location of your wedding. Allow several months lead time, if you can.

What's Cookin'?

Known for your good cooking? If you'll be having a small wedding at home or in a local rented hall, you and a few good friends can always decide to cook! Prepare foods you can cook in advance and freeze. Naturally, you'll be leaving the serving to others.

Is your groom a cookout king? If you're having an informal reception, why not combine previously prepared home-cooked or take-out dishes with the groom's grill cooking? Of course, on this special day, he will probably be willing to pass the spatula to a good friend or professional chef.

If you want to include homemade touches such as cookies, the cake, or your signature dish, but are hiring a caterer to provide the balance of the meal, discuss your plans with the caterer before you sign the contract. Ask how the items you bring in will be stored and served and whether this will entail an extra service charge.

Selecting the Caterer

Finding a caterer can be a matter of finding your reception site and using the in-house caterer, or choosing from a panel of approved caterers for that facility.

If your options are wide open, get referrals from friends or look up caterers who handled the wedding food you enjoyed as a guest. You can also log on to the Internet and find an abundance of caterers ready to please you. Look in regional and local wedding magazines, yellow page listings, and the ads in your local newspaper.

If you're investigating a caterer you aren't personally familiar with, be sure to check with the Better Business Bureau and consumer agencies in the company's area to make sure there are no unresolved disputes. You might also plug the name into your Internet search engine to see if any articles or background information come up. You will be asking for references, but these may come from relatives or friends, so take them with a grain of salt.

When selecting a caterer, there are several factors you'll need to keep in mind relating to the food service. Let's go through some of them.

Kosher or Not

Your Jewish community, your personal practices, and the practices of your family members and other guests will help determine whether you'll be serving kosher food and wine. For those who observe the rules of *kathruth* (kosher food), kosher or *glatt* kosher food service is a given.

Others may serve kosher food to accommodate their guests. There are may regulations for serving kosher food and varying levels of observances. This can be a touchy situation fraught with the possibility of offending some guests. Check with a rabbi for guidance.

If many of your guests are observant, serving a kosher meal should be mandatory. If only a few of your many guests keep kosher, you may be able to arrange to have previously prepared and double-sealed *glatt* kosher dinners brought in from an outside kosher facility. You can have the food served on attractive paper plates with brand-new plastic utensils, or have brand-new china and silverware used that can later be rotated into the caterer's stock.

Serving a dairy, fish, or vegetarian meal prepared at your wedding site's kitchen and presented on disposable or new dinnerware is another option acceptable to some—but not to others. Your best bet would be to check with the individual guests and ask their preferences and requirements. Don't be offended if an observant Jew feels uncomfortable with the available choices and prefers to pass on your kind invitation to dinner.

Those who do not observe *kathruth* but enjoy the tradition of kosher food may opt for "kosher-style" but *treif* (nonkosher) catering. As such, the caterers should not serve pork products, shellfish including shrimp, or fish that does not have scales and fins (such as swordfish), nor mix meat and dairy foods at the same meal. The food will not be authorized as kosher, however, having not met the stringent *kathruth* requirements.

If you plan to use a caterer in a setting other than a synagogue, you'll want to determine if the kitchen is under rabbinical authority and if the *mashgiah*, a kosher supervisor, will be present while the food is being prepared and served. Some caterers will charge an additional fee to cover these costs.

Looking Beyond Yourselves

In addition to considering your guests' need for kosher dining, there are other considerations you should check into with your caterer. If you have many older friends or relatives, you may want to avoid featuring steak or prime rib on your menu—or at least offer "softer" choices along with them.

Most caterers can easily offer a vegetarian entrée for guests who prefer this to a meat dish. And inquire about sugar-free and salt-free alternatives for those guests who may require them. A fresh fruit dessert and some sugar-free pastries or cookies can replace fancy desserts for a diabetic, and sugar-free soda, and seltzer should be available for those who require it.

Be sure to give your caterer, as soon as possible, a list of the people who will be requiring special meals and the table at which they'll be seated. Hopefully, this will eliminate the delay some special-order guests experience in getting their meal served.

In addition, if you, as a bride or groom, really, *really* want a particular entrée served at your wedding, but you realize it would not be welcomed by the majority of your guests, ask your caterer about having that dish made up just for you. It may be possible, and it may not. If you're talking about a nonkosher entrée brought into a kosher service, it might not be feasible. Should that happen, think of the greater good. After all, your guests are coming to wish you well; they've dressed up, traveled, and will be bringing gifts. Perhaps you can reserve the seafood for that special honeymoon dinner the next evening. And keep in mind, between photography, dancing, and greeting guests, most brides and grooms hardly get to eat a bite of their wedding meal, anyway.

About the Little Folks

If you're planning to invite children to your wedding, be sure to ask the caterer about the policy on kiddie food. Some caterers charge full price even for children above the infant/toddler stage; others come in at half price. Some will even prepare kid-friendly food such as fish sticks, hot dogs, hamburgers or meatballs, and french fries.

The Care and Feeding of Your Vendors

Ask your caterer what the policy is regarding the feeding of your musicians or DJ, photographer(s), videographers, and other vendors and professionals who will be working the wedding. Many caterers will provide food for the "crew" as a courtesy or at a reduced price. They may, instead, tell you to advise your vendors to help themselves to the cocktail buffet if you are including that in your plans.

My Kind of Style

The "style" of your wedding will also be a consideration. Some caterers specialize in upscale, formal, and very elegant food service; others offer home cooking, barbecues, and simple service. You may want to serve *Sephardic*-type dishes rather than "Jewish-style" *Ashkenazik* food. This could include hummus and pita, couscous, shish kebab, lamb tajin, different varieties of Israeli-style salads, and ethnic foods from the Mediterranean region.

Or, you may want your food to reflect other ethnic dishes to celebrate your roots, interests, or even the place you met. This could include Indian, Russian, French, Chinese, Mexican, and other types of cuisine.

The Tasting

You'll want to actually taste the food prepared by the caterer you're considering before making any final decisions. Most caterers will arrange for you and a guest to sample various foods they prepare. Come with someone who cares about food to get a second opinion. This may or may not be your honey. As one groom said, "I don't care what food is served—whether it be fish or something else. I want to make sure I like the DJ." If you, as a groom, echo that sentiment, perhaps the bride's mom or her maid of honor should go to the tasting instead. Sample several dishes from the various meat groups. A caterer may have many different ways to prepare chicken, for example.

The Presentation

The food tastes fantastic, but that's only one part of the equation. Presentation is another. How the food *looks* as it's served is important, too. On the other hand, beautifully presented food that looks good but lacks taste is just not going to cut it for *your* wedding.

Food should be presented in an attractive and pleasing manner. The style should also match the venue to some extent. The presentation at a country wedding, for example, should reflect the country: baskets with gingham touches, perhaps. More dramatic designs could be incorporated in a big-city hotel reception.

Garnishes are an important element, not only on the food platters but also around the table and at the base of the dishes set out on a buffet. Some elegant touches include ice sculptures, chocolate sculptures, cornucopias spilling with dinner breads and rolls, round baskets filled with various items, filled squash or melon shells, and carvings made from fruits or vegetables. Built-up displays on buffet tables add eye appeal.

Some From Column A and Some From Column B

What will the caterer be offering you? Are you both on the same wavelength? Listen to the chefs' ideas and see if they mesh with your own. But don't be stubborn. They are professionals and may have ideas that improve on your own.

Comparison-shop among caterers if you can. For the same all-inclusive price, one caterer offers a wedding party of 250 guests the following at the cocktail hour: an open bar with premium liquors, a raw vegetable platter with a dip, a fruit salad bowl, two hot chafing-dish choices, and a choice of five hot and/or cold butler-passed hors d'oeuvres to be selected from long columns listing hot and cold items; the other offers the same but with an added platter of assorted smoked fish, a bowl of chicken liver pâté, assorted breads and crackers, a choice of six *additional* hot chafing-dish items, and a combined hot and/or cold choice of twenty-five butler-passed hors d'oeuvres. So, in addition to great taste and attractive presentation, you'll want to compare the quantity of food offered between the various caterers you interview.

When looking over the list of choices included in the per-head price, watch carefully for those little asterisks. They may denote that one type of hors d'oeuvre, for example, counts as two selections due to its expense or complexity. And certain choices may require an additional price over the standard all-inclusive rate. An extra dollar for an entrée you may be considering doesn't seem like much, until you multiply it by the number of guests, and tack on the additional costs of tax and gratuities.

You'll also want to check the "refill factor." You'll want your buffet items to "keep on coming" for the entire designated time of the buffet. There's nothing worse than a guest coming back for one more chicken wing only to find a large, empty, gaping chafing tray denoting: "Sorry, all out!"

Belly Up to the Bar

The type of bar service the caterer offers is another factor to look into. Will there be a full-service bar offering scotch, rye, vodka, gin, bourbon, rum, white wine, red wine, bottles of beer, champagne, club soda, and diet and regular soft drinks? What about mixers, including juices, flavorings, and garnishes such as lemon, lime, cherries, and olives? Are the liquors "top-shelf" or premium, or lesser or unknown brands? What name-brand wines will be served? If it's "house wine," be sure to buy a drink and sample both the red and white. Some house brands are wonderful, others barely drinkable.

The Challah

If you are holding a traditional Jewish wedding meal, you'll be opening the dinner with *H'Moize*, the blessing over the *challah*. It's usually a photo opportunity moment, so you'll need to have your caterer provide a large, nicely baked loaf of this traditional braided egg bread, along with a small covered table and a bread knife.

Dining With Dollars

When hiring a full-service caterer, the per-head cost you'll be paying includes much more than just the food. It can include the cost of service (wait staff, bartenders), place settings, silverware, tablecloths, garnishes, and liquor. It may even include the centrepieces. Make sure you get complete costs, not just costs of food.

Discuss how your caterer works the finances of your food. Is the wedding food service all-inclusive? If so, are there any items to be billed as extras? Is your entire food service itemized instead? Your budget comes into play here, so you'll want to make sure there are no surprises. Norm, for example, was shocked to find that the appetizers he and his bride selected from the caterer's menu choices required that they be passed butler-style. As such, he was faced with additional costs for this service.

Prices for catering can vary by more than a hundred dollars per head. It stands to reason that a caterer specializing in sandwiches and salads, for example, will differ dramatically in price from an upscale kosher caterer serving a full buffet with carving stations, followed by a sit-down dinner with choices of sea bass, prime rib, or duck à l'orange, along with an open bar of premium liquors, and followed by dessert and a Viennese table.

The quality of the food is another consideration. You can be serving cold-cut platters, but is the corned beef first cut or second? And within the same level of food service, kosher catering usually comes in at a higher price tag. Remember, you're also paying for the kosher supervision.

The number of courses, the number of salad and entrée choices your guests can have tableside, and the extras you add will also affect the price. A six-course dinner will cost more than an entrée and a slice of wedding cake for dessert.

Do you want your guests to be asked for their choice of a chicken, fish, beef, or veal dish by a waiter who comes around to the table? You'll most likely be paying more per head for each additional choice you make available, although your guests will only select one. And the base price of the meal may be set at the most expensive of the entrées.

One option that you may have is for your guests to select their entrée choices at the time they are invited. Thus the kitchen will not have to prepare extra portions of food. From the standpoint of weddings, however, that's not considered terribly gracious.

Post-entrée selections can affect your cost per person as well. Are the coffee and tea included in your price, or are they additional? While you're thinking of coffee, you may have the option of serving international coffees, but that may be extra again. So, too, the Viennese table, which can add anywhere from four to more than ten dollars to the per-person charge.

Drinks can dramatically affect the budget, too. Are you having a five-hour open bar serving top-shelf liquors? Are you paying for an open bar by the hour, or is liquor being billed on a per-consumption basis?

The level of service is also paramount. How large is the kitchen staff? Is the dinner sit down, buffet, stations, or a combination of several styles? How many waiters are there per guest at a sit-down dinner, and how many chefs will service the various food stations?

The style of service may also affect the price. Will you be having French, Russian, or American service? These terms are often bandied about erroneously, so make sure that you and your caterer are on the same "service" page.

French service. The waiter sets up a stand or cart near each table, prepares or garnishes the food, and serves each individual guest's plate from the cart. Pros: Fancy, elegant, showy. Cons: Slow. Imagine being the last guest at a table of ten to be served!

Russian service. Often called French by mistake. Be sure you clarify this with a caterer who says it will be "French service." In this type of service, waiters carry out food on large silver platters and serve each guest individually, item by item. Wearing white gloves, one waiter will carry the meat platter, for example, and make the rounds, placing the slices on each guest's plate. Another waiter will follow with the vegetables, serving each person individually. Pros: Elegant and pampering. Guests can ask for a particular slice of meat, pass on the gravy, or what have you. It's also faster than French service. Cons: Food can get cold (or lukewarm) by the time it's individually served. The waiter can spill food on the guest. The guest may need to move or bend to clear room for the waiter to serve.

American service (also known as "plated"). Sometimes considered to be a less expensive or less elegant way to serve, but this is not necessarily so. The plates are arranged in the kitchen and waiters bring them out and place one at each guest's setting. Some plates may be covered with a metal dome to keep the contents hot. Other dishes may come in an oval- or boat-shaped casserole-type plate. Pros: Food may arrive hotter than if delivered Russian service. The food can be artfully arranged in the kitchen, including fancy garnishes and drizzles of sauce. Sometimes waiters wear white gloves to add an element of class. Cons: If the food isn't creatively arranged, the service tends to lack luster.

Family-style. Best suited for cookouts and other informal events. Food is brought to the table in large serving platters. Guests help themselves and pass it around.

Ask your caterer how long it takes to serve all guests by each method and find out how many guests are assigned to each server. You'll want a mix that's affordable—but don't scrimp on the help. There's little worse than people waiting and waiting for their meal to arrive.

The Wedding Cake

The wedding cake, or *gâteau* (French for "cake"), is one of the most traditional elements of the wedding. But wedding cakes have lately become sophisticated and make trendy fashion statements. The type and color of the icing, how the cake is decorated, and even its shape can change with the times and personal preferences. The wedding cake has become a showpiece in itself, with a lot of detail and planning involved.

The bride-and-groom statue that normally graces the top of the wedding cake has become somewhat passé of late. Still, trends being what they are, they may be back on the guest list soon. Place the "little newlyweds" under a *chuppah* atop the cake and the old standby has a new twist. The little bride and groom, if made of fine porcelain instead of plastic, can become a permanent addition to the lovely knickknacks that can decorate a new home.

And a cake needn't be a cake at all. It could be a collection of cupcakes mounded together to form a multitiered "cake."

Although some caterers include a basic wedding cake in their per-head cost, others charge a separate fee. Of course, the latter holds true if you're bringing in your own wedding cake from an outside caterer. Depending on the reputation of the baker, the ingredients, and complexity of the design, prices can range from several dollars a slice up to more than ten dollars. Sometimes you can buy a wedding cake for a set fee—two hundred to five hundred dollars, for example. You'll also want to ask your caterer or baker about any delivery and setup fees that may be tacked on as additional expense.

Counting Your Crowd

Your contract with your caterer will include the number of people you guarantee, with the final head count coming in anywhere from two weeks to a few days before. You'll be paying for the number of guests you state, whether your invited guests accept or not—so reduce the number of people you guarantee at this point. Keep in mind, if your caterer has more than one affair going on at once, the room you're assigned is based on the number of guests you guarantee. Undercount and you might run into problems; overcount and you'll be paying big bucks needlessly.

Signing Off on the Contract

Look over your catering contract carefully and make sure it includes:

- ❦ The name, address, telephone number, and e-mail address of the caterer

- ❦ The name of the person or manager who will be overseeing your wedding

- ❦ The responsible party at your end: name, address, phone number, e-mail address

- ❦ The date, day, time, and number of hours of your party

- ❦ The exact location and number of rooms, and exact name or identification of the room

- ❦ Whether you will have the exclusive use of the facility or share with other affairs—and if so, how many

- ❦ The elements of your wedding and their order

- ❦ Costs per hour for overtime

- ❦ The exact menu, including number of choices of all items

- ❦ The hours of the open bar or other drink arrangements; if the caterer is providing liquor service, the exact brand names of the liquor and wine available, and whether a champagne toast is included

- ❦ The type of service (French, Russian, American)

- All other inclusions or costs for extras—itemized, as you discussed with the caterer—including color and fabric of table decor, chair styles, amenities, floral arrangements if any, valet parking, outdoor use of terraces, and so forth

- The payment schedule

- Cancellation policy. Note that most caterers' contracts state that deposits are nonrefundable. Try to insert a clause that allows you to claim a refund or apply it toward another date if you must back out or change the date.

- When the final payment is due and how it must be delivered (cash, certified check, debit or credit card, or the like)

- Final head-count date

- Taxes and gratuities

- Caterer's proof of license and liability insurance

Look the contract over carefully once again. Make sure it includes everything you've discussed with your catering representative. Don't let anyone brush you off. It's your money and it's big money. If you should run into any problems, your contract can be the final say.

A Word About *Benchen* and *Sheva Brachot*

You may want to distribute *benchers*—cards or booklets printed with the grace after meals prayers—so that guests can chant the grace at the conclusion of the wedding feast. Made up through the caterer or obtained from a Judaic shop or through sources found over the Internet, they can be artistically rendered and beautifully illuminated. Your names and wedding date can be included; guests can keep these as a reminder of your wedding day.

The *Sheva Brochot* (Seven Blessings) are said immediately after the grace at the end of the wedding dinner. A father, grandfather, or other honored guest can lead the *benchen* (grace), and other guests can be called up to recite each of the seven *brochot*. The people to be so honored are decided in advance, and a list of their names should be given to the person leading the grace.

Reminders and Tips

- It's imperative that everything you've discussed with your caterer be indicated on your contract.

- When giving your initial deposit, always count fewer people than you invite to account for those who decline.

- Refine your head count and let the caterer know by the designated time.

- Make sure there's an oversight person, maître d', or manager who will stay with your wedding throughout your cocktail hour and reception.

- Check with your caterer for proof of licensing and liability insurance.

- Ask your caterer if there will be a corkage or cake-cutting fee if you bring in your own wedding cake and/or liquor.

- When calculating your catering costs, don't forget to include service charges and tax.

- Caterers may refer you to other vendors such as florists and photographers. Will you be paying more (or less) if you use these referrals? Have another person cold call and see if you can get nonreferred prices to compare.

♥ Check your contract for anything *not* in it. You want to be totally specific. It's the little "left-outs" that can hit you financially at the end.

Insider's Interview: Kosher Caterer

Jeffrey Becker, president, Foremost Glatt Kosher Caterers, Westwood, New Jersey, www.foremostcaterers.com

Background: Foremost Glatt Kosher Caterers, often referred to as the "caterer to the caterers," provides kosher catering at top New York establishments such as the St. Regis Hotel, the Waldorf Astoria, the Plaza Hotel, and the Russian Tea Room, as well as in homes and synagogues.

"The first step, before choosing a caterer, would be to identify the venues you would consider for your wedding reception," says Becker. "Then, you would meet with the catering managers of those facilities. If you are planning to hold your wedding at a synagogue, ask what the process would be to book a wedding there. They will often have recommendations of caterers who have worked there, and will provide you with the name of the caterer who is exclusive to their facility or one on their catering panel.

"If you plan to marry in a neighborhood without many kosher caterers, seek counsel of the rabbi at the nearest *shul* there; the rabbi will know who is available in the area.

"The interview process is by far the best and most reliable way of finding out if somebody's services are right for you. It's the same as buying anything very important to you: you don't do it by phone and you don't do it by recommendation alone. Meet in person and talk about your needs, your expectations, and your budget. Then, based on the answers you receive, it will either prove or disprove that this caterer is the right one for you.

"If you contact me to cater a wedding at a particular facility, I would meet you there, walk through it with you, and explain how I would set it up, what I might serve, how I would envision the room to be laid out. I would show you the china. At the same time, I would ask many questions, because it's not so much what *I* see as what *you* see. Weddings are very personal. We don't have a set menu you must use. Rather, we discuss what *you* really want served. Are you a poultry person? Or do you prefer veal or lamb? Do you want fish as an appetizer, or not? If yes, do you want salmon or sea bass? Hot fish or cold? If you have no clue, we'll sit until we figure it out. What else? How about a soup course? In this way, the party and dinner is most reflective of the client, rather than the caterer. That's a very important thing.

"If you cannot meet me at the facility, we'll go to your home. People are also welcome to come in and see a wedding at one of our sites.

"Once the event is booked, we hold a tasting. You can come to our headquarters, or we'll find a facility close to you where we'll do it. There is no charge for the tasting since the wedding is already booked. The bride and groom, and the parents of the bride, will come for the tasting—sometimes the parents of the groom join in, too. Here's where we finalize the menu.

"Upon booking, we ask for an initial deposit, then payment is due one week prior to the event based on the estimated balance. By then, you'll have all of your R.S.V.P.'s in; you'll know how many people you'll be having, although you may still be waiting for Uncle Bill to respond. Let's say you have 285 people. We know how much it costs per person, so we ask for that amount less the deposit. We can accommodate up to an additional 5 percent, even guests showing up unexpectedly that day. We never turn down anyone who is hungry.

"Although you will be responsible to pay for the estimated number of people, if you have more, we'll send a bill for the difference after the party. You don't have to have the money on the wedding night (although some caterers ask that you do). We feel you have enough things to be concerned with the night of the party; you should not have to worry about bringing a check for the caterer."

Quiz: How Much Do You Know About Gracious (and Kosher) Grub?

Are you an epicure, a gourmet, aware of life's varied gastronomical delights? Or do you basically wonder if there are fries with those yummy burgers? When planning the menu for your wedding reception, you may find yourself right at home conversing with caterers—or sitting in a daze, wondering what in the world they're talking about. Take this quiz to discover how much you really know about food terminology, kosher selections, and wedding cuisine. For each statement, circle the letter that correctly completes the sentence or provides the correct answer.

1. *Hors d'oeuvres* are:

   a) fancy napkins folded into interesting shapes and placed at each table setting.
   b) bite-sized, elegant, iced, mini cakes served on platters for dessert.
   c) bite-sized, flavorful, hot or cold appetizers served before the meal.
   d) thin strips of veggies used to tie asparagus together on the dinner plate.

2. *Kasha* is another name for:

   a) a home-style, cheese-filled dessert cake.
   b) buckwheat groats.
   c) sesame seed and honey candy.
   d) mashed potatoes with fried onions.

3. If you're serving a kosher *meat* meal, you *cannot* include:

   a) chicken cordon bleu, escargots, or coquilles Saint-Jacques.
   b) dipless crudités, escarole, or king salmon.
   c) pasta, roulades of veal, or vegetable soup.
   d) hard-boiled eggs, *kreplachs,* or *matzo* balls.

4. If you're serving a kosher *dairy* meal, you *cannot* include:

   a) American golden caviar, fruited blintzes, or *pain perdu.*
   b) bagels, lox, or cream cheese.
   c) lobster bisque, salami and eggs, or shepherd's pie.
   d) tempeh, basmati rice, or café au lait.

5. Which of the following would you *not* serve for dessert?

   a) sweetbreads.
   b) halvah.
   c) wedding cake.
   d) petits fours.

Answers: 1—c; 2—b; 3—a; 4—c; 5—a.

Scoring: Give yourself 5 points for each correct answer.

0–5 points: Do you want ketchup on those fries, too? You may know what you like, but usually, you'll want to do a little something special for guests on your wedding day. If you enjoy only a limited menu of simple good ol' standbys, ask your caterer to prepare this just for you and provide a wider selection for your guests. Of course, it wouldn't hurt to branch out a bit yourself. Read some cooking or food magazines, talk to a rabbi about kosher food, and try sampling a few new things. It may expand your good taste.

10–15 points: Perhaps the French terminology throws you off (after all, not everyone knows that *pain perdu* is simply French toast). Or, beyond knowing that one does not mix meat and dairy, the intricacies of serving a kosher meal may escape you. But you do have the basics down. Don't be afraid to ask or check when you hit a snag. In most cases, your caterer will be happy to explain. Then you can make intelligent decisions based on fine food and what you feel your guests will enjoy.

20–25 points: Congratulations—you're a connoisseur of fine (as well as kosher) dining, and your guests will surely benefit from your expertise. Talk freely with your caterer, exchange ideas, and together you'll delight your guests with a meal that will perfectly complement your very special day.

12

Name That Tune

THE MUSIC FOR YOUR ceremony and reception sets the tone as well as moves the crowd. It can bring tears of joy, stomping feet, fun, and elegance to an affair. So be sure to choose your music, and those providing it, with care.

Your musical taste can range from Israeli, *Sephardic,* Eastern European/klezmer, and world music to classical, pop standards, country and western, rock, easy listening, or a mixture of many types. At your wedding, you can play prerecorded tapes or hire a string quartet, a guitarist, one or two instruments, a DJ, or a live band. And since your wedding takes place in various "segments," you can mix and match music.

Before the Wedding Ceremony

The Chossen's Tish *(The Groom's Party)*

Singing and dancing by the men marks this groom's party where the *ketubah* (marriage contract) is signed and witnessed. According to tradition, after the signing the groom attempts (unsuccessfully) to deliver a serious speech on a topic from the Torah or Talmud. But the guys don't let him. He gets interrupted by celebratory singing and dancing each time he attempts to delve into his speech. Finally, the groom abandons the effort, and, all the men sing and dance their way from the room to visit the bride. The singing can be a cappella, or accompanied by musicians. A klezmer band is particularly suitable to lead or accompany this segment of the activities.

The Callah Bazetsn *(Seating of the Bride)*

While all of the fun and excitement is going on at the groom's party, the bride's gathering is taking place as well. Here, her female friends come by to greet her while more serious background music provides a backdrop for contemplation. A poignant song is either sung or played.

And now the guys, singing and dancing their way to the bride, join the girls. Together they watch as the groom places the veil over his bride's face, and then, with music and dance, they all make their way to the ceremony.

If you choose a more egalitarian version of the *ketubah,* the bride and groom will sign it together, and music can be incorporated here as well.

Seating Guests

Classical pieces or soft Hebrew arrangements are the perfect accompaniments to the reserved muffle of chatter as guests quietly greet each other and take their seats. Depending on your mood, the location, and your budget, you can have several instrumentalists providing the melodies—such as a string quartet, or a soloist playing a flute, violin, or electronic keyboard. If your sanctuary has an organ, you may want to have the organist who plays at services play for your wedding, too. In place of live musicians, you can play a cassette or CD of your favorite wedding music.

The Processional

The door to the sanctuary opens, and all eyes turn to catch the first glimpse of the wedding party. The processional is about to begin.

If a cantor will be officiating or co-officiating, he or she enters first, singing a beautiful Hebrew song to lead the way. Often this would be a selection from the Song of Songs. His or her voice fills the sanctuary and heightens the moment during the march down the aisle. Or the same instrumentalists who played during the seating can provide your music. The selections or medley of songs you choose can be classical, Hebrew, or something totally different.

If a cookie-cutter wedding isn't your piece of cake, you can toss tradition in favor of a more personal statement. Combining different types of music in the same ceremony is popular, but you should be sure that they flow well together. An exception would be the moment the bride is introduced, when a change in musical style can prepare the guests for the bride's entrance. A harpsichordist and a flutist playing Renaissance and Baroque music can backdrop your processional, for example, and then a solo trumpeter can herald the bride's grand entrance.

When selecting music for your ceremony, think "mood" and "imagery":

- Cantorial selections lend lush imagery, with a favorite song, *"Erev Shel Shoshanim,"* evoking the feelings of a romantic and fragrant evening.

- Broadway show tunes or movie theme songs make a big, bold statement—but can be expressively romantic, too. Songs from *Fiddler on the Roof* can be particularly appropriate to the Jewish wedding.

- Jazz is sophisticated and spontaneous. There are many variations from which to choose. You can try klezmer music and Jewish jazz as well.

- Classic rock offers lots of romantic songs. You might find one that features the bride's name (Diana, Michelle, Donna) or one with meaningful lyrics.

- Want to be way different? How about a rap song written specifically for you with lyrics referencing your lives and love?

Some of today's more memorable wedding ceremonies do march to the beat of a different drummer. There is a wide margin of acceptance in wedding music today, but be sure to check with your officiant. He or she may have some restrictions. Some synagogues allow Hebrew music only during the ceremony, although secular music can be welcome during the reception.

Under the *Chuppah*

If you do have a cantor, he or she can add musical moments to the ceremony, chant the Seven Blessings, and offer a benediction after the bride and groom have been pronounced husband and wife. And after the groom stamps on the glass, the joyous music once again begins as the newly married couple and their wedding party prance back up the aisle. A popular song for the recessional is "*Mazel Tov* and *Siman Tov,*" with the entire "audience" joining in singing and clapping to the upbeat melody. Of course, other songs can be used in a medley or by themselves. You may wish to carry out the theme of the earlier processional, whether it be classical music, show tunes, jazz, or what have you.

The music should continue until all of your guests have left the ceremony area.

Cocktail Hour

Whether you're holding a cocktail hour before or after the ceremony, the music during this period is usually sophisticated background music. Brides and grooms on a limited budget can forgo the music during this period, or they can play some background CDs. For live music, hire a strolling violinist, a string quartet, or two or three instruments that will provide sweet harmony together. Should a baby grand piano be available, a pianist can tickle the ivories for your guests' listening pleasure. If you're hiring a band for the dinner dance to follow, you could have a few musicians arrive earlier to cover the cocktail hour.

And if you go all out, you can have a band or society orchestra play for the cocktail hour, too. Standards such as Frank Sinatra and Tony Bennett tunes are popular during this time.

For a more *haimish*-style wedding, an accordian player can add the perfect touch. And if you're having a theme wedding, this can be carried out during the music of your cocktail hour as well.

The Main Reception

Once the guests are seated, the DJ or bandleader calls everyone's attention to the magical moment: the wedding party's entrance into the reception area. Perhaps you've selected individual songs for each person in your bridal party. The song can have a particular meaning related to the person. The selected tunes can be woven through the generally upbeat *horah* tunes in a medley.

As the emcee announces each member of the wedding party, he or she makes a grand entrance amid clapping and singing. Each bridesmaid will arrive on the arms of an usher, and your maid or matron of honor on the arm of your best man. And then, the emcee will make the announcement everyone is waiting to hear: "Let's give a warm welcome to our bride and groom, the new Mr. and Mrs. _____!"

The music picks up amid wild applause, and continues. As the couple make their entrance, they circle the room in time to the music, accepting the good wishes of all the guests as they pass by. And often the couple will weave their way under and through a living arbor: the bridesmaids (holding their bouquets) and groomsmen face each other in a row, raising their arms above their heads and touching hands to form a flower-covered walkway through which the bride and groom stroll in time to the upbeat music.

And soon, after everyone has settled down, it's time for the first dance. This is the moment when all eyes are on the bride and groom as they dance together for the first time as husband and wife. With the music rising, and tears of happiness welling up in guests' eyes, the groom sweeps his bride across the dance floor in an image of grace and beauty, perhaps even ending in a dramatic dip. Some brides and grooms, aware of the importance of this first dance, even take dancing lessons to prepare them for this moment.

The music continues as the bride dances with her father, the groom with his mother. Again, the songs are carefully selected to reflect the sentiment. Next, the best man takes the floor with the maid or matron of honor. Then all the others in the wedding party are asked to join in. Bringing in the guests, the emcee may ask everyone to now dance, or call couples up by how long they've been married. "Will everyone who has been married twenty-five years or more join us on the dance floor," is a common request.

Other "special events" accompanied by music follow.

The Horah

Danced at least several times during the wedding reception, this lively circle dance encourages participation by everyone. The bride and groom are lifted high on chairs held up by four people each, as the dancers circle around them. The bride and groom can hold a kerchief between them as they are held aloft. Guests who can't keep up with the heart-pounding pace stand at the rim of the circle and clap and stamp to music such as *"Havah Nagilah," "Shovtah Mi'em,"* and long-lasting medleys of joyous music. Often guests break away from the main circle and form circles within circles, and also honor parents by dancing around them as well. There are other variations as guests weave through each other, close a circle tighter and then open it wider.

The Mezinka

This is the dance honoring the mother who is marrying off her last daughter. The typical song played is *"Die Mezinke Oysgegeben."* The mother is seated on a chair in the middle of the room and everyone dances in a circle around her, giving their best wishes. She wears a wreath of flowers in her hair placed on her head by the bride and groom for this occasion. Today, the *mezinka* dance is often invoked for the mother marrying off her last son as well. In this case, the lyrics of the song can be changed to reflect the change in gender. Other songs can be used instead, including any *horah*.

Cutting the Cake

This is where the bride cuts the wedding cake and the bride and groom feed it to each other. The song usually played here is a version of "The Farmer in the Dell," with lyrics changed to, "The bride cuts the cake, the bride cuts the cake . . ." but other songs can be used as well.

The Garter Toss

Here's where the groom reaches *way* up under the bride's gown to remove the garter from her leg and tosses it to the single men gathered nearby. One lucky fellow catches it. Songs such as "The Stripper" are traditionally played during this time.

Specialty Fun Dance Numbers

These can include the song "One" or "New York, New York" for a chorus line; "The Electric Slide" dance; "Who Let the Dogs Out"; "Y.M.C.A."; the "Twist"; the "Macarena" (on its way to becoming a much-loved cliché); and traditional groaners such as "The Hokey Pokey" and "The Bunny Hop." For additional variety, there's the limbo and conga-line dances. Some bands or DJs distribute oversized fun items—inflatable musical instruments, huge sunglasses, lightsticks, and other "toys"—during some of the specialty fun numbers. This could be considered a contemporary version of the ancient practice of entertaining the bride and groom with jesters, hand-painted masks, and other props.

The Last Dance

And just when you were having fun! The wait staff has just served coffee and tea and is passing around slices of wedding cake. The dessert and/or the Viennese table has been attacked and demolished, and it's getting to be time to say good-bye. The band or DJ strikes up a signal song and may offer a few words to the departing guests.

Separate Dancing

For those who eschew mixed dancing, the music (live or recorded) plays and men and women have separate dance areas. A clarinet's buoyant notes may rise to a crescendo with guests dancing the *horah* in joyous abandon—in two separate areas of a large room, or even in two separate rooms simultaneously. Outdoor weddings can separate the male and female groups by a curtain hung from poles or another type of divider. Despite the restriction against males and females dancing together, a *mitzvah-tants* is permitted. The bride can dance with her father and grandfather, or even her father-in-law, by each holding the end of a kerchief between them. So, too, the groom can dance with his mother, and so on.

Booking the Music

Band or DJ

So will you hire a band or DJ for your main musical entertainment? There are advantages to each. While there's nothing more elegant than a live band, a DJ may be able to provide a larger selection of music. And as far as finances go, you'll have to do some comparison-shopping. A good DJ may not necessarily be less expensive than live music.

Once you've decided on the type or types of music you want, it's time to hire the musicians. Perhaps you've been to weddings and have enjoyed a band or DJ. That would be the first place to start. But in actuality, it's only the beginning of your research.

Many bands are not comprised of the same members. Some bands are run by a company that has hundreds of musicians at its disposal, and could have thirty or more bands under its banner. Musicians can be mixed and matched. Some may play together consistently and work in harmony; others are slapped together at the last moment and wing it from there. That's not to say they aren't talented or that they won't do a great job for you, but you can see the risk.

Then there are the other bands or musical groups that stay together always. You're hiring exactly the group you've heard. No surprises here—unless one of the members gets sick or has an emergency that keeps him or her away. Check in advance about arrangements under these circumstances.

Asking friends or relatives for recommendations is another option—but if you don't know their taste, this could prove problematic. If you hear the band and hate it, that might be considered a direct insult by your friends, who'd feel you shunned their choice as "the best band in the world."

You can locate other bands or DJs by checking out regional bridal magazines or your local phone book, by attending bridal showcases, asking your caterer for advice, checking your local newspaper's classified ads, reading special wedding sections in newspapers, or doing an Internet search for "wedding music."

Once you've made a list of bands or DJs, check out their reliability. Ask the Better Business Bureau or local consumer groups if they have had any unresolved complaints against them. If all seems okay, it's time to get in touch.

You and your honey will set up an appointment with the band. Often, they'll have video- or audiotapes of their music for you to peruse. If you don't like the tapes or the type of music they present, don't waste time. Move on.

Your best bet is to find out where the band or DJ will be playing. Go down there. Listen to the reaction of the crowd. Then decide if this is the group or DJ you truly want at your wedding. Another choice is to find out about other weddings where they are playing, dress up enough to mingle with the guests, and go down and check them out. Do *not* help yourself to food or crash the party, however!

Depending on your time frame and style, you may want to hear five or more groups, or perhaps three will do. Next, sit down and talk with them. Can you communicate? Do they understand what you want? Do they have the instrumentalists you want or the type of instruments the music you want requires? Can they work your location? What are their fees? How do they compare with other bands you've seen? You don't want to necessarily hire the musicians who are the least expensive—you want musicians whose music you love!

Does the Music Sing to You?

Armed with a listing of your favorite tunes and "must-haves," you start planning your music. A year before the big day is not too soon to start. Popular bands get booked early, especially during popular wedding times. Can the band deliver? Be leery of promises such as "Oh, we can play anything you want." Be specific and get your band's representative to be specific as well. You don't want to find out at your wedding reception that the band that could play "anything" is clueless about klezmer.

In most cases, you'll work with the band or DJ to select the type of music they will play at your wedding. Their ideas can be invaluable. Bands have play lists, which actually are the songs they usually do and can do well. If band members aren't familiar with your choices and have to learn new numbers, get sheet music if you can, or at least a tape or a CD. You may have to pay an additional fee if they need to practice the number.

If you don't see a good deal of Jewish music on their play list, ask them how many Jewish weddings they've actually played. You don't want them to learn the ropes at your wedding!

In addition to satisfying your own musical tastes when selecting music, consider those of your guests. Consider the age group of the majority of your guests as well. Most people feel comfortable and come alive with the music they danced to when they were young adults, so think in eras: big band, 1940s classics, classic rock, disco, club, and all the current styles. If your guest list is top-heavy with a particular generation, increase the music of that era accordingly.

Perhaps you want to hire a DJ for your reception. You'll want to know about availability on the date, time, and place you're holding your wedding reception. Is the DJ playing another gig after yours? If so, what if you want to extend the music for another hour since everyone is having so much fun?

Check out the personality of the actual DJ covering your event. Is this someone who just puts the discs on and lets the music roll, or does he or she act as an emcee? How much effort does the DJ make to get people up on the dance floor? Is there one DJ who spins the discs and another who acts as an emcee? Look over the song collection and ask if you can provide additional tunes, for specific songs you want to play.

In addition to dance numbers, consider music to dine by. Or you can ask the band or DJ if they do their own specialty set (perhaps a medley of show tunes or a *doina*) during the main course as well.

Then, too, there may be songs that you absolutely *do not* want included anywhere in the ceremony or reception. Perhaps a song brings up bad memories, or it's just a tune that you absolutely hate. And finally, ask the band or DJ about the type of specialty numbers they normally would include. You may not think about ruling out Musical Chairs until the band or DJ mentions it.

Contracts

When signing a contract with a band or DJ, you will most likely give a deposit, make another payment along the way, and offer the final payment at or before the event. If possible, pay your deposits with a credit card; in case of a future problem, you may have some recourse through the credit card company. In most cases, deposits are nonrefundable. Make sure everything you want is written into the contract. This includes:

- The name of the bride and groom

- The contact and who is paying for the services

- The date and day of the week of the wedding

- The start and finish time of the wedding

- The location of the wedding

🍂 The breakdown of the segments of the wedding (ceremony, cocktail hour, reception) with start and finish times of each

🍂 The names of musicians and instruments/vocals for each segment. For example, which musicians and what instruments will play at the cocktail hour, the ceremony, and the reception? This includes the names of all the musicians, and the names of backups in case of emergency. You'll want all the instruments listed, and the total number of musicians indicated.

🍂 The number of guests you expect, and the size of the wedding venue. Let them know if it's an outdoor or indoor affair. The size of their sound system needs to be considered. If you're hosting a wedding for five hundred people in a vast outdoor area, the sound equipment will be different from those of a wedding for fifty in the back room of a restaurant.

🍂 The amount of the deposit and the installments and the dates they are due

🍂 Overtime fees

🍂 Travel fees

🍂 Cancellation policies. What is the responsibility of the band if they must cancel and your responsibility if you cancel? What is the policy regarding acts of nature that prevent the band or DJ from performing?

🍂 Will you be feeding the band or DJ?

🍂 A list of any special songs you want played, and those you absolutely don't. Later on, you'll provide the band with the names and relationships of the bridal party, those honored, birthdays, anniversaries, and so forth.

The List

Well in advance of the wedding day, you'll provide your band or DJ with an index card (maybe a large card!) or sheet with the names of guests whom the emcee will call up to honor, as well as the names of the bridal party. In addition to the names, write out their pronunciations phonetically. You may want to call your musicians' office to verbally go over any difficult-to-pronounce names, or even make a short cassette tape or e-mail sound bites for them. You'll also provide them with a general "order of the day" schedule outlining the special events. With the details all arranged and the contracts signed, there's only one thing left to do: dance the night away at your wedding and have a wonderful time!

Wedding Music Play List

Following is a list of songs you might decide to play at your wedding. They have been divided into sections by event. You can take this list to heart, or you can use it as a sounding board to inspire you to find your own favorite songs and artists.

Prelude: As Guests Are Being Seated

"Sunrise, Sunset"	*Fiddler on the Roof* soundtrack
"Sabbath Prayer"	*Fiddler on the Roof* soundtrack
"Evergreen"	Barbra Streisand
Four Seasons	Vivaldi
Romeo and Juliet Overture	Tchaikovsky

Callah Bazetsn, Bedecken, and Tish

"Erev Ba"	David and the High Spirits
"Kale Bazetsn"	Itzhak Perlman
"Badeken Di Kalleh"	Giora Friedman
"Erev Shel Shoshanim" (instrumental)	David and the High Spirits

Processional

"Mah Tovu"	Shoshana Damari
"Dodi Li"	David Shneyer, David & the High Spirits
"Flatbush Waltz"	The Andy Statman Klezmer Orchestra
"Partos Trocados"	Ensemble Accentus
"Shalom Aleichem"	Traditional rendition
"Wedding Processional"	*The Sound of Music* sound-track
Wedding Cantata no. 202	Bach
Canon in D Major	Pachelbel
Processional Klezmer Suite	Itzhak Perlman
Trumpet Voluntary	Jeremiah Clarke

Ceremony

"Introduction to Ceremony"	Danny Albert & His Orchestra
"Oyfen Prepichik"	David and the High Spirits
"Wedding—*Sheva Brachot*	Complete Marriage Service for Hazzen
"Blessing Over Wine"	Abraham Lopes, Cass Cardozo

Recessional

"Dovid Melech Yisrael"	Andy Statman and David Grisman
"D-Aynu"	Traditional rendition
"Mazel Tov" and *"Siman Tov"*	David and the High Spirits
"Hevenu Shalom"	David Shneyur
Wedding March	*The Marriage of Figaro* (Mozart)

"Havenu Shalom Aleichem"   David and the High Spirits
"We've Only Just Begun"   The Carpenters

Cocktail Hour

"I Could Write a Book"   Ella Fitzgerald
"Night and Day"   Frank Sinatra
"You're Nobody Till Some-   Frank Sinatra
   body Loves You"
"I've Got You Under My Skin" Frank Sinatra
"Isn't It Romantic"   Ernestine Anderson
"Fascination"   Billy Vaughn & His Orchestra
"The Look of Love"   Kenny G
"One Hand, One Heart"   *West Side Story* soundtrack
"For Once in My Life"   Tony Bennett
"Embraceable You"   Duke Jordan

Dinner

"If I Were a Rich Man"   *Fiddler on the Roof* soundtrack
"Parents of the Kid in Love"   Mike Douglas
"Hey, Big Spender"   Peggy Lee
"Everything's Coming Up   Bette Midler
   Roses"

Announcing the Wedding Party

"Gonna Fly Now"   *Rocky* soundtrack
"Hey, Look Me Over"   Bing Crosby and Rosemary Clooney
"You're My Best Friend"   Don Williams
"I Get By (With a Little   Beatles
   Help From My Friends)"

Announcing the Bride and Groom

"Here Comes the Bride"	Traditional
"Fly Me to the Moon"	Frank Sinatra
"Love and Marriage"	Frank Sinatra

First Dance (Bride and Groom)

"Breathe"	Faith Hill
"When I Fall in Love"	Natalie Cole
"Grow Old With Me"	Mary-Chapin Carpenter
"Through the Eyes of Love"	*Ice Castles* soundtrack
"True Companion"	Marc Cohn
"It Had to Be You"	Harry Connick Jr.
"Endless Love"	Diana Ross and Lionel Richie
"As Time Goes By"	Rudy Vallee

Father/Bride Dance

"Daddy's Little Girl"	Al Martino
"The Way You Look Tonight"	Frank Sinatra
"My Heart Belongs to Daddy"	Mary Martin
"Thank Heaven for Little Girls"	Maurice Chevalier
"A Song for My Daughter on Her Wedding Day"	Ray Allaire

Mother/Groom Dance

"Sunrise, Sunset"	*Fiddler on the Roof* soundtrack
"A Song for Mama"	Boys II Men
"What a Wonderful World"	Louis Armstrong
"A Song for My Son on His Wedding Day"	Mikki Vierick
"Through the Years"	Kenny Rogers

Garter Removal

"The Stripper"	David Rose
"Do Ya Think I'm Sexy"	Rod Stewart
"You Sexy Thing"	Hot Chocolate
Mission Impossible: theme	Danny Elfman

Bouquet Toss

"Girls Just Wanna Have Fun"	Cyndi Lauper
The Dating Game: theme	Herb Alpert's Tijuana Brass
"Hands Up"	Ray Anthony

Group, Line, and Specialty Dances

"One"	*A Chorus Line* soundtrack
"New York, New York"	Frank Sinatra
"The Alley Cat"	Lawrence Welk
"The Bunny Hop"	Ray Anthony
"Limbo Rock"	David and the High Spirits
"Macarena"	Ray Anthony
"Y.M.C.A."	Village People
"The Hokey Pokey"	Ray Anthony
"The Electric Slide"	Marcia Griffith

Last Dance

"Last Dance"	Donna Summer
"The Party's Over"	Ray Anthony
"I've Had the Time of My Life"	Bill Medley and Jennifer Warnes
"Thanks for the Memory"	Bing Crosby
"The Best Is Yet to Come"	Tony Bennett

Tips

- ❦ Go over your play list with your music provider.

- ❦ Go over the date and times of your various wedding segments that call for music (prelude, cocktail hour, and so on).

- ❦ Tell the band or DJ if any of the wedding segments for which you're hiring music will be held outdoors (including on a terrace or patio).

- ❦ Make it clear that the band or DJ cannot drink liquor, wine, or beer before or during your event, nor can they indulge in any recreational drugs.

- ❦ If you're holding your wedding in midafternoon, ask your music provider if there will be additional charges. (It may prevent them from doing another job before or after.)

- ❦ Does your facility have a bandstand available for your band? Is it large enough to accommodate the number of pieces you've hired?

- ❦ Check the size of the dance floor at your reception facility. Is it large enough to accommodate the number of guests you expect will be dancing?

- ❦ Find out what the musicians will be wearing. Most come in tuxedos, females in gowns. But ask, and request any changes you may want.

- ❦ Will they be available for overtime and, if so, how much do they charge?

- ❦ Will they be providing continuous music? If not, will they play taped music during breaks? You don't want dead air.

- ❦ Before hiring a band or DJ, check out their style. Some are high energy, others refined. Does their style match your vision?

- ❦ Before hiring a band or DJ, make sure they carry insurance and show you their certificate of insurance.

- ❦ If hiring a DJ, does he or she have backup in case of emergency?

- ❦ If you're hiring a group, how many musicians and singers are there?

- ❦ Do they need any special equipment, such as musical stands or chairs? Do they bring their own? If so, do they charge extra?

- ❦ Do they come with backup equipment and instruments in case of a problem?

- ❦ How much setup time do they need? Can they get into the facility in time to set up?

- ❦ Have you included some line dancing or group dancing so that those who aren't ballroom dancers or who don't have dance partners can join in the fun?

- ❦ If you're having separate dancing for men and for women, alert your music provider.

- ❦ Don't try to micromanage your band or DJ. Leave them room to do their jobs as they know best.

> ℬ When you go to see the DJ or band at a live performance, check out their ability to "read" the crowd and get everyone up and dancing.
>
> ℬ Ask your band or DJ if they are members of a professional organization.
>
> ℬ Has the band or DJ played the room before? Are they familiar with any particular sound problems the venue may present, and do they know how to overcome these?
>
> ℬ Does the DJ have professional-level equipment? Find out what type he or she uses and check it out—perhaps with a music equipment store, a knowledgeable friend, or a university music department.
>
> ℬ If a band's or DJ's fee is significantly less than the general price ranges, they may be amateurs or part-timers. Find out how many gigs they play a month. Four or five should be a minimum number.

Quiz: Are You in Step With Wedding Music?

Selecting the music for your wedding is an important decision. Not only does music enrich your marriage ceremony, but it can also be one of the key factors that makes or breaks your reception. How knowledgeable are you when it comes to selecting the music for your wedding? Take this quiz to see if you're in step or off the beat. For each statement, circle the letter that represents the best answer.

1. You love Brahms; your honey loves Britney. So you:

a) play a recording of the Violin Concerto in D Major as people are gathering for your ceremony and ask the DJ to play "Baby One More Time" at your reception.

b) play a recording of the Violin Concerto in D Major as your guests gather and ask your band to play their version of "By Your Side."

c) ask the band to play a medley composed of the *Four Seasons'* "Walk Like a Man" and The Four Seasons: Concerto in E, "Spring": Allegro.

d) invite Mr. J. Brahms and Ms. B. Spears to be your guests of honor at your wedding reception.

2. Both a rabbi and a cantor are officiating at your wedding ceremony. So:

a) the rabbi walks down the aisle, followed by the cantor.

b) the cantor walks down the aisle, followed by the rabbi.

c) both the cantor and the rabbi walk down the aisle together holding a kerchief between them.

d) the cantor walks down the aisle singing the Seven Blessings and the rabbi follows repeating it in Aramaic.

3. You and your honey both agree that your first dance should be a beautiful classic waltz. You select:

a) "Tea for Two"

b) "Blue Danube"

c) "Yellow Submarine"

d) "It's Raining Men"

4. For a disco segment at your reception, you ask the band to play:

a) "I Love the Nightlife"; "Get Down Tonight"; "Shake Your Booty."

b) "Castle on a Cloud"; "The Sun Will Come Out Tomorrow"; "I Got the Sun in the Morning."

c) "The Look of Love"; "Raindrops Keep Fallin' on My Head"; "Bridge Over Troubled Waters."

d) *"Hinei Mah Tov"; "Osah Shalom"; "Avadim Hayinu."*

5. When making up your seating plan for dinner, you:

a) place your older relatives at the table closest to the band; with declining hearing ability, they should be right on top of the music to better enjoy your event.

b) put teens and twenty-somethings alternating between every guest over fifty at the tables, so the younger generation can explain the meaning behind the rock lyrics to their parents and grandparents.

c) seat the teens and twenty-somethings closest to the band so they can enjoy the music—the louder the better.

d) have the band change their location to different quadrants of the room so that each table can have a chance at being near the music.

Answers: 1—a; 2—b; 3—b; 4—a; 5—c.

Scoring: Give yourself 5 points for each correct answer.

0–5: Face the music, buster! You've got a lot to learn. It's time you bought or borrowed a stack of CDs and invested time in some serious listening. And if you go to another's wedding, or a *bar* or *bat miztvah,* pay attention to how it's done. Although you'll need to leave most of the musical moments to the band or DJ you hire, you'll still need to know enough about music to hire the right people to make your wedding a success.

10–15: You can use a little tune-up, but you're not badly out of step. Perhaps you're familiar with one or two musical styles, but can expand your knowledge into different areas. Since you'll most likely want to include many different types of music to match the tastes of all of your guests, now's the time to get a sampling of what the wide world of music has to offer.

20–25: You're a musical maestro who not only has mastered the art but is also in touch with the way music will enhance your wedding. Your choices, coupled with those of your music provider, should ensure that your guests will be moved, swayed, and able to fulfill their *mitzvah:* to celebrate and dance at your wedding!

13

Flowers

IT IS AT LAST time to take your walk down the aisle. Yes, you're nervous, and so you take a deep, calming breath. Talk about aromatherapy! As you inhale, the wondrous fragrance of fresh flowers fills you and lifts your spirits even higher than you thought possible. Before you, twin flower girls are making their way down the white runner, tossing rose petals for you to walk upon. And although your hands may feel shaky, the beautiful bouquet of carefully selected flowers you hold before you lends a certain steadiness to your heart.

Here goes! As you take your first steps forward, your bridesmaids, holding their own matching bouquets before them, are ready to greet you. You pass by the floral arrangements sitting high on pedestals along the aisle. As you approach the end of your walk, you'll see the baskets or urns of arranged flowers standing majestically on each side of the *chuppah*. And oh! The *chuppah* itself, bedecked with garlands of greenery and flowers, is a sight to behold. It welcomes you and your honey as you join together to become husband and wife.

Flowers hold the power to transform the ordinary into the extraordinary. They have a language all their own and make a powerful statement in their gentle way. Walk into an empty room and you have, well . . . an empty room. Fill it with flowers and you have a fantasy come true.

Undoubtedly, flowers for your ceremony and reception—as well as personal flowers—will consume a large part of your wedding budget. Prices can range from mildly expensive to "the sky's the limit." You can go with in-season florals or exotic flowers imported from around the world. If you have your heart set on a specific type of flower and have the time, you can even grow them!

"If someone says, 'we love this rose and want it in our wedding,' they may need to work to get it," says Barry Collins at Timeless Roses. One couple wanted a particular type of garden rose for their wedding, he explains, and they wanted ten of them. So they decided to grow them in their garden and have them ready in time for their wedding. "But if you want to do this, always have a back-up plan because it's very difficult to make it work out, especially for an amateur," he warns. "If you don't have a back-up you may not have flowers for the wedding."

Know My Flowers, Know Me

Flowers can act as your signature and reflect your style. Carrying that style throughout your wedding festivities mark a united look that tells a great deal about your personality. Your choice of flowers and colors can show you as a drama queen, a country girl, an exotic type, or a true unadulterated romantic. You can be an old-fashioned girl at heart, or a cutting-edge contemporary woman. Consistently carrying your theme from your personal flowers to your ceremony and reception spaces stamps your signature on the entire event.

Flowers, Flowers Everywhere

When thinking flowers, you need to think beyond just your walk down the aisle. Flowers will enhance the many events associated with your big day, starting with your pre-wedding events, and continuing right on through the wedding itself.

Meeting the Parents

If you've been invited to dinner, bring flowers or send an arrangement afterward with a "bread and butter" note thanking them for the evening.

Engagement Party

If you're setting up round tables for eight or ten people, flowers make the perfect centerpieces. Long tables are enhanced with long, low floral arrangements as well. Cocktail tables can be charmed with candles decorated with rings of flowers, or the tables can hold bud vases with one or two flowers that match or complement the tablecloths or decor. If you want to go for the unusual, small pots filled with exotic fruits and flowers make an interesting statement.

Bridal Shower

If the shower is held in a home, flower arrangements strategically placed in the party areas enhance the feeling of festivity. In a restaurant or party space, you may be able to bring in your own flowers—or the establishment may provide them. A corsage for the bride-to-be is always appropriate. A wrist corsage may work better than a pin-on type because the bride will be getting lots of hugs that might crush her flowers if they are pinned near her chest and shoulder area. The wrist corsage will look lovely as she opens gifts, waves, or shows her ring during the party.

Ufruf

Twin flower arrangements for the *bima* make a nice offering to the temple or *shul*. If you're holding a *kiddish* after, flowers can decorate the buffet or wine table. If individual tables are being used, arrangements as centerpieces or in bud vases for small tables are in order. Rose petals can be scattered on the tables for extra ambience.

Bachelorette Party or Bridesmaid Party

Depending on the facility, flowers may be used to enhance the event. If the shindig is being held in a nightclub or bar, area flowers are pretty much out of your hands. In a restaurant, the facility may take care of the flowers, or you can bring in your own. The people hosting the event may want to provide the bride with a corsage, however.

Rehearsal Dinner

Centerpieces for the tables are a given, unless the dinner is held in a restaurant. Either the restaurant will provide table flowers, or you can talk to the staff about bringing in your own.

Guest Quarters

If you're hosting out-of-town guests at your home, brighten up the main rooms and your guests' bedrooms with flowers—either a formal arrangement or loose flowers arranged artfully in a vase. These can be ordered from a florist or handpicked from your garden, if you have one. If your out-of-town guests are booked into hotel or motel rooms, placing a small floral arrangement there along with a basket of yummy snacks will be a pleasant surprise for them.

The Ceremony

If you're holding your wedding ceremony indoors in a synagogue, decorate the entrance and the lobby areas. It's the first impression your guests will have of your wedding. Depending on the building itself, and the time of year, you may want to have several pots of flowers placed at the outside entranceway to the building or along the sides of the front door. Spring annuals are lovely and cheerful, and containers of mums are nice in the fall. Make sure, however, that they don't block or otherwise get in the way of your guests as they walk up the steps or enter the front doors.

You might opt to have a trellis or two woven with greenery and flowers to set area boundaries or highlight specific spots. You can also fill a vacant area with topiaries. A small arrangement of flowers will enhance the little table that will hold *kippot* for your guests. In fact, if the *kippot* are placed in a basket, the handle can be decorated with a garland of greenery and some small flowers.

The sanctuary of the *shul* or temple is where you will want to invest your flower power. Be sure to check with your rabbi for any rules as to flower placement and allowable delivery times. Remember that someone has to be in the building to let the florists in.

When you're planning flowers for the sanctuary, the room itself will lead the way. You'll want flowers on the *bima*. If your *bima* is offset with railings, garlands of greenery and flowers may "ride the rails" if you like. And with the *chuppah* taking center stage, flowers here get the most attention.

Chuppahs can be vastly different in design, ranging from stationary types to those made of a *tallit* stretched over four poles. If your *chuppah* is stationary, it can be made of wood in a lattice design. In this case, you can decorate the entire top, sides, and poles with flowers and greens. If it's made of cloth, garlands of flowers can be strung across the edges and down the sides. And if your *chuppah* is being made from a large *tallit,* garlands of greenery and flowers can be coiled around the poles. Potted flowers or floral arrangements can also stand at the foot of the poles, or be placed on pedestals in front of each pole. If the rear poles will be facing a wall or otherwise out of view, you can save dollars by decorating the front poles only.

A low arrangement of flowers can also be placed on the table under the *chuppah* that holds the wine and glasses, so that the guests see the flowers rather than the items set out for use during the ceremony.

In addition to the up-front flowers, pedestals topped with floral arrangements should be situated along the aisle that the wedding party uses for the march. Starting at the front row, they can be placed on both sides of the runner, every second or third row. If the aisle is long, the pedestals can stop halfway down the aisle, giving their attention to the front of the *shul*. Tulle, the all-purpose wedding fabric, can be made into large bows and attached to the individual pedestals, or draped and looped from pedestal to pedestal after guests have been seated (and removed before they exit).

If you're holding your ceremony in a catering hall or other indoor space, the same holds true—minus the *bima,* of course. Your caterer or space manager will form an aisle by the way the seating is placed, and your florist can set arrangements along the aisles just as in a sanctuary. The more ornate the space, the fewer flowers you'll need; the greater the expanse of simple space, the more flowers or indoor trees you'll need to fill the area.

Marrying outdoors is a long-held Jewish tradition, and the topography as well as landscaping itself can determine your need for additional flowers and foliage. If your ceremony is being held in a flat, grassy area set with chairs and a *chuppah,* you can add florals just as you might with an indoor ceremony. Should there be natural flower beds, trees, or bushes on the property, try to shape your seating to take advantage of the setting. Flowers in stone urns sitting atop pedestals can be placed along the aisles; without pedestals, they can sit at the foot of the *chuppah*'s poles. And for a romantic touch, a carpet of flower petals strewn in front of the *chuppah* adds elegance.

If you're incorporating a gazebo into your ceremony, it can be decorated with garlands of flowers and greenery draped around the outside, and plantings or flowers set along the foot of the structure. Pots of flowers can be set inside, as well as flowers for the *chuppah* and the table beneath.

Setting up trellises here and there to create boundaries can confine a vast outdoor space to create a more intimate area. Weave them with flowering vines.

The Reception

Your guests can spend up to six hours at your reception, and flowers set the mood, provide the eye candy, the fragrance, and the lavish look of luxury. If the florist you select has worked in the space before, he or she may have ideas that worked well and know just what to do. But of course, you'll want to personalize your selections. If you're booking a wedding reception hall, the price of the catering as well as the floral arrangements will be all-inclusive with the per-head price you'll pay. Usually, however, you'll have the option of upgrading the flowers, and often this option is actually an understood necessity!

Entranceway. If your reception is in a location separate from your ceremony, you may want to greet your guests with urns of flowers at the front door. If you've booked a hall that caters to weddings on a regular basis, hallway decor is generally provided.

Rest rooms. If not provided by the reception hall itself, you can place an arrangement of fresh flowers on the countertop in the bathrooms, along with a basket filled with appropriate toiletry amenities.

The cocktail area. Bud vases with one or two flowers can be placed on each small, round cocktail table. Buffet tables can be decorated with sumptuous fruit and floral arrangements, and garlands of greenery and flowers can be attached as well. Garlands can also be hung along the bar. And if the wait staff is passing hors d'oeuvres, each tray can be decorated with a single perfect flower.

Your room space can be addressed with trellises and topiaries, both to hide service areas and to decorate the space in general. If your musicians sit on a raised bandstand, this, too, can be edged in garlands.

The reception space. Again, your space can be decorated with trellises and topiaries, even palm trees or ficus, depending on your theme. This is where your floral designer can fully unleash his or her creativity.

Reception table centerpieces need to be low enough so that your guests can converse over them, or tall enough so that guests can see each other under them.

Since guests like to take home the table centerpieces, why not ask your florist to make them out of separate clusters of flowers so that each female at the table can get a breakaway piece to take home? Or you can have the florist arrange for paper wrap and have the wait staff pull and wrap separate flowers from the centerpiece to hand to the ladies at the end of the evening.

For the Bride

The bridal bouquet is your all-important piece of "artwork." It helps decorate your personal moment, finishes off your look, and is a major player in your wedding pictures. The key, however, is that no matter how much you love flowers, and no matter how much effort you put into selecting them, *you* are still the star of the show. Your bouquet should complement you, but never overpower you or hide your gown.

Bridal bouquets can be styled to set the tone of your gown and wedding theme. Is your dress influenced by the Victorian look? Have the floral designer make a tight, clustered, Victorian-inspired bouquet to match the spirit. Exquisite ribbons can enhance your fresh flower bouquet, or an old-fashioned tussie-mussie—a horn-shaped vase in silver, colored glass, porcelain, or gold—can replace the standard plastic bouquet holder.

On the other hand, unstructured bouquets with stems tied in luscious ribbons made of fabrics such as organza or velvet create a relaxed but elegant look. Lisianthus in clusters has a gardenlike effect.

For a winter wedding, bouquets can be enhanced with pine, ornamental berries, and even coffee beans. And for spring, bouquets using garden flowers such as lilies, hydrangeas, and peonies are popular. Roses are always in style. Some brides enjoy the look of combining different types of roses. Tropical flowers such as birds-of-paradise make for dramatic visions, as will mini callas.

Colors can reflect the season. Flowers are popular in soft pastels and pale creams or white, but starting in late September the hues can go vibrant.

Still, with today's fast overnight shipping, seasons have pretty much melted away. You can get out-of-season flowers shipped here from South America, for example.

Some brides also like to incorporate flowers into their headpiece. A flowered bun wrap, for example, can complement the bouquet, as can a headband of flowers or a single flower pinned to your bridesmaids' hair.

Flowers for the Women

Your bridal attendants' bouquets should work with the colors of their gowns. Soft touches of color can be picked up to highlight the shades they're wearing, and they can even have their lipstick or eye shadow reflect the floral palette. Textures can also match the fabric of the gowns to some extent. For a winter wedding feel, the rose 'Magic' offers the look of burgundy velvet, which can tie in to the bridal party gowns.

Instead of holding bouquets, bridesmaids can wear their flowers. A wreath of flowers can encircle each bridesmaid's head while she holds a ribbon-tied scroll or little soft drawstring pouch in a fabric matching or complementing her dress.

The bouquet for your maid or matron of honor can match those of the other bridesmaids or be slightly different to set her apart. Your flower girl or girls can hold baskets of rose petals or a bouquet of roses. They can pull petals from the roses and drop them as they walk, or just walk down the aisle holding the bouquet intact. In fact, in ancient times, the flower girl actually carried wheat (a symbol of fertility), which through the years was transformed into flowers. If you're having a winter wedding incorporating pinecones, coffee beans, or woodsy looks, you can add some wheat springs to decorate the flower girl's basket or even her hair.

The mothers of the bride and groom, as well as grandmothers, can wear corsages that tie in with the general look and feel of the floral signature you've created. Or you can find out each parent's or grandparent's favorite flowers and incorporate those into their individual corsages to make them feel especially loved. And if either mother is "marrying off" her last child, order a wreath of flowers to crown her head during the *mezinka* dance.

If you're incorporating the bouquet toss into your wedding plans, have the florist make up a tossing bouquet—which is usually smaller than the bridal bouquet, maybe six inches in diameter. You'll want to keep the original bouquet for yourself, and perhaps have it preserved as a wedding remembrance.

Blooms for the Grooms

Some men do actually *like* flowers. And they may have definite opinions about what they don't like. Their boutonnières should, however, reflect the overall style of the wedding. They can wear a carnation, stephanotis, hydrangea, a single rose, double roses (a large rose sided with a tea rose), calla lily, alstroemeria with touches of greenery, or even ornamental berries. The groom can wear a different boutonnière than the rest of the men, as can the best man. One suggestion is that the groom wear triple roses, the best man double, and the groomsmen a single rose. And don't forget flowers for Dad, Gramps, the ring boy, and the pageboys.

Say It With Silk

If just the *thought* of being surrounded by fresh flowers and greenery starts you sneezing, consider holding your wedding indoors during allergy seasons. And to ease your sinuses, you may want to indulge in silk flowers instead of fresh. Silk flowers also have the advantage of holding up in all kinds of weather. They don't need watering, of course, so they won't wilt. They can be particularly effective if you're having a destination wedding and would like to know you have just the bouquets you want with you when you arrive.

If using silk flowers, check out your source carefully. See the kind of stock available, if the staff can get the flowers you want, and, most important, the level of craftsmanship: it must be superb. Look at actual pieces your craftsperson has done—not just at pictures. And if you've seen silk flowers beautifully done, ask for the name of the person or company that made them.

Hiring Your Florist

Before meeting with your florist, check with your local Better Business Bureau and ask around to make sure you're dealing with a reputable company or individual. You may want to interview several florists until you find one with whom you feel comfortable working, and whose designs reflect your style. Some lean toward dramatic minimalism, others sumptuous European looks. Ask to see a portfolio of work they've actually done; don't settle for stock photos of bouquets and arrangements they say they can copy.

Do they have any fresh bouquets ready that you can see? Whether they are bouquets or centerpieces, look at the workmanship of items they have on hand. Can you see spots of foam sticking out? That's a no-no! Hopefully, the piece will look full and lush.

Also check if the flowers are in some way hydrated. You don't want half-dead blooms drooping about. If you're holding an outdoor summer wedding, you'll want to select flowers that hold up well in the heat. Speak to your florist to get ideas of those that can be serviceable and match your vision at the same time. The last thing you want to worry about is wilted flowers on your wedding day.

You'll also want to check the shops' staffing. If you're having a lot of floral work done, can a shop handle it? Will there be a florist to arrange the pieces at the site upon delivery, and if so, is there an extra charge for this service?

Before your first visit, you should know the date, day of the week, time, and location of your ceremony and reception. You should also have an idea of the type of reception you're planning. Flowers for a full-scale formal Saturday-night hotel affair will be quite different from those for an afternoon outdoor western-themed party. You should also know the color of your bridesmaids' and parents' gowns so that your florist can coordinate personal flowers. A swatch of the fabric as well as a photo of the gowns—both the bride's and those of the wedding party—can help your florist work best for you.

You'll want your meeting to be a two-way street, so come with ideas. Clip pictures, jot down favorite flowers, and discuss the possibilities with your florist, who can help mold your dream into reality.

Also discuss your pocketbook. If your florist is suggesting exotic, out-of-season flowers and your budget is limited, don't feel shy about putting the brakes on runaway expenses. Ask what you can substitute instead.

Before you leave, make sure to get a written estimate outlining all the arrangements needed and the cost. You'll have to refine this after the florist has seen your venue. Remember that you are paying not only for the flowers, but for the labor and florist's expertise as well.

Your first consultation should bring you to a meeting of minds about your personal style and the style of your florist. Designs can include traditional, contemporary, and garden-style. And unless your florist has worked the space before, provide the name and location of your ceremony and reception sites, and expect him or her to pay a visit. It's also a good idea to have the florist look at the *chuppah* you will be using, to measure it and get decorating ideas. Ask if the florist can provide the *chuppah* and see what might be available. Many synagogues and reception halls may also have them on hand for rental.

Your second consultation can refine details, now that your florist is familiar with the space and layout. At this time, you'll review your florist's recommendations.

Keep in mind that the larger the space, the more you may have to fill. Talk to your caterer or the people in charge of your reception space about the number of people you expect. Ask your florist how much time he or she will need to set up at the ceremony as well as at the reception site, and make the proper arrangements with the facilities.

Before the wedding, make sure you have provided your florist with a contact list and delivery information. You may be having the personal flowers sent to your home so you can have them available for photography. The groom may want the boutonnières delivered to his place for the same reason. In addition, the florist will need directions to the ceremony spot as well as the reception location, the name and phone number of a contact there, the location of the doorway to use for delivery, and hours deliveries can be accepted.

Some Floral Tips

❦ Use flowers set at different levels and heights to add visual interest.

❦ Use candles to enhance flowers and add a glow.

❦ Placing mirrors behind flowers sitting on a table against a wall will seem to double their effect.

- ♥ Have the bridesmaids place their bouquets along the head table to add flower power during the reception.

- ♥ Decorate the edging of the head table with garlands of foliage, dotted with flowers.

- ♥ Use ribbon to enhance bouquets.

- ♥ Entwine candelabras with foliage and mini flowers.

- ♥ Decorate the cake-cutting knife with flowers—it's especially effective in photos.

- ♥ Make centerpieces by placing three to six votive candles on the table with rose petals strewn about.

- ♥ Don't forget to assign someone to help your bridal party pin on corsages and arrange the boutonnières for the men.

- ♥ Check into buying or renting bowls, containers, and vases to house the flower arrangements, or ask your florist if these are provided with the arrangements.

- ♥ When talking about the shape or design of your floral arrangements, talk directly to the source: the floral designer at the place you purchase your flowers—not a salesperson.

Money-Saving Ideas

- ♥ Ask your florist about substituting less expensive flowers that can achieve the same "feel" as more expensive varieties.

- ♥ Choose flowers that are locally grown; you'll avoid shipping charges and find they will be more readily available.

- ♥ Select flowers that are in season.

❦ Although some may suggest you share the cost of flowers with the wedding coming into your space directly before or after you, it may not be the best thing to do. Some guests tend to pick flowers out of the arrangements, so you don't know the shape the flowers will be in when it comes to your wedding.

❦ Remember, the more complex the arrangement, the more it will usually cost. You're paying for labor.

After All Is Said and Done

Many brides and grooms donate their flowers to area hospitals after the wedding. But before you make that decision, check with the hospital administration. Believe it or not, some may refuse your offer!

Do you have any relatives who would have loved to have come to your wedding but were too ill, confined, or unable to make it? If they live in the local area, ask one of your bridesmaids to deliver some flowers to them as a way of sharing your wedding day.

If you'd like to have your bouquet preserved, ask your florist if he or she does preservation work, and if not, see if he or she can recommend someone. Contact the person or company that will be preserving your flowers to reserve the date. Make sure the time right after your wedding day is available.

Your flowers can be preserved under a dome, or pressed along with a keepsake copy of your invitation and put under glass. You may want to press some flowers into your wedding sign-in book if you have one.

Quiz: How Much Do You Know About Flowers?

Flowers have the power to lift the spirits, beg forgiveness, entice, enchant, enrich, delight, and make the world a sweeter, prettier place in which to live. For each statement, circle the letter that represents the best answer.

1. Who said, "Life without love is like a tree without blossoms or fruit"?

   a) Kahlil Gibran in *The Vision*
   b) Dorothy Parker
   c) King Solomon
   d) Homer Simpson in *The Simpsons*

2. A boutonnière is:

   a) the buttons on a tuxedo's shirt.
   b) a white, thigh-high boot worn with a tight, ultramini wedding gown.
   c) a flower worn in a buttonhole.
   d) a wedding bouquet made from tight little flowers.

3. The flower most associated with love is:

   a) Baby's breath.
   b) Geranium.
   c) Oleander.
   d) Rose.

4. The bridal bouquet should:

   a) make a more intense statement than those of the bridesmaids.
   b) be the largest of all the bouquets because it's for the bride.
   c) not steal attention from the bride or her gown.
   d) be used to hide a bride's bulging belly.

5. Reception table centerpieces:

   a) are removed when dessert is being served.
   b) must be a different style for every table.
   c) should not block the guests' views of each other.
   d) must all be taken home by your mother-in-law.

Answers: 1—a; 2—c; 3—d; 4—c; 5—c.

Scoring: Give yourself 5 points for each correct answer.

0–5 points: Wake up and smell the roses! Flowers can add a wonderful dimension to your life—all you have to do is take notice and enjoy. Start to build a mental list of blooms you love. And don't forget to have a *serious* talk with your florist before your wedding day.

10–15 points: Flowers *do* make their way into your life, and you enjoy them on special occasions. But unless you want to leave the statement they reflect to someone else, take some time to explore their meanings and how your personal style is best reflected in the flowers you select.

20–25 points: You won't settle for just any petal. Flowers are an important part of your life, and you know how to orchestrate a look that will enhance the ambience of all your wedding-related activities. Congratulations!

Insider's Interview: Floral Designer

Heather Hendrickson, Floral Designs by Heather
www.floraldesignsbyheather.com

Background: Heather provides wedding flowers in the wine country, Sonoma County, and San Francisco's North Bay area, in California.

"When I meet with brides, we start with the date of the wedding so that I know the time of the year it will be and the types of flowers that are available," says Hendrickson. "Although most flowers are available year-round, if you know the date right away you can work with the availability of the product. Before meeting the florist, the bride should also have the location set, and an idea of the number of guests coming so the florist knows how many centerpieces she will need. She should also have some idea of the color of the bridesmaids' dresses. We take it from there.

"Since this area—the wine country—is a destination site for weddings, brides come in and have to meet several vendors in one day. So I either meet them at their hotel's lobby or at the site and we can walk through it together.

"There are two kinds of brides: one who knows nothing about flowers so I have to guide her and show her pictures, and one who has some idea and I fine-tune it and go through all the details. If she has one favorite color, we work out the other flowers that will complement that. I always explain to a bride that flowers are a commodity that have to be grown. If we can't get exactly what she wants, she'll have to leave it to my discretion as a professional to find a substitute.

"The whole wedding starts with the bride's bouquet. She decides on the type she wants, and what she would like in it. Does she want a cascading bouquet or a hand-tied bouquet? In a hand-tied bouquet, the stems are cut very short and the flowers are bound together with ribbons or wire; it has a round effect rather than a cascading effect. The round, hand-tied bouquets are much more popular now. If the bride wants a natural look for flowers, I can use those I grow in my garden. If she doesn't know what type of bouquet to select, she can look at pictures to help her make a decision.

"Some brides want an all-white bouquet, but if she wants color, it has to complement or work with the bridesmaids' dresses. The groom's boutonnière complements the bride's bouquet. If the bride carries white or cream roses, for example, that will be the flower for the groom.

"When planning flowers for the bridesmaids, I look toward their dresses. Do they turn toward pastels or jewel tones? That determines the shades in the bridesmaids' bouquets. For the groomsmen, we will choose something out of the bridesmaids' bouquets so that their boutonnière will complement them.

"Flowers for the fathers will match those of the groomsmen. For the mothers, I tell brides to choose something in a neutral color so no matter what color dress the ladies wear that day, it will work.

"I'll ask the bride, 'Do you want a toss bouquet?' She'll generally say yes. However, some brides think it's tacky and don't do it. Nowadays, we always make a separate bouquet for the bride to toss. It's a scaled-down version of the bride's bouquet. Usually, the toss bouquet is kept in the refrigerator, or it can decorate the cake table until the bride does the bouquet toss.

"When holding an outdoor wedding, you have to make sure the *chuppah* is secured to the ground so that it doesn't blow away. For one wedding, held outdoors in a winery in August, for example, it took two assistants and myself an hour to decorate it. We did garlands of greenery and roses on the posts and along the top and sides of the *chuppah*. We used roses in four colors, and a light fern. All the roses were in water vials so they wouldn't dry out in the afternoon sun. We added a decorative carpet of rose petals for the bride and groom to stand on. And although it couldn't be seen, *tallitot* were placed on top of the *chuppah,* as a symbolic gesture.

"To decorate the aisle, we tied tulle at the chairs along the aisle. At the first two rows we had roses in the four shades and the greenery, and then repeated it every second row along the aisle.

"At the reception, we had two sets of decorations for the tables. The tables during the hors d'oeuvre hour were decorated with edibles. Because the wedding was being held at a winery, we created a living doily of grapevine leaves for the center of each of the ten cocktail tables. Then we added a grapevine wreath. Inside the wreath I placed grapes, apples, pears, and a smattering of edible flowers such as pansies, and nasturtiums.

"Then, inside, for the reception, we had seventeen round tables decorated with platinum containers. At the base we used green hydrangeas and, coming up out of them, a dozen roses in the same colors as the bridesmaids' bouquets. Because it was a late-afternoon wedding, we used three votive candles to add a little ambience, and sprinkled rose petals on the table. I try to use containers that the guests can take home with them at the end of the event."

14

Your Chariot Awaits

TRAVELING THE ROAD FROM love to marriage is one of the most exciting journeys of your life. Although at-home weddings are the dream of some, many marriage ceremonies and receptions are held miles from home. And those marrying at home often need a lift to the airport after the big event. Although the best man can be enlisted to play chauffeur for the day, the majority of couples generally hire professional transportation.

When planning your wedding, be sure to consider how you will travel throughout your special day. It is more than just getting from one place to another in an expedient manner. It's a way to fulfill a vision and a dream that will forever become a part of your wedding memory.

Often the traditional white chauffeur-driven stretch limousine arrives in all its glory to whisk the bride and her party in fairy-tale fashion to her dream wedding. Neighbors and passersby ogle as, ever so carefully, the bride enters the back of the limo. Gently, her maid of honor manages to tuck the opulent fabric of the wedding gown into the car, carefully arranging it to avoid wrinkles. A meticulous bride may ask a member of her bridal party to spread a clean white sheet on the seat before she steps inside.

With her bridal attendants surrounding her, the ride to the ceremony offers a chance for last-minute chatter or for finalizing arrangements for the umpteenth time. It can also be a time to calm nerves, or to reflect on the future. After all, it's the last time the bride will be traveling as a single woman.

Sometimes the limousine makes a scheduled stop along the wedding route to take advantage of a beautiful spot for a photo opportunity. Perhaps the bride will pose amid lush foliage. Then it's on to the ceremony site, where the arrival of the bride is an eagerly awaited event.

Hiring a limousine or other specialty form of transportation is not just appropriate for the wedding day itself. Consider this option for bachelor and bachelorette parties as well to safely transport guests to and fro. And the standard dark-colored nonstretch luxury car makes an ideal choice for picking up out-of-town guests at the airport, if no one else in the bridal party is available to do so.

Since most chauffeur-driven vehicles are rented by the hour, and many have multihour minimums, plan the use of the car carefully and be sure to tell the company and your individual driver your requirements. Unlike church weddings, Jewish ceremonies may be completed quickly. If you're then moving on to another location for the reception, you want to be sure your car and driver are ready for you. Although you may expect that the car and driver will be outside the *shul* waiting at the ready (after all, you're paying for the waiting time), in reality this may not be the case. The chauffeur may have moved to another location to be out of traffic's way, or might even meet his or her buddies at the local doughnut shop for coffee while you're inside taking your wedding vows. If the driver is planning to move away from the *shul* or ceremony spot, ask for his or her cell phone number or beeper, and make sure to give it to the best man and maid of honor.

What if you're holding the ceremony and reception at the same site, and it's rather local? You don't want to hire one limo to transport the bridal party to the ceremony site, and another for the groom's group. And you don't want to incur the unnecessary expense of having the cars wait outside for five or more hours to then take you to the airport and your attendants back home. One couple arranged to make best use of their car's three-hour minimum rental time by having the car make multiple trips.

First, the limo was scheduled to pick up the groom, his parents, and his attendants at his parents' home. After delivering them to the wedding hall, the car then went back to the bride's house and picked up the bride, her parents, and her attendants, dropping them off and staying until the ceremony was under way before taking leave. The couple also hired other transportation to arrive at the end of the wedding reception to take them to the airport and their wedding parties back to their respective starting points.

Ensuring the Good Ride

Before hiring a limousine or transportation company, check out its insurance. Operators should show you proof of valid and current insurance coverage for their fleet or vehicles. Commercial "passenger for hire" insurance can be very expensive. Thus some companies may insure their vehicles under their personal auto policy, and this may not cover you. According to the National Limousine Association, there are cases where clients have been successfully sued for negligence attributed to a vehicle under their hire.

Since many states do not regulate limousine service, it's up to you to be diligent. Get a copy of the limousine company's certificate of insurance.

In addition to insurance, you'll want to make sure that the vehicle or vehicles you hire are operating under the proper authorities and that the driver is properly licensed. While some states or municipalities have no regulations, others tightly enforce both vehicle and chauffeur licensing.

If the vehicle you hire will need to cross municipal or state lines, make sure that the company's in compliance with all necessary authorities. In some places, vehicles can actually be stopped and impounded if found not to be in compliance, the National Limousine Association reports. The association can assist you in determining the regulations in your area, and can also provide you with member companies in your neighborhood.

If your budget is limited or you eschew the drama of statement-making transport, be sure to enlist the help of your best man, a member of the wedding party, a friend, or a family member who can get you to the ceremony, from the ceremony to the reception space (if held in a different place), and to your postreception location with ease. If your designated driver's vehicle is too small or too unsteady, consider renting a more appropriate car for the wedding day. Although you may love to drive, this is not the time for a do-it-yourself trip. And for peace of mind, enlist a backup driver and car. You never know when a guest will have "too good a time" and be unfit to drive, or have to leave in an emergency.

But even when hiring a limousine or other form of professional transportation, you want to take steps to help ensure that all goes according to plan. And doing so takes more than a quick call to a phone number listed in an advertisement.

You might start by asking friends for recommendations. Your caterer might have suggestions as well. And you should speak to several different companies and make a personal visit to their facilities. In most cases, you'll be signing a contract; if one isn't offered, it's a good idea to write up one of your own and get it signed by the appropriate individual at the company.

The contract should include the date of the wedding, the number of hours the car(s) will be hired for, the number and locations of the stops each will make. It should specify the type of vehicle(s), size, and color. You should also include identifying characteristics of the vehicle, including the license plate. Other things to look into: you might want to specify the type of uniform the driver will wear, and the amenities offered. Prices vary by the type and color of the vehicle, as well as the time of year or day you'll be hiring the car for. And gratuities may or may not be included with the contracted price. Be prepared to leave a deposit at the time you sign the contract.

For those holding their wedding at home or at a friend's house, you'll need to consider making proper parking arrangements and perhaps hiring an auto wrangler or two to guide your guests as they arrive. And whether held at a home or another location, you may want to offer valet parking for your guests. The hosts of the wedding should consider this expense as part of the deal if it's not included in the catering hall or hotel package. Guests should never be asked to pay for their own parking or valet fees, nor should they be required to tip the valet staff.

Have the best man or another wedding party member run a spot-check on the valet staff as they park and then retrieve cars. Although the majority of valet services are totally honest and helpful, some might try to play both ends. With their fees and tips already paid for by the wedding host, the valet parkers might post an elegant sign outside the door of the reception hall right before the affair ends, which stipulates that there is a per-car charge upon retrieval.

But whether renting professional transportation, asking a ride from your best man or another member of your circle, or arranging for guest parking, the key is to take the time to do a little legwork and planning beforehand. Taking these steps well in advance will help ensure that come your wedding day, you, your wedding party, and your guests will all have smooth rides and wonderful memories.

FROM OY VEY TO OLÉ

It was a rainy, stormy night, but Susan and Jonas were having such a good time at their wedding, they wanted to be the last to leave. So after a large Saturday-night affair, all the guests, parents, and wedding party members left for home, assuming that the bride and groom had arrangements made to get to their post-wedding destination.

Alas, the usher who had volunteered to be chauffeur for the night (he had the nicest car of the group) had to leave the wedding reception early. His wife developed one of her migraine headaches, and he had to rush her home. He did quickly mention this change of plan to the bride, who was more concerned about her new relative's headache than the headache she would later be facing.

So as the catering staff collected the last of the dinnerware, rolled up the tablecloths, and dimmed the lights, there stood our bride and groom, alone in the center of the cavernous catering hall with no way to leave.

Due to the inclement weather, there wasn't a taxi to be found—

not even for a just-married bride and groom. Finally, and quite reluctantly, our resourceful groom called his brother-in-law, who by now was home and just about asleep. Since he lived the closest to the wedding hall, he was "elected" to drive the couple for the almost one-hour trip to their overnight accommodations, and then back to his own home. In the raging storm.

Poor Marty. Good Marty. He dragged himself out of bed, threw some street clothes over his pajamas, and once again went out in the pouring rain to rescue our stranded, woeful, and slightly drenched bride and groom.

Although their post-wedding hours were surely a washout, the couple got to their overnight destination safely—and in time to see the morning sunrise together as husband and wife.

Insider's Interview:
National Limousine Association

Bruce Cottew, past executive director
www.limo.org

Background: The National Limousine Association is a voluntary, nonprofit organization responsible for, and dedicated to, representing and furthering the interests of all aspects of the limousine industry.

"Booking a limousine is pretty much like booking a synagogue," says Cottew. "If you are getting married at a peak time, you'll need six or more months out. If you want a June wedding, for example, there are very few weekends available. If you want a stretch limousine or a fancy car, you'll have to allow more time than that.

"There are a lot of different types of limousines out there. Each one will be rated for a certain number of passengers. You will have to talk to the limousine company's people to find out what the car is rated, because different ones will be stretched for different lengths.

"A lot of times a limousine company will show you a vehicle—but it will not necessarily be the one they'll be using. I advise, 100 percent, that you go down and take a look at the *actual* vehicle you are reserving. Take a look at how well it's maintained, see if it's the right age, the right color, and if it's really what you want. An immaculate white limousine is a lot different from one that's dirty or showing a lot of wear. There is nothing wrong with a ten-year-old limousine that looks brand new, but there *is* something wrong with a two-year-old limousine that looks ten years old. The biggest mistake people make is that they don't get terms and conditions in writing. They need to discuss what happens if the car breaks down or gets into an accident before the reserved date. They need to make a detailed list of items of service they are promised, such as a red carpet to roll out from the vehicle so the bride and groom can walk along it getting into the car, complimentary champagne, and other items provided in the package. If you have particular services and items you want, make sure it's in writing and in the contract. In addition, if complimentary champagne is part of the contract, the bride and groom have to be of legal drinking age.

"The minimum booking time varies by company, but it's usually about a four-hour minimum. But if you get into the busy season, you may get less favorable terms, as you'll be competing for the vehicles with other weddings, proms, [and] graduations.

"The number one thing is to give the limousine company written details, including what time the limousine needs to be there, and *where* it needs to be. If possible, provide a map—even a hand-drawn one—of all the stops and pickups: from the bride's house to the synagogue, from the synagogue to the reception hall, from the reception hall to the hotel where you are going to stay. It makes for a nicer experience than it would if the limousine were to show up late.

"The driver may be picking up five or six members of the wedding party from all over town. Drivers will need detailed directions and the times when they'll need to be at each location. The biggest cause of problems is lack of communication. One company, for example, didn't realize that one of the people they had to pick up was forty miles away!

"Know your cancellation clauses in case some emergency should happen, or if the wedding should not come off. You have to realize that these limousine companies are, in many cases, turning away other customers. There will be some cancellation penalties. However, if you cancel a long, long time in advance, and the company is able to re-book in that time frame, you can generally get your money back. If the company can't recapture the business, you'll end up paying a steep penalty.

"Before contracting with a limousine company, check to see if they are a member of this association. We do some background checks and insurance checks. Call the Better Business Bureau to make sure there are no outstanding complaints about the company's service."

15

Picture-Perfect

"OH, GRANDMOTHER, YOU WERE such a beautiful bride," you exclaim. Lovingly, you admire the framed heirloom treasure you hold in your hands—her exquisite wedding day portrait taken so many years ago. Now as *you* prepare to marry, you'll also want to immortalize your day with photography.

And, in addition to still photography, you may wish to have a video made. Not only will you get to relive your wedding and share it with others, but you might actually get to "see" parts your wedding for the first time! Perhaps you missed your honey's expression when they hoisted him up on a chair during a lively *horah*. Or the tears of happiness welling up in your mother's eyes as she walked you down the aisle toward the *chuppah*.

Ideally, you should start your search for your photographer and videographer from twelve to eighteen months in advance, as soon as you become engaged. Professionals with good reputations book up early, especially during the prime months of April through June, September, and October. When booking early, ask about a hold on any price escalations between the date you sign the contract and your wedding date.

Types of Studios

Some studios are considered "volume" studios, in which the owner has several photographers available. Since you may not know which photographer will be assigned to your wedding if you book far in advance, ask to see a variety of the photographers' work. That way, you'll get a general impression of the standards held by the studio. With a wide variety of photographers available, the owner of a volume company may be able to make the best match for you. If you know the work of a particular photographer within the company and want that person, speak to your contact at the studio; most likely this can be arranged as long as the photographer is free on your wedding date. In any event, you should be able to meet with your assigned photographer about two months before your wedding. An advantage of a volume studio is that there should usually be a well-qualified professional available as a backup photographer in case of an emergency. This should be stipulated in the contract.

You may prefer to hire a photographer who works independently. You know the photographer's reputation, and no one else will do. If you hire an independent, make sure that he or she has a trusted professional backup available in case of emergency. If possible, get this backup person's name written into the contract after reviewing his or her work and finding it acceptable. This may be easier said than done, especially if you're booking a long time in advance.

Double Duty

Some brides and grooms hire *two* photographers or *two* videographers to cover their wedding. It's not that they're worried about no-shows—they simply want to ensure that every aspect of their wedding is documented. They may also want to have shots taken from different angles to make the album or video edit more interesting.

For still photography, one photographer might take posed pictures of guests at each table during the reception while the other photographer snaps candid shots of reception events at the same time. Dual videographers can shoot your wedding from different vantage points. If you're walking down the aisle in a synagogue with a balcony, one can shoot from overhead, while the other can catch the processional from the front.

Check With Your Synagogue

If you're marrying in a synagogue, there may be special regulations your photographer or videographer will need to follow. Some congregations will allow photos and videos but limit them to certain areas of the building or sanctuary. Some *shuls* will not allow flashes to be used in the sanctuary. Others won't permit photography of any kind during the actual wedding ceremony. If this is the case, you may need to have a "dress rehearsal" and shoot the photos and video beforehand. Be sure to check with your rabbi or synagogue official and provide the information to your photo people.

Special Considerations

Wherever you're getting married, ask your photographer/videographer if he or she has worked that site before. Each venue has its own lighting situations and spots that might be perfect as backdrops. If new to the venue, ask that he or she visit the site before your wedding day to take a look around.

Also be sure that they become familiar with key people in your life. Usually he or she can tell by the flowers: special people may be wearing corsages or boutonnières. To be safe, a bridesmaid and groomsman should be assigned to "coach" the photographer to ensure that the key folks get caught on film.

Do you have a special idea or event you want captured on film? Make sure you give your photographer a list. Perhaps it's the *mezinka* dance or the musical set where the band gives out hats or blow-up toys.

Where and When

Where and when your photo shoot begins has a lot to do with whether the bride and groom will see each other before the ceremony. In the Jewish tradition, this indeed is the situation for those participating in the *bedecken* ceremony. Photography-wise, this can work out wonderfully. The formal photography can start about three and a half to four hours before the ceremony. In that way, everyone is fresh, makeup and hair are in place, and the bride's wedding gown is in perfect condition. Photos can also be taken to capture the bride readying for her big day, the *bedecken* ceremony, and the groom's table. And then, with the "formals" out of the way, the bride and groom can happily mingle with their guests throughout their wedding.

If the bride and groom don't want to see each other before the ceremony, the photographer will usually photograph the bride, her parents, and her bridesmaids first, then switch to the groom's side. The photos with both bride and groom together are done after the ceremony, which will take time away from the celebration.

Proof Positive but No Negatives?

Once the photos have been taken, you'll be getting back the preview prints, also known as proofs. These are all of the actual pictures snapped at the wedding. Some photographers have them available for the bride and groom within a week; others may not have them ready for months. Property of the photographer, the proofs are loaned to you for picture selection purposes.

Consider having a proof party to which you can invite your parents, close family members, and friends to help you select the pictures that will make up your wedding album.

Once you have the selections, you'll meet with the photographer to put together your final album. Your photographer can help you arrange the order of the photos within your album so they will tell the story of your wedding day.

You can usually make arrangements with the photographer to purchase the proofs as well. They may run one to two hundred dollars, depending on the quantity and the photographer. Some photographers will give them to you free of charge if you order a certain dollar amount of photography. If your budget is really tight, you may order the proofs alone, with or without an album.

The negatives are another matter. By law, they belong to the photographer, as does the copyright on the photos. Some photographers may be willing to sell you the negatives immediately, others after so many years, with the price dropping as time progresses. Generally speaking, they stay with the photographer. Be sure to ask how long your photographer keeps them in case you want additional pictures in future years.

Questions to Ask Your Photographer

1. Will you personally be photographing my wedding, or will you be assigning another photographer?

2. If you are assigning an "associate," may I select the photographer or do you make the decision?

3. Are the sample albums and portraits I'm looking at the actual work of the photographer who will be covering my wedding? If not, when I can meet with the associate and see samples of his or her actual work?

4. Do you have a backup photographer available in case of an emergency? Can I see his or her work as well?

5. What type of work does the photographer do best? Does he or she tend toward broad overviews or focus on details?

6. Will the photographer be taking photos at the ceremony, cocktail hour, and reception? Does he or she stay for the entire time? Is there a time limit after which there will be overtime charges? If so, what is it?

7. Do you maintain liability insurance? Workers' compensation? Also, what recourse do we have if for some reason you fail to show or the pictures don't come out? Do we reschedule at your expense?

8. Will the photographer come to both of our homes prior to the ceremony? Meet us at the synagogue or catering hall?

9. Is the photographer familiar with my wedding venue(s)? If not, will he or she visit prior to my wedding?

10. Can we get black and white instead of color? What about

sepia tones? If we *do* want black-and-white photography, is it taken from the color shots or is it shot in black-and-white film?

11. What, if any, special effects are available? Do you have samples? Which are included in the price and which incur extra charges?

12. Exactly what are we getting for the contracted price? How many photos do you shoot? How many go into the album? What style are the finished photos? What kind of album? Any portraits? What upgrades and additions will be available and what will they cost?

13. Can we buy the proofs? If so, how much will they cost?

14. Can we buy the negatives? How much would they cost? How long do you maintain the negatives? How much would it cost for us to buy extra pictures later on?

Questions to Ask your Videographer

1. Will the video be edited or unedited? Do I get both versions, or only one? If it's edited, will there be an additional charge or is the stipulated price based on the edited version? Does the price include a prologue and a recap? How long will the edited tape actually be?

2. Do you have one videographer or more? Can I see samples of their work and, if available, book a particular person?

3. Can I see proof of your company's liability and workers' compensation insurance?

4. Will there be a "prologue" with pictures of us growing up?

If so, will there be an extra charge? What do I need to provide you with? Can you use old video or film or just stills?

5. Will there be music in the prologue? Who provides it? If you do, do we get a choice of music or is it standard fare? Is there an extra charge for this?

6. Will there be a recap of moments to highlight? Is that included in the price or is there an extra charge?

7. Do you give individual guests the opportunity to send wishes or to say something special (or even lovingly stupid)?

8. Do you shoot the entire wedding—getting ready, ceremony, cocktail hour, reception? Do you stay for the entire deal or leave after some point?

9. Do you do special effects? What types are available? What about fancy scene transitions? Do we have our choice as to style? (Fade-in or -out, slides, combinations?)

10. When will we get the final tape?

11. Do we get the digital master? How many copies are included in the price? If you maintain the master, how long do you keep it? What would it cost to have additional copies made later? Can you make a DVD from the digital master?

12. Will the videographer talk with my venue about shooting and lighting restrictions?

The Contract

The contract must include the date and day of the wedding, including the year, both the bride's and groom's addresses and phone numbers, and future address if known. It should also stipulate where the photographer or videographer should first report, including address and phone number, the time and location of the ceremony and reception (don't forget to stipulate A.M. or P.M.), key contact people, the number of people in the wedding party and names of parents and other important members, the name of the photographer (if known at this point), the studio services contracted for such as portrait sittings, the package and its contents including number of photos, album style, and more (be very specific), the total price of the package purchased, taxes, payment schedule, and due dates. Review the fine print and discuss any changes you'd like to make in the "boilerplate" such as ownership of proofs and negatives, exclusive photography and videography rights, and others.

Friends in the Act

If you don't have the budget for professional video, a friend may volunteer to play videographer. If so, be sure the camcorder has a fresh tape inserted. In haste and excitement, you don't want to discover your amateur videographer recorded over an important tape left in your camcorder.

A fun addition to your still photos are candids taken of your guests by your guests with disposable wedding cameras placed on each guest table.

16

Destination Weddings and Honeymoons

THE WEDDING MAY BE OVER, but your lives together have just begun! Is it real? Are you actually married? You bet! After all the planning, the whirlwind of joyous activities, the tensions and tribulations, you've managed to ride the roller coaster that culminated in this very special lifetime event. And now it's time for the honeymoon . . . that is, unless you subscribe to the Orthodox Jewish post-wedding practice. If you do, the partying doesn't end quite yet—for there's another week of celebration ahead of you. Remembering the seven-day celebration after Jacob married Leah, the newlywed couple arrive at their new home and for the next seven nights are guests of honor in various homes, being wined and dined by relatives and friends within the community.

As an alternative, you may decide to partake of this pleasure for two or three days and then go off to visit family in other locations or go to a kosher hotel or resort for the balance of the week. Here, the joyous good wishes continue: everyone loves to celebrate with the new *chossen* and *callah*.

The majority of Jewish brides and grooms, however, leave for their honeymoon either directly after the wedding or on the following day. It's a personal choice.

If your travel plans include catching a plane, train, or bus directly after the wedding, you'll turn your gifts over to your parents or to the best man. After changing out of your wedding clothes, you'll leave the best man, maid of honor, or your parents in charge of your bridal outfits.

Many newlyweds opt to leave for their honeymoon the next day, especially if the reception is held at night. As one groom-to-be put it, with a smile, "I wouldn't dream of leaving right after the reception, before checking off and depositing our gifts. What if my best man runs away with the cash?"

With the popularity of the weekend wedding, the partying doesn't necessarily stop at the end of the wedding day. With events that include a breakfast or brunch the next morning for out-of-town guests, some brides and grooms decide to stay and share in the fun. If your honeymoon plans have you ready for takeoff directly on your wedding day, apologize not. Your parents or members of the bridal party will see to it that stay-over guests enjoy the next day.

By Prior Arrangement

With so much planning focused on the wedding itself, don't let your honeymoon take a back burner. Planning should start about six months in advance; in fact, the earlier, the better.

In the past, planning the honeymoon was almost exclusively the groom's department, and often the location was kept a big secret—even, at times, from the bride herself. Although surprising the bride by whisking her off to an exotic place unknown may seem like a romantic idea, it's not highly recommended. The groom's concept of a perfect honeymoon could be skiing in Aspen while the bride, trying to second-guess the location, packed for a trip to Hawaii.

Today things tend to be a little different. Usually both of you will decide where you would like to go, aided by your dreams, a knowledgeable travel agent, and a plethora of brochures. You can spend quality time together poring over Internet vacation sites, talking to friends, and generally exploring the myriad choices available to you. Let your fantasies loose and follow where they take you. But keep your budget in mind.

Do you want your honeymoon to be a quiet time for you to spend alone with each other, or do you want to go sight-seeing in a city you've both dreamed of exploring? Do you love the sun and beach and look forward to relaxing in a vacation paradise? How about a cruise that combines the amenities of a resort with the excitement of travel? Perhaps a quaint bed-and-breakfast turns you on. Or is exotic adventure travel, such as whitewater rafting, kayaking, going on an African safari, or joining an archaeological dig, more your speed? Do you want to stay in the country or travel abroad? So many choices! So much fun deciding!

If you're booking your "home away from home" through brochures, take the beautiful pictures of the rooms with a grain of salt. And read the fine print. That luxurious room with a king-sized bed and balcony may be one of a kind. And probably the most expensive. You want to know what's included in the room you book. In most cases, if you book the bridal suite you'll get one of the best rooms—but don't count on it 100 percent. You may enjoy a standard room in a luxury hotel more than the bridal suite in a crumbling old relic of a building.

Also consider the practical aspects when making your choice. You may imagine a bed-and-breakfast to be totally romantic, warm, and cozy. But the reality may be different. Do you want to spend your first nights together in a place that may have a nosy proprietor or a pesky guest? How much privacy will you have? How soundproof are the walls?

If you want privacy, on the other hand, you may choose to stay at a mega-hotel, but you'll need to decide if such a large complex is the right choice for you. Whatever you decide, when booking your haven, let the folks there know that you're on your honeymoon. They may surprise you with some extra perks—such as a complimentary bottle of champagne or a celebratory cake.

Destination Weddings

Destination weddings combine your wedding and honeymoon into one singular event. It can resemble an elopement in some ways, although in this case everyone is in on it, and may even come to see you off, or even travel with you. There are many ways to structure this type of event.

You can get married at a location you've both always dreamed of, and then spend the rest of your time there on your honeymoon. Or you can have your family and friends join you for the wedding and even come along on some or all of the celebratory trip!

Perhaps you and your beloved were raised in different cities and want to go back to one of your hometowns to marry. In other cases, you may be living in one city while many of your relatives live in another. You decide to hold the wedding where it's most convenient for the majority of your guests.

In any event, having a destination wedding is a wonderful way to solve wedding situations, such as an overbloated guest list, if that's your choosing. And unless all your friends are doing the same thing, it's a way to avoid the cookie-cutter weddings that seem just like all the others you may have attended recently.

The logistics of planning a destination wedding can be awesome or simple; all depends on the type of wedding you want, where you plan to marry, and whether you're planning to bring guests along. You can travel to a city or town within the United States or to a foreign destination—perhaps a place you've always wanted to visit, or where you have family roots. Cruises are also popular for destination weddings, as are resorts within the country or in a foreign location.

Getting Married Overseas

If you're an American citizen and plan to marry outside the country, the U.S. State Department advises that generally, marriages legally performed and valid abroad are also legally valid in the United States. The attorney general of the state where you live may be able to provide you with specific information.

Since each country has its own rules and regulations for marriage, the embassy or tourist bureau of the country in which you plan to marry is your best source of information. Looking outside this country, the American embassies and consulates abroad often have information about marriage within the country in which they're located.

According to the State Department, most countries require that a valid U.S. passport be presented. In addition, birth certificates, divorce decrees, and death certificates (of former spouses) are frequently required. Some countries require that a consular official of that country first authenticate the documents in the United States, which can be expensive and time-consuming. Some countries require that documents presented to their marriage registrar be translated into the language of the country.

The State Department further advises that civil law countries require proof of your legal capacity to enter into a marriage contract. A competent authority has to certify that there are no impediments to the marriage. No such documents exist in the United States. What to do? Some foreign authorities will allow a statement to be executed before one of their consular officials in the United States. If not, you will need to go to the American embassy or consulate in the country in which you plan to marry. There you'll execute an affidavit stating that you are free to marry. Called an "Affidavit of Eligibility to Marry," the fee for the American consular officer's certification of this affidavit is fifty-five dollars, subject to change. Some countries also require witnesses who will execute affidavits to the effect that the parties are free to marry.

Some countries require blood tests, so be sure to ask about that when you contact the authorities. Will you need a physical and, if so, would a letter from your doctor at home be accepted instead?

Marriages abroad are subject to the residency requirements of the country in which the marriage is to be performed. Some countries require a brief waiting period; others a lengthy one. So before you decide on a quickie wedding abroad or plan to dash off a cruise ship to say "I do" on the beach, you'll need to get the facts.

What Else Should You Know?

Will the country you wish to marry in marry noncitizens? Do you need to have a civil as well as a religious ceremony for your wedding to be recognized as legal in that country? What type of documentation do you need? Do you need witnesses and, if so, how many? Can they be supplied at the wedding site?

Some countries make it relatively easy for you to marry; others do not. Once you've decided on your locale and checked with the U.S. State Department for safety and health information, you can get information on the country or island's official Web site.

Your next step is to find a wedding planner or coordinator in the foreign country who can guide you through the maze of rules, regulations, and documents. A good wedding coordinator can actually do just about everything you need at the location to make the event a success—right down to finding an officiant, renting chairs, and arranging for a *chuppah*.

Contact the tourist office of the country in which you plan to marry. If you tell the staff members you're planning a wedding, they may be able to put you in touch with local wedding planners and vendors. In your search, also check with an experienced travel agent who may have contacts. Some travel agents specialize in a particular country or region and can have a fully packed Rolodex. Hotels and synagogues in the area in which you plan to marry may be able to help you find a coordinator as well. *The Jewish Travel Guide,* published by Vallentine Mitchell Publishers, can be a helpful starting point. It includes descriptions of sites of Jewish interest, hotels, restaurants, and *shuls* in two thousand towns and cities in 110 countries.

Another resource for Orthodox *shuls, Chabad* centers, and lists of *shuls* in *Sephardic* countries is available on the Internet at www.kashrut.com.

If you have relatives who live in your destination country, you may want to enlist them to either help with the actual planning or help find a suitable coordinator.

Are you planning to find a rabbi at your destination who can perform your marriage? If so, ask your local rabbi for a letter of reference for you, and ask if he or she knows and could recommend a rabbi in that locale. Getting married in Israel may be particularly difficult, and your letter of reference should come from an Orthodox rabbi who can vouch that you are both Jewish. It may take some time to work things out, so you must plan far ahead. And although your dream may have always been to marry in Israel, pay attention to travel advisories.

If your local rabbi doesn't know who to recommend in your designated country, contact that country's synagogues on your own. For *Chassidic* information, *Chabad* houses are available worldwide. Hillel, the largest Jewish campus organization in the world, embraces all streams of Judaism and is available on college campuses. The theology department of a university in your destination country may be able to help, as well.

Hiring a Coordinator

Making the arrangement for your destination wedding can challenge even the best party planner—especially when guests are involved. You will need to coordinate travel and pickups for your guests, who may be coming from various locations and arriving at different times via different airlines or modes of transportation. Lodging arrangements will have to be made. Transportation to your wedding site will need to be provided. If you come up with some fascinating ideas, such as transporting guests to the top of a Greek island mountain by donkey, have alternate arrangements for the less adventurous of your guests. Depending on your location of choice, you might even need to provide a translator or local guide.

Some countries, some resorts in foreign countries, and even some cruise ships have wedding planners available at your destination to help make all of the legal, spiritual, and party arrangements in advance. You might also get recommendations from cruise ships, hotels, the tourism bureau of the country, or by doing a Web site search. Before hiring a coordinator, check out references and make sure you both speak the same language—literally and figuratively. Hopefully you'll both have e-mail access, which can facilitate back-and-forth notes, sharing photos of wedding sites and elements, and even hearing clips of music. Remember, if you can't communicate, or if your ideas of wedding style are totally different, continue your search for another planner.

As you plan your event, you should consider the Jewish culture and customs of your local country and incorporate as many as you would like into your ceremony. This can be reflected in the food, the music, and specific wedding customs. Your wedding coordinator can best advise you on the practices of the country and region you select.

Bringing the Party With You

If you're bringing your guests along, whether to a foreign or a stateside destination wedding, be sure to give them plenty of notice so that they can plan their vacation around the event. Sending hold-the-date cards, along with some preliminary information such as the locale, eight months to a year in advance is a good idea if your invitation includes foreign travel. You can later provide updates for your guests as you refine your plans.

If your destination has a tourist office, ask if it can supply you with a quantity of information packets about the location; you can include them with your hold-the-date cards. If supplies are limited, you can send them out later, only to those who have actually agreed to attend your wedding.

And Wedding Gown Makes Three

If you're planning to marry in full regalia, think about how you'll get your gown to your destination. If you're flying, new regulations limit you to one piece of carry-on luggage, and that would be your wedding gown. You do not want to put it in the plane's belly for fear of it getting lost, as luggage sometimes does. If you bring it aboard, it must fit into an overhead compartment or under the seat in front of you. Squish! Total horror, especially if others are sharing the overhead compartments with their coats, bags, or computers. First-class passengers may have the use of a small closet, but again, you'll be sharing this small area with garment bags and other stuffed-in items.

One option, suggested by an airline clerk, is to talk to your dry cleaner about having the gown encased in plastic with all the air pushed out. Once you get to your destination, you can hang it and shake it open again. If money is not the object, you can also book a seat just for your gown, with it wrapped in loads of acid-free tissue and covered in plastic on a padded hanger.

Another option: you can ship it to your location ahead of time by guaranteed delivery if there is someone at the other end to receive it. The dress would have to be packed without folding and loaded with acid-free tissues and bubble wrap. It should be packed in a box big enough for it to be spread out but with no extra room for movement. Veiling fabric, although light, can wrinkle as well. Take the same care with it as you would with your gown.

In any event, if you *do* find wrinkles, don't you *dare* let anyone near your gown with an iron. Steaming would be your best bet. You may want to take a small steamer with you, along with an electricity converter if you are traveling to a foreign country that requires it. If you engage the help of a dry cleaner at your destination, ask him or her to hand-steam your gown and veil.

Resorting It

If you love the idea of a resort that can cater to just about your every whim, you can find many to choose from. You can get married and have your honeymoon at the same place in many of the facilities. They include Disney World Resort, Sandals, Beaches, SuperClubs, and Club Med, for example. Some, such as Sandals, Beaches, and SuperClubs, offer complimentary weddings. The details vary, and weddings may be offered at selected facilities only, so you'll have to check with them for details. Some will not allow children if they are couples-only resorts. Depending on your choice, they can be your perfect private getaway or a fun-filled honeymoon/destination vacation to be shared with family and friends. See your travel agent for more information.

Cruise Control

Could there be anything more romantic than cruising into the sunset with the love of your life? Yes: actually getting married at the same time! Cruise lines can arrange the wedding of your dreams to be held aboard the ship during a stop at a port of call, or on land at some ports, as well. A local officiant will perform the ceremony. Several cruise lines offer full-wedding packages. Contact your travel agent for details.

Saving Money While Traveling

❦ Register for your honeymoon. Today engaged couples are adding contributions toward their honeymoon to their gift registries.

❦ If either of you is a student, ask about student discount fares.

❦ Check plane, train, and bus fares by calling toll-free numbers. Ask whom the company is partnered with and check rates with partners, too. Next, check the transportation company's Web site, which may offer less expensive fares than its toll-free number. Also look at general travel Web sites and compare with the price available through your travel agent.

❦ When booking a stateroom on a cruise ship, decide if a porthole or window is important to you. For people who get claustrophobic, the window or porthole could be mandatory; for others, it's just extra money. There are plenty of opportunities to view the water from seats in public areas. If you have the romantic notion of watching the water from your room at night, keep in mind that it may be too dark to see anything out there at all. No matter which room you book, the amenities of the ship are usually the same.

❦ Ask about package deals. Sometimes the transportation combined with a hotel or land package will be less expensive than booking them separately, and sometimes not.

❦ Call back again, and again, and again! Rates change by the minute. It's like a wild gambling game—how cheap can you get before you're knocked out of the game (seats all booked up)? When do you quit and take the rate, knowing it could be higher or lower with the next call?

❧ When calling for a fare, ask for the best possible fare right up front, then ask what restrictions apply and what you get for your dollar.

❧ Since you're booking in advance, ask for specials such as fourteen- or thirty-day advance notice fares.

❧ Pull out your memberships: many organizations offer discounts on car rentals and hotel and motel reservations, and sometimes even cruises. Do you belong to AAA? Professional or community organizations? Inquire with the carrier or check with information provided by your organization.

❧ Have frequent flier miles? Don't forget about them. It pays to join a frequent flier club even if you rarely fly. Some are tied in to hotels, as well.

❧ Do you have a credit card tied to a frequent flier program? Paying for your wedding-related expenses on your card could get you lots of points toward free or upgraded travel. Watch the interest rates on the card, however. It's not a good idea to charge more than you can pay at the end of the billing period.

❧ Charging your trip on a credit card (frequent-flier-type or not) may get you coverage for travel insurance free of charge. Check with your credit card company for details (and read the small print).

❧ Book your honeymoon during off-peak times. Transportation may be less expensive. Some attractions may be closed, however, and you could be facing extreme heat, cold, or the rainy season. Check out information in a guidebook or with the country's tourist bureau.

- Ask for special offers and deals. You may get a companion discount or companion free deal.

- Beware of come-ons that offer you free vacations or honeymoons. You may have to pay your own airfare to get there. It may also include your having to sit through a pitch to buy land or invest in time-share property.

- Tell them you're newlyweds when booking your transportation, including car services. Who knows? You might get lucky.

- Try again *without* telling them you're newlyweds. See if there's a price difference. Who knows? Maybe they hear *honeymoon* and mistake it for *money-moon!*

- If renting a car, check with your credit card company and auto policy first to see if you're covered for collision on the rental vehicle. Most car rental places sell it under the name of "loss damage waiver" for extra bucks that can sure add up. It's important to have the coverage, but why pay twice if you're already covered?

- Ask your employer's travel service (if there is one, and you're permitted to use it for personal service) if it can help you plan your trip and get a better rate.

Kosher Corner

Keeping kosher while on your honeymoon can be a bit of a challenge unless you're staying at a kosher hotel. If you've traveled before, you probably know the ropes. Here are some suggestions for the uninitiated.

Airlines

If an airline would normally offer food service during your flight, you can often request kosher food. Make your request at the time you book your flight, or shortly thereafter. Some airlines can fulfill your needs within a day's notice, but why take a chance? If your trip involves stopovers or changing planes and carriers, make sure that the carrier of each leg of your trip is notified of your kosher food request. For more information about eating kosher while flying, log on to www.star-k.com.

Restaurants

The *United States Jewish Travel Guide* lists kosher restaurants, synagogues of all denominations, *Chabad* houses, *mikvahs,* and Jewish sites around the country. Another choice: log on to www.kashrut.com and click on "Kosher Travel." It includes the Shamash Kosher Restaurant Database, as well as lists of *shuls* and *Chabad* centers. Another good Web site: www.kosherfinder. com. It lists kosher bed-and-breakfasts, cruises, resorts, hotels, and restaurants around the world. A kosher restaurant database can also be found at koshernic.com.

Prepackaged Kosher Meals

If you're honeymooning in Puerto Rico, you can get prepackaged kosher meals delivered to you from Chabad Lubavitch of Puerto Rico. They can arrive hot, or packaged so that they can be reheated at your hotel. You can order by e-mail, fax, or phone. For further information, call (787) 727-2709 or (787) 724-1680.

And if you want to carry your own kosher food with you, or have it shipped by

United Parcel Service to your honeymoon location, My Own Meals provides main-course, refrigeration-free, packaged kosher food in boil-in-bag pouches or in microwavable and boilable plastic trays. They are fully cooked and ready to eat. E-mail myownmeals@worldnet.att.net or visit www.myownmeals.com.

Home Again

Your honeymoon is over—but at the same time it has just begun. Well rested or happily exhausted, you've made it home. The groom may carry the bride over the threshold (to protect her from evil spirits, or just for fun!). You put down your bags and look at your home, apartment, condo, or room in your parents' house. Somehow it looks a little different then when you left it before your honeymoon. Whether you've lived there before or just spent time fixing it up, it seems to hold a new meaning. It's now the residence of a newly married couple.

But somewhere in another place, whether near or tucked far away, there may be a band of people waiting to welcome you home. Now is a good time to make those phone calls to let those near and dear know you're home and ready to start your new life.

Starting tomorrow, your life will be filled with writing thank-you notes, unpacking gifts, and probably running around to stores to return or exchange duplicates or "white elephants." You'll also be accepting continued rounds of good wishes and enjoying visits with family and friends while catching up on work and/or your studies at school.

For now, just take the moment to rejoice in each other. You've made it through the planning, the chaos, the blunders, and blessings to become a married couple, united as one.

MAZEL TOV!

FROM OY VEY TO OLÉ

Ever since she was a little girl, Melanie, who grew up in New Jersey, dreamed of having her fairy-tale wedding at Disney World. Her family used to visit there for a few days each year on the way to see her grandfather, who lived in southern Florida. And when Melanie met Howie, her prince charming, and they fell in love, she knew her dream would soon become a reality.

At first, Melanie's mom was not happy about her daughter's decision to marry so far way. As a result, Mom didn't want to fully participate in the early wedding plans, Melanie relates. "It was a horrible year—we didn't speak often. Usually I'd speak with her every day, but that year I only spoke with her once a week." Melanie did a lot of planning with her father, but missed sharing things with her mom as well. "I did all the invitations myself, did the wording, the calligraphy. Everything I would have turned to my mother for," she says. But Melanie stood firm.

Planning the destination wedding took several trips to Florida, and although her mom did not go along on one of the trips, she eventually was won over. "Once she got down there, she was okay," Melanie says.

Back in New Jersey, her mom helped her get her bridal gown—a very princesslike, custom-made dress with a tank top and a big tulle skirt. And planning went on, much of it by telephone and FedEx packages.

The wedding coordinator at Disney World gave Melanie the name of a rabbi, who was also a cantor. She and Howie met with him several times as they planned their Conservative wedding ceremony. They would use a *tallit* as their *chuppah,* and the rabbi would explain the traditions of a Jewish marriage for the benefit of some guests who were not Jewish. With approximately 210 people invited, 74 family members and friends would be joining Melanie and Howie for their dream wedding to be held outdoors, backdropped by the Disney castle. They planned an exciting weekend for their guests, including a "kosher-style" dinner for Friday evening and a whole night of events. The wedding would be held on Saturday night, followed by the reception and a Sunday-morning brunch. "People were very excited," Melanie says.

Arriving at Disney World the Tuesday before the wedding, Melanie had consultations for hair and makeup, and firmed up the final arrangements, including a special surprise finale.

Come Saturday night, Melanie and Howie arrived at their wedding in a Cinderella-like coach. The rabbi performed the ceremony as guests sat on chairs set up by the Disney staff.

And shortly after the rabbi pronounced the couple husband and wife, the sky lit up with the majestic Disney fireworks display. The photographer captured the happy couple at this perfect moment— and Melanie's dream did indeed come true.

Epilogue: . . . And They Lived Happily Ever After

THEY WERE BOTH YOUNG, but Abe Rabinoff met the love of his life when she walked through the door in his workplace—more than eighty years ago. Having come to the United States from Russia at an early age, he became a bicycle messenger, delivering telegrams for Western Union in Denver. And Rae, who had arrived in Denver from West Virginia just two years before, got a clerk's job with Western Union, too.

"I saw that gal from the mountains when she opened the door," says Abe, his voice reflecting the awe he felt the first time he set eyes on his wife-to-be. "We got acquainted, and—here we are!"

After dating for a few years, they married on September 18, 1920, despite the fact that Rae was an "older woman": she was born one year before him. "And he's been trying to catch up ever since," jokes Rae. "But I don't let him!"

Now, at ages ninety-eight and ninety-nine, Abe and Rae have been married for more than eight decades. They still hold hands and share loving kisses. Their secret for success?

"We always respected each other," says Rae.

"We never fought with each other or anything," adds Abe, reflecting back over the years. "She held my hand so I couldn't," he says with a laugh.

"Yes, we were happy," Rae relates. "If we were fussing or fighting it wouldn't have been as nice."

Wedding Planning Timetable

Eighteen Months to One Year
Before the Wedding

Bride (to catering hall manager): *Do you have June 16th available?*
Caterer: *June 16th of which year? Next year or the year after?*

    Early birds can get a wider choice of venues and vendors. So, if you've announced your engagement at this point—start getting busy. Make sure to check cancellation clauses before signing contracts.

❑ _____ Announce your engagement
❑ _____ Decide how many printed announcements you'll need
❑ _____ Order engagement announcements—contact newspapers
❑ _____ Start your diet (if necessary!)
❑ _____ Interview officiants and select

- ❑ ____ Develop/sign pre-nuptial agreement
- ❑ ____ Shop for, appraise and buy engagement/wedding rings or stones and settings
- ❑ ____ Pick up rings
- ❑ ____ Take out insurance for engagement and wedding rings or jewelry
- ❑ ____ Check marriage requirements in the state and town
- ❑ ____ Set tentative wedding date (may change due to site availability)
- ❑ ____ Talk to your families about wedding styles and finances

Relax! Time Out!

- ❑ ____ Decide on the style of wedding
- ❑ ____ Consult with rabbi or officiant you selected
- ❑ ____ Consider (and implement) premarital counseling session(s)
- ❑ ____ Formulate a wedding budget
- ❑ ____ Decide on the size of wedding
- ❑ ____ Pick up, address and stamp envelopes and mail out engagement announcements
- ❑ ____ Determine number of attendants
- ❑ ____ Select and ask attendants
- ❑ ____ Visit a bridal show to check out vendors
- ❑ ____ Develop your "dream" wedding invitation list
- ❑ ____ Ditto your honey's list
- ❑ ____ Visit ceremony sites
- ❑ ____ Visit reception sites

Take a breather—no wedding talk for a week!

- ❑ ____ Refine combined wedding lists
- ❑ ____ Refine it once more
- ❑ ____ Firm up actual wedding date and time
- ❑ ____ Secure ceremony site

- ❑ ____ Secure reception site
- ❑ ____ Arrange for alternate sites if wedding and/or reception are outdoors
- ❑ ____ Interview caterers if not tied into reception site
- ❑ ____ Book caterer
- ❑ ____ Audition/view tapes of bands, DJ's, string quartets, and other musicians
- ❑ ____ Book all music
- ❑ ____ Interview photographers
- ❑ ____ Book photographer
- ❑ ____ Interview videographers
- ❑ ____ Book videographer
- ❑ ____ Interview florist
- ❑ ____ Book florist
- ❑ ____ Interview wedding cake bakers if cake is not provided by caterer
- ❑ ____ Secure wedding cake baker
- ❑ ____ Interview other entertainers
- ❑ ____ Secure other entertainers

Another breather! Absolutely no talk of wedding arrangements!

- ❑ ____ Start looking for wedding gown
- ❑ ____ Decide on style of wedding party attire
- ❑ ____ Discuss honeymoon destination
- ❑ ____ Visit travel agent
- ❑ ____ Check passports, visas if necessary
- ❑ ____ If you're planning a destination wedding, check out residency and marriage requirements there
- ❑ ____ Dig up birth certificates (and, if applicable, divorce papers or a death certificate). Order replacements, if necessary
- ❑ ____ Register for china, household things, and so forth
- ❑ ____ (fill in) _____
- ❑ ____ (fill in) _____
- ❑ ____ (fill in) _____

One Year to Six Months Before the Wedding

❑ ____ Complete any tasks you haven't finished from the above list

❑ ____ Decide if you're having a pre-wedding dinner (rehearsal dinner)

❑ ____ Book venue and menu for pre-wedding dinner

❑ ____ Book block of hotel rooms for out-of-town guests

❑ ____ Decide if there will be a morning after breakfast/brunch

❑ ____ Check out venues and menus for breakfast/brunch

❑ ____ Secure venue for breakfast/brunch

❑ ____ Book bridal suite

❑ ____ Select and put deposits on your wedding gown and accessories; arrange fitting schedule

❑ ____ Choose and purchase garter (if using), cake topper, guest book, imprinted ribbons, imprinted cocktail napkins, and so forth

❑ ____ Select and order imprinted *yarmulkas* (*Kippot*)

❑ ____ Make up ceremony programs if using

❑ ____ Select or make glass bag holder if using (to break glass)

❑ ____ Select or design *chuppah*

❑ ____ Decide upon and purchase favors

❑ ____ Order room decorations or hire wedding decorator

❑ ____ Meet with your bridal party to discuss price range and style of their dresses, tuxedos, accessories

❑ ____ Select wedding party attire—choose rental shop, dressmakers, stores, place orders, arrange fitting schedules

❑ ____ Talk to your attendants about things you'd like them to handle for you

❑ ____ Buy lingerie and bridal gown underpinnings

❑ ____ If wedding will be held at home or photographs to be taken at home, consider refreshing or improving your home decor and property

❑ ____ Order and arrange delivery/implementation of home improvement/decor

❑ ____ Tell parents/grandparents of level of formality for their wedding outfits

❑ ____ Work out ceremony arrangements with clergy/officiant

- ❑ _____ Start shopping for a house or apartment
- ❑ _____ Start shopping for furniture
- ❑ _____ (fill in) _____
- ❑ _____ (fill in) _____
- ❑ _____ (fill in) _____

Six to Three Months Before the Wedding

- ❑ _____ Complete any tasks you haven't finished from above lists
- ❑ _____ Finalize your guest list—count and recount
- ❑ _____ Arrange for activities for out-of-town guests (golf, tennis, swim club, and so forth)
- ❑ _____ Order wedding invitations, table cards (if not provided by caterer) and other stationery
- ❑ _____ Find calligrapher and get her/him started on the envelopes or start addressing them yourself
- ❑ _____ Arrange for vacation time from work

Remember: delegate tasks to bridal party members; parents, each other

- ❑ _____ Take out wedding insurance
- ❑ _____ Order an artistic *kutubah* with your rabbi's advice about the content
- ❑ _____ Rent/buy a house or apartment
- ❑ _____ Order household furniture
- ❑ _____ Change addresses on magazine subscriptions
- ❑ _____ Do a trial run commute from new address to work/school
- ❑ _____ Write any wedding vows you plan to include in the ceremony—check with officiant
- ❑ _____ Take one complete invitation set and enclosures to post office and weigh for

postage. Add response card postage. Order special theme stamps you may want

❑ _____ After speaking to your rabbi, select Jewish customs you'll include in your wedding ceremony

Learn to compromise on the above

❑ _____ Arrange for *shaytl* or *teichl* if you'll be wearing them
❑ _____ Develop and reproduce direction sheets to include with invitations
❑ _____ Develop and reproduce activity sheets of things to do in the area
❑ _____ Look into transportation for yourself, bridal party, and out-of-town guests
❑ _____ Sign wedding transportation contract(s)
❑ _____ Arrange for valet parking; check parking facilities at both ceremony and reception sites
❑ _____ (fill in) _____
❑ _____ (fill in) _____
❑ _____ (fill in) _____

Two Months Before

❑ _____ Complete any tasks you haven't finished from above lists
❑ _____ Pick up or arrange delivery for any items on order so far
❑ _____ Buy and wrap gifts for bridal attendants
❑ _____ Buy wedding gifts for each other
❑ _____ Put together invitations and enclosures, stamp and mail invitations
❑ _____ Get marriage license if within your state's time framework
❑ _____ Organize wedding responses
❑ _____ Write thank you notes for gifts as they arrive; keep track of gifts
❑ _____ Make medical appointments; get any necessary blood tests, medical clearance notes; birth control; see eye doctor for new contacts or glasses

- ❑ _____ Visit dentist
- ❑ _____ Look into stress reduction methods
- ❑ _____ Arrange for household help if needed for day of wedding
- ❑ _____ Arrange for home catering if having houseguests or bridal party preparations at home
- ❑ _____ Discuss hair/make-up/nails/skin care with appropriate professionals
- ❑ _____ Go for almost final fittings
- ❑ _____ Order any rental items necessary
- ❑ _____ Open necessary bank accounts
- ❑ _____ Finalize menu for wedding reception, pre-wedding dinner, post-wedding brunch
- ❑ _____ Have wedding photo taken for newspapers
- ❑ _____ Send wedding announcement and photo to newspapers

Time out—Take a breather!

- ❑ _____ Confirm and make final arrangements with all vendors and travel agent
- ❑ _____ Shop for honeymoon clothing; buy luggage if necessary
- ❑ _____ (fill in) _____
- ❑ _____ (fill in) _____
- ❑ _____ (fill in) _____

One Month Before

- ❑ _____ Complete any tasks you haven't finished from above lists

Stop procrastinating—time is getting short!

- ❑ _____ Finalize your after-marriage house or apartment and furnishings
- ❑ _____ Visit deceased parents graves (if applicable)

- ❑ ____ Buy homeowner/renter's and content insurance
- ❑ ____ Arrange for dressing space for bridal party
- ❑ ____ Give musicians list of special songs; names of people and your relationship to them for acknowledgment or calling up for activities
- ❑ ____ Go over special requests with all vendors including photographers
- ❑ ____ Gather items for bridal emergency basket, such as needle and thread, and toiletries
- ❑ ____ Make arrangements for *ufruf* and *kiddish* afterwards
- ❑ ____ Invite people to *ufruf* and provide head count for *kiddish*
- ❑ ____ (fill in) _____
- ❑ ____ (fill in) _____
- ❑ ____ (fill in) _____

Three Weeks Before

- ❑ ____ Follow-up on non-acknowledged invitations
- ❑ ____ Order any extra items such as wedding cameras for tables
- ❑ ____ Arrange reception seating; consider taking a headache remedy
- ❑ ____ Pick up wedding rings and try on for size
- ❑ ____ Buy insurance for wedding ring
- ❑ ____ Have a luncheon for your attendants
- ❑ ____ Make appointments for hair, nail, skin salon or day spa
- ❑ ____ Go for all final bridal and attendant fittings
- ❑ ____ Arrange for pick up and return of all rental items and rented clothing
- ❑ ____ Purchase candy or nuts to toss at *chossen* after *ufruf*
- ❑ ____ Purchase candles; also rice, birdseed or bubbles to release after ceremony if appropriate and permitted
- ❑ ____ Finalize menu including challah with caterer
- ❑ ____ Discuss processional and under-*chuppah* positions with clergy/officiant
- ❑ ____ Go over all checklists

❑ ____ Gather something old, something new, and so forth

❑ ____ Organize jewelry to wear with bridal outfits/groom's jewelry

❑ ____ Make out wedding announcement cards if you're using them

❑ ____ Arrange for your transportation after wedding and to honeymoon locale

❑ ____ Inform all household workers you may have of your new address

❑ ____ Look into hiring new service workers at new address if necessary

❑ ____ Arrange to bring or ship personal effects, any furniture and other items you're taking to your new home

❑ ____ (fill in) _____

❑ ____ (fill in) _____

❑ ____ (fill in) _____

Two Weeks Before

❑ ____ Confirm and tie-up loose ends with all vendors

❑ ____ Give caterer final head count if necessary. If not, hold off one more week

❑ ____ Implement all necessary name changes: driver's license, credit cards, bank accounts, insurance policies, credit cards, personnel/school records

❑ ____ Shop for last minute personal items, medications, contact lens solution, birth control needs, sunscreen, and so forth

❑ ____ Start packing—for honeymoon, for after wedding get-away and for items you'll need to bring along to your wedding

❑ ____ (fill in) _____

❑ ____ (fill in) _____

❑ ____ (fill in) _____

One Week Before

Delegate Delegate Delegate

- ❑ ____ Pick up your wedding gown, shoes and accessories
- ❑ ____ Give caterer final head count
- ❑ ____ Arrange for a post-*mikvah* party for women if you are having one
- ❑ ____ Visit the *mikvah* (within four days of the wedding) if applicable to you
- ❑ ____ Enjoy a post-*mikvah* party if applicable
- ❑ ____ Arrange envelopes with wedding-day payments and tips for vendors
- ❑ ____ Arrange for gifts/cash brought to reception to be taken home or put in designated place
- ❑ ____ Break in wedding shoes
- ❑ ____ Gather outfit for pre-wedding dinner
- ❑ ____ Purchase any hair items needed such as clips, and so forth
- ❑ ____ Prepare a white sheet or tissue paper to spread on the car seat while you are in your wedding gown
- ❑ ____ Organize all bring-alongs you'll be providing (wine glass cloth or bag; *yarmulkas;* personalized goblets; handkerchief; table cloth; wine; candles; pen; matches; and so forth)

Stifle the urge to cancel the whole wedding
Practice stress relief techniques
Practice some more

- ❑ ____ Confirm travel, hotel and all honeymoon arrangements
- ❑ ____ Confirm salon/barber appointments
- ❑ ____ Buy film, videotapes, batteries, and other related needs
- ❑ ____ Finish packing
- ❑ ____ Confirm hotel arrangements for bridal party
- ❑ ____ Pick up wedding clothes and try on to insure fit
- ❑ ____ Pick up any dry cleaning needed/do last minute wash

- ❑ ____ Give post office(s) your new address
- ❑ ____ Put out any fires and loose ends—review all checklists again
- ❑ ____ (fill in) _____
- ❑ ____ (fill in) _____
- ❑ ____ (fill in) _____

Try to get to bed early

The Day Before

Don't panic!
Practice stress relief

- ❑ ____ Touch base with clergy/officiant
- ❑ ____ Load luggage and necessities in post-wedding car
- ❑ ____ Gather passports, travel documents
- ❑ ____ Give best man envelopes with vendor and officiant's payments and tips
- ❑ ____ Arrange for food you'll share during *yichud*
- ❑ ____ Make sure tuxedos are picked up
- ❑ ____ Get jewelry, stockings, undergarments, veil and headdress, personal bag ready for the next day
- ❑ ____ Gather your going away outfit, handbag and shoes and arrange for someone to bring it to the reception hall
- ❑ ____ Have garment bags or extra suitcases ready to put your wedding clothes in after you've changed out of them
- ❑ ____ Arrange for someone to take you and your honey's wedding clothes home after you've changed out of them
- ❑ ____ Make all last minute confirmations
- ❑ ____ Talk to your parents and loved ones
- ❑ ____ Give your mother or maid of honor the announcement cards to mail out a day or so after the wedding

- ❑ _____ Have out-of-town guests picked up at airport
- ❑ _____ Attend pre-wedding family (rehearsal) dinner
- ❑ _____ Arrange for pick up of non-delivered items
- ❑ _____ Arrange for the groom's table/chair for signing the *ketubah*
- ❑ _____ (fill in) _____
- ❑ _____ (fill in) _____
- ❑ _____ (fill in) _____

Try **to get some sleep**
Try again
Stop dreaming of "things to do"

Wedding Day

- ❑ _____ If you're not fasting, remember to eat breakfast
- ❑ _____ Have cars driven and left at reception location for those arriving by one-way limousine
- ❑ _____ Prepare food/snacks for wedding party arriving to dress and help you dress
- ❑ _____ Take a relaxing bath or shower

Think calming thoughts
Think about how much you love your honey

- ❑ _____ Have hair, nails, make-up done
- ❑ _____ Don't forget to shave

Prepare to welcome wedding party

- ❑ _____ Give bride's ring to maid of honor
- ❑ _____ Give groom's ring to best man

❑ ____ Get into your wedding gown and put on accessories
❑ ____ Get into tuxedo or other wedding attire

Find your lost shoe

❑ ____ Gather personal flowers; pin on flowers
❑ ____ Take a last look around. Get misty-eyed
❑ ____ Check your make-up
❑ ____ Check your tie and cufflinks
❑ ____ Travel to ceremony site

**If you needed this check list for the last item,
consider having someone *carry* you to the alter!**

❑ Sign the *ketubah*
❑ Perform the handkerchief ceremony (*Kabalat kinyan*)
❑ Perform the veiling ceremony (*be'decken*)

**Stop your knees from knocking—SMILE—then . . .
10—9—8—7—6—5—4—3—2—1. . . .
May the wedding procession begin! MAZEL TOV!**

Index